The OSS in
World War II Albania

The OSS in World War II Albania

Covert Operations and Collaboration
with Communist Partisans

PETER LUCAS

Foreword by Fatos Tarifa

McFarland & Company, Inc., Publishers
Jefferson, North Carolina, and London

LIBRARY OF CONGRESS CATALOGUING-IN-PUBLICATION DATA

Lucas, Peter, 1934–
    The OSS in World War II Albania : covert operations and collaboration with communist partisans / Peter Lucas ; foreword by Fatos Tarifa.
        p.   cm.
    Includes bibliographical references and index.

    ISBN-13: 978-0-7864-2967-7
    softcover : 50# alkaline paper ∞

    1. World War, 1939–1945—Underground movements—Albania. 2. Albania—History—Axis occupation, 1939–1944. 3. Anti-Nazi movement—Albania. 4. United States. Office of Strategic Services—History. I. Title. II. Title: Office of Strategic Services in World War Two Albania. III. Title: Office of Strategic Services in World War 2 Albania.
D802.A38L78 2007
940.54'8673094965–dc22   2007006379

British Library cataloguing data are available

©2007 Peter Lucas. All rights reserved

No part of this book may be reproduced or transmitted in any form or by any means, electronic or mechanical, including photocopying or recording, or by any information storage and retrieval system, without permission in writing from the publisher.

On the cover (left to right): Enver Hoxha, Captain Tom Stefan, Dr. Omer Nishani, Helmës, Albania, August 1944 (National Archives)

Manufactured in the United States of America

McFarland & Company, Inc., Publishers
  Box 611, Jefferson, North Carolina 28640
    www.mcfarlandpub.com

To Madeleine, Maya and Ava

Acknowledgments

I would like to thank members of the OSS, especially Nick Kukich and Kostas "Gus" Routsis, for the help they gave me in writing this book. They helped me find OSS Captain Tom Stefan, the man I went looking for. Along the way, the two provided me with some important and wonderful stories about their experiences behind enemy lines in World War II Albania. I am also grateful for the help provided by OSS Captain James Hudson.

I need to give special thanks to Larry McDonald of the staff at the National Archives in College Park, Maryland. Larry expertly, and kindly, guided me through a maze of documents to get me where I needed to go in order to write this story. The road would have been much more difficult without his help, and I am grateful to him.

I must also thank my friends and companions in Albania—Edi Kortezi, Agim Prodani and Fatos Tarifa. I have had the good luck to have gone through many adventures in Albania with these three fine men. I could not have written this book without them.

Lastly, I must thank my long-suffering wife Paddy for putting up with me and Albania for longer than a long time.

Table of Contents

Acknowledgments	vii
Foreword by Fatos Tarifa	1
Preface	5
Note on Pronunciation	9
Key People and Organizations	11
1. Tank	15
2. Nick	38
3. Hudson	63
4. Tom	80
5. Nick, O'Keefe and Tom	104
6. North	120
7. Tirana	136
8. Victory	156
9. Home	184
Epilogue	196
Chapter Notes	199
Bibliography	205
Index	207

Foreword by Fatos Tarifa

This is an outstanding work and the first of its kind.

It is a breathtaking account of what took place in Albania during World War II. And it is objective. Not only is it extremely well documented, but it is also crosschecked with field work and long conversations with eyewitnesses to events.

The author is a veteran journalist, not an academic. Yet he has given us a history as it was not written before; a history as it was not known; a history that was not told, neither to Albanians nor Americans nor anyone else.

While several British authors (Anthony Quayle, Reginald Hibbert, Julian Amery, and David Smiley) have published books on the British presence in Albania during World War II, no American has. Lucas is the first. And his account is brilliant.

As of today, all that Albanians know about the role of the United States in Albania during World War II is primarily what a highly ideologized text on the history of the Labor [Communist] Party of Albania has said, and what has been written in the memoirs of Albania's communist dictator Enver Hoxha, published in 1982 under the title *The Anglo-American Threat to Albania.*

A book by Albanian scholar Arben Puto, *Through the Annals of British Diplomacy*, published in the mid–1980s in Tirana, made extensive use of archival documents of the Foreign Office, as did half a dozen of British authors who published their personal accounts. Lucas knows all of this, but he also reveals information that none of the other authors knew. And he does it with much accuracy.

Other writers, too, have portrayed Enver Hoxha and Mehmet Shehu, the two chief figures in Albania during World War II, but none has portrayed them more realistically and thoroughly than Peter Lucas in his *The OSS in World War II Albania*. His descriptions combine both the accuracy of thousands of papers of original documents that are preserved in the National Archives of the United States, and with the personal accounts by individuals who knew Hoxha and Shehu during the war, individuals he has interviewed.

Lucas catches the reader with the caves at Seaview along the Karaburun Peninsula where the first U.S. mission of men from the Office of Strategic Services (OSS) first set foot. He then takes us through Italian Fascist and Nazi occupied territories of Southern Albania and through towns and villages whose people were stringently divided on both sides of the war. On one side were the Reds (the Communist Partisans) fighting the Italian army and the Nazi invaders, while at the same time fighting those who collaborated with them, the Balli Kombëtar and the Legaliteti. Further, Lucas takes us to Communist Partisan headquarters, to Labinot and Çermenikë, to towns and cities that were just liberated (Përmet and Berat), and to where the Albanian Communists laid the foundations of Albania's post-war government.

Later Lucas leads us to the most remarkable event of the anti–Fascist war in Albania, the liberation of its capital city Tirana, engaging us cogently as well as emotionally in the dramatic and joyful atmosphere of those days. Following the liberation of Albania, Lucas's story finally and naturally leads us to what Albania became under Hoxha's communist rule. He does this first by telling us why and how Hoxha's relations with the OSS mission in Albania deteriorated, and then by describing in a realistic manner the way in which Hoxha's Communist Party–led National Liberation Movement transformed itself into a political force that established a communist dictatorship in Albania. The tragedy is that Hoxha's National Liberation Movement, which had fought the Nazi occupation in alliance with the United States and Great Britain, ended up be coming what it had fought against.

Lucas's book starts with just one man, the first American OSS Secret Intelligence officer who landed in Albania on November 18, 1943, and goes on to describe how the entire mission of some twenty-five men was built during the course of the war. His last pages tell us about the brief stint of the United States diplomatic mission in Tirana after the war, a mission that was forced to leave Albania shortly after the war ended, leaving the two nations with no diplomatic ties for forty-five years.

Lucas takes no sides. Instead he tells a mesmerizing story about how the United States' OSS mission performed its task in an extremely hostile and complex environment. It is beyond a black and white picture, to be sure.

Lucas is an investigator. He carefully collects all the pieces of the puzzle—individual stories, episodes, historical events, archival records, old photographs, written accounts, oral histories—and brings them all together. His account unveils a mystery and discovers the truth, which has not been told until this account. He explores a rich gallery of characters acting in various settings and in a variety of circumstances brought about by the war. And he makes a number of points:

First, Americans did not want to take sides in the civil war, the war within the war, that took place in Albania during the Nazi occupation. The Americans, however, were inclined to support those who were willing to fight the Nazis. This turned out to be the communists. Of the five OSS Secret Intelligence units that were sent to Albania from November 1943 to the end of the war, all were eventually attached to the Communist Partisans since the communists clearly were the only resistance group in Albania determined to fight the Nazis.

Second, Enver Hoxha and his Communist Partisans had different goals from the British and, later, the Americans. The Allies had a war against the Germans to win. Hoxha also had a war against the Germans to win. But he also had a civil war against the Balli Kombëtar and the Legaliteti to fight at the same time. Hoxha wanted to fight his war on his terms, and not the terms of the British or the Americans. Hoxha tolerated the Americans. But he hated the British and never trusted them.

Third, Albania and the Balkans historically came under the British sphere of influence. The United States was the junior partner in the British/American Balkan coalition. However, at no time did the American OSS mission in Albania come under the command of the British. Although the men of the OSS frequently cooperated with their British counterparts in the Special Office Executive (SOE), they often also competed with each other over the gathering of intelligence. Hoxha, meanwhile, skillfully played one group off against the other.

Fourth, Enver Hoxha was a politician who successfully used his combative instincts to fight intra-party battles leading to his control of the Communist Party of Albania. Whether through cunning, vituperation or plain outright backstabbing, Hoxha was able to out maneuver all of his opponents in the battle for power and rule for forty-five years. He understood from the beginning that the man who controlled the Communist Party controlled the army, and whoever controlled the army controlled the country.

Lucas captures the story.

I know of no foreign writer—let alone any American writer—who has more knowledge about Albania or who has spent more time in Albania than Lucas. *The OSS in World War II Albania* speaks of that deep understanding and experience.

Fatos Tarifa
Former Ambassador of Albania
to the United States
Washington, D.C.

Preface

This is the previously untold story of the secret operation of the American OSS (Office of Strategic Services) in Albania during World War II, and how the United States—along with the British—helped the Communists defeat the Nazis and take over the country.

Made up of a handful of resourceful officers and some thirty enlisted men (many of them Albanian immigrants), the OSS successfully infiltrated its men into Albania at night, crossing the Nazi-patrolled Adriatic Sea on captured Italian torpedo boats and fishing vessels. There they operated out of coastal caves along the isolated Karaburun Peninsula, dodging German patrols before joining forces with the only Albanian resistance group willing to fight the Nazis—the Communist Partisans.

It was this OSS mission that, along with the British, helped Enver Hoxha and his Communist Partisans defeat the Nazis and liberate the country. The Americans and the British supplied Hoxha with weapons, food, intelligence, fighting men and advisors. They called in air strikes to help Hoxha's forces, and fought with the Partisans when the need arose. Despite the fact that Hoxha worshiped Soviet dictator Joseph Stalin and the Soviet Union, the Soviets failed to provide the Partisans with any military assistance throughout the war. Yet this lack of material support did little to diminish Hoxha's admiration of Stalin.

Although the Allied operation (minus the Soviets) was a success, it later proved to be an embarrassment to the United States because the American-supported Communist victory emboldened Hoxha to turn his back on the west, seek a Cold War alliance with Stalin, and establish a diabolical police state in Albania that lasted for close to fifty years. After the war the OSS mission was classified and forgotten.

While Hoxha launched a guerrilla war against the Nazis, he also fought a civil war against the nationalist Balli Kombëtar, a war he won. After its defeat, Hoxha executed many of its members, while others fled to Italy and the United States, where they were welcomed as anti-Communist freedom fighters. That the Balli Kombëtar collaborated with the Nazis was somehow forgotten. Given the anti-Communist climate of the times following the war, it was enough that these Nazi collaborators had fought the Communists, the very Communists that the United States had previously supported.

One of the aims of the United States and its Allies was to keep the several German divisions in and around Albania under constant Partisan attack so that they could not be sent as reinforcements against the Allies who were battling the Germans up the boot of Italy. Another goal was to keep the Germans off balance with the possibility of an Allied invasion along the Albanian coast. This the British did well, as its Long Range Desert Group (LRDG) launched raids along the Albanian coast as well as inland. A third challenge was the rescue of downed Allied airmen forced to bail out of their damaged planes returning from bombing raids on the oil fields of Romania.

Little is known about these events in Albania or in the United States. Records of the OSS, which later became the Central Intelligence Agency (CIA), did not start to become public until 1975 when the CIA began turning them over to the National Archives and Records Administration. In Albania Hoxha destroyed all evidence that did not enhance his role or the role of the Albanian Communist Party. He had the American OSS written out of his vitriolic, revisionist history of the war. And he ridiculed the role of the British. Hoxha disliked Americans, but he hated the British. Although several British officers who played important roles in Albania published books about their experiences, they too generally wrote the Americans out of the story. Hoxha, upon assuming power, rid himself of the Americans and the British. He turned Albania into a vast prison. No one could get out and no one could get in. In 1986, a year after Hoxha died, I became the first American journalist to visit Albania in thirty years.

Although there are many fine books about the OSS in World War II, this is the first book about the OSS operation in Albania. It is also the first book to tell the story about what the OSS did in Albania to help Enver Hoxha and the Partisans win the war against the Nazis in that country.

Throughout the secret mission, American OSS officers like Captain Thomas E. Stefan of New Hampshire, who spoke Albanian, and Marine Corps. Lt. Nick Kukich of Ohio, who was fluent in Serbian, worked with Enver Hoxha during the most crucial months of Hoxha's war against the

Germans. These men, along with OSS Capt. James Hudson, another most able officer, set up a series of intelligence rings that provided the Allies with priceless information about the Germans. These men also crossed paths with American actor Sterling Hayden, an OSS Marine Corps captain who piloted schooners from Italy to the Balkan coast, and Major Anthony Quayle, the British actor, who shared a cave with the Americans.

Captain Stefan, who was born of Albanian immigrant parents and could speak Hoxha's Tosk dialect of Albanian, got to know the Communist dictator better than anyone else. The British, whose relations with the Americans remained testy throughout the Albanian campaign, resented his closeness to Hoxha. The high point of Stefan's military career came when he marched into Tirana with Hoxha after the city was liberated in November 1944. Stefan's life after the war was an unhappy one and he died in sad circumstances.

Much of the material for this book comes from many trips to Albania, where I interviewed aging Partisans who had fought with Hoxha, as well as witnesses to events that took place during the war. I have visited scores of villages like Dukat, Tragjas, Borsh, Dhermi, Kuç, Himarë, and others where many events took place. I have been over the Dajti Mountain up to the rugged Çermenikë where Hoxha was almost captured by the Germans. I have traveled in northern Albania from Shkoder up to Boga and the isolated mountain village of Thethi. I have been up and down the Karaburun Peninsula, both by land and by sea. I have been in the caves known as Seaview along the coast that the OSS occupied, as well as to Grama Bay. I have spent time at the Xhelil Çela's farmhouse along the coastal road that the OSS used as a safe house, and have driven the coastal road from one end of Albania to the other. I have followed the routes the Partisans took in their pursuit of the enemy and have lingered in cities like Saranda, Vlora, Përmet, Korcë, Berat, Gjirokaster, Tirana, Elbasan, Peshkopi, Pogradec and elsewhere. I have ridden by donkey up though the mountains of southern Albania where Hoxha made his headquarters.

In Tirana I was able to access information from the National Library and the National Museum of History and was fortunate enough to obtain a copy of General Mehmet Shehu's *Lufta për Çlirimin e Tiranës* (*The Battle for the Liberation of Tirana*), Shehu's first-hand account of the battle that has yet to be translated from Albanian. Access to the Boston Public Library provided me with microfilmed copies of several Albanian-American newspapers that were published in Boston in the decades leading up to World War II and after. My research took me to the Laconia Public Library in New Hampshire, the Museum of World War II in Natick, Massachusetts, the Massachusetts State House Library, as well as to the archives of the *Boston Globe* and the *Boston Herald*, having worked at both newspapers.

This book could not have been written without access to the records of the OSS at the National Archives at College Park, Maryland. There in boxes upon boxes were thousands of first-hand reports and documents sent by OSS agents in Albania to Harry T. Fultz, head of the OSS Albanian Desk at headquarters in Bari, Italy. Much of this material is quoted in the book. I also relied heavily on in-person interviews with the few of the OSS men still alive. One key source of many interviews, both at his home in Delaware, by phone and on the Internet, was Nick Kukich, who served with Stefan and was on hand with General Shehu at the Battle of Tirana. Another important source was Kostas "Gus" Routsis, who I interviewed at his home in Naples, Florida, as well as many times over the telephone and by mail. Routsis and his late brother George were radio operators who worked with Hudson and Stefan. Both Kukich and Routsis were not only generous with their time, but both provided me with pictures as well as documents. I also interviewed Semeon Simallari, another radio operator, at his home in Wayland, Massachusetts, and talked with Hudson over the Internet.

These men and the Albanians who worked with them—some at the cost of their lives—deserve to have their story told. I consider myself lucky to be the person to tell it.

Note on Pronunciation

In Albanian the letters "xh" are pronounced as a "j" as in the name Jason or Jeff. Thus first names like Xhavil and Xhevit are pronounced as Javil and Jevit. Enver Hoxha's last name would sound like Hoja, or Hodja. In addition, the letter "x" in Albanian is also pronounced like a "j," only harder. Koçi Xoxe's last name would be pronounced Joe-Gee.

Various Albanian cities, like Vlora, Durrës and Shkodra, were given different names by the Italians. The Italians called Vlora Valona, called Durrës Durrazzo and called Shkodra Scutari. I have used the names of these cities interchangeably in this book, as did the people at the time.

Key People and Organizations

Americans

Harry T. Fultz, code name Gates or *Plak* ("Old Man" in Albanian), was the civilian head of the OSS Albanian Desk in Bari, Italy. Fultz, an expert on Albania, had run the Albanian Vocational School (known as the Fultz School) in Albania, before the war. He was well respected and knew the Albanian leaders, many of whom had attended his school.

Dale McAdoo, code name Tank, led the first OSS Special Intelligence mission to Albania, setting up headquarters in a coastal cave called Seaview. He was a civilian with the equivalent rank of major. He became friendly with SOE Major Anthony Quayle, the British actor.

Captain Thomas Stefan, code name Art, was chief of the OSS Mission in Albania. Born of Albanian immigrant parents in Laconia, New Hampshire, Stefan was fluent in Albanian. He became intimate with Enver Hoxha and was a key source of wartime intelligence for the OSS.

Captain James Hudson, code name Bill, made numerous forays into Albania. He collected intelligence pouches dropped off at secret coastal locations by OSS Albanian agent rings he helped set up.

Captain Sterling Hayden, known as John Hamilton, was a strikingly handsome and flamboyant actor who was also an expert seaman. Hayden, a U.S. Marine Corps officer, captained ships that crossed the Adriatic from Italy to Yugoslavia and Albania.

Lieutenant Nick Kukich, code name Galba, was a U.S. Marine Corps gunnery sergeant from a coal mining town in Ohio. He won a battlefield promotion to lieutenant in Albania. He spoke Serbian and was close to both Hoxha and General Mehmet Shehu.

Lieutenant John O'Keefe, code name Venol, was born in Lonoke, Arkansas. O'Keefe parachuted into Albania and worked with Colonel Myslim Peza and General Shehu during the Battle of Tirana.

Master Sergeant Stephen Peters was an Albanian-born Harvard College graduate. He was a teacher and an intellectual who in 1945 filed a series of comprehensive OSS reports on Albania for the State Department.

Corporal Kostas "Gus" Routsis, along with his brother **George,** was born in Albania but reared in Middleton, Connecticut. Both were OSS radio operators fluent in Albanian and Greek, and both handled radio operations for Stefan at Hoxha's headquarters.

British

Brigadier E.F. "Trotsky" Davies, head of the British SOE (Special Operations Executive) Mission, was wounded during a firefight in the bitterly cold Albanian mountains. His capture by members of the collaborationist Balli Kombëtar in December 1943 dealt a serious blow to the British. Turned over to the Germans, Davies spent the rest of the war as a prisoner of war

Major Billy McLean was the first member of the SOE to enter Albania, in April 1943. McLean helped organize the Communist Partisans. Later he failed to get Abas Kupi and the Legaliteti to fight the Germans.

Major Anthony Quayle, a distinguished British actor, was the ranking SOE officer at the caves at Seaview. He went into Albania on the same schooner as Kukich. Quayle and Kukich did not get along. Quayle later wrote a novel about his Albanian experience.

Albanians

Enver Hoxha, the leader of the Communist movement in Albania, and commander in chief of the army, took over Albania in November 1944 following the liberation of his country. He was aided in his rise to power during World War II by both the British and the United States. He ruled Albania as a dictator until his death in 1985.

General Mehmet Shehu, a battle-hardened Communist, returned to Albania after fighting in the Spanish Civil War on the side of the Republicans. He quickly rose in the ranks of Hoxha's Communist army and became a top field commander. He was a graduate of Fultz's school and was fluent in English.

Ismail Carapizzi (Karapiçi) was an Albanian Communist from Vlora. He was hired by the OSS after he was freed from an Italian prison in Bari by the Allies. He became an important agent for the OSS until he was assassinated by a double agent on what the OSS believed were orders from Hoxha.

Xhelil Çela, an Albanian OSS agent, had a farm just over the Dukati Mountains from Seaview. His home, which was close to the coastal road, was a center of OSS and SOE agent activity. Çela was educated at the Fultz School and spoke English. He was later abandoned by the Allies and was murdered in Rome on Hoxha's orders.

Abas Kupi was a monarchist tribal chieftain who failed to fight the Germans, although he was supplied with arms and money by the British. Kupi, an anti–Communist, sought to husband his strength and take over the country. He was overrun by the Partisans and abandoned by the British. He fled to Italy.

Factions

Albanian Communist Party. The party was co-founded in Albania by Enver Hoxha, who united several party factions under his leadership. The party was nurtured by Yugoslav Communists sent to Albania by Tito. With the help of the Yugoslavs, Hoxha elbowed his way to the top position in the party.

Balli Kombëtar. The BK (National Front) was an anti–Communist nationalist organization that sought to take over the country. The BK collaborated with the German occupiers and fought the Communists in a civil war.

Legaliteti. The Legaliteti (Legality Party) was a collection of mostly northern mountain tribes that made up a third group that sought to take over Albania. Headed by Abas Kupi, the Legaliteti sought the return of King Amhed Zog, who had fled the country on the eve of the Italian invasion on Good Friday 1939. Despite the urging of Major McLean and a faction of the British SOE who sought to thwart the Communist takeover of the country, the Legaliteti failed to fight.

"If the American ladies would like to know what we have learned from our fathers, who learned it from their fathers and their fathers' fathers, I will speak. All these things are very old, and none of them are written in books, therefore they are true. I am an old man, and I have seen that when men go down to the cities to learn what is in the books they come back scorning the wisdom of their fathers and remembering nothing of it, and they speak foolishly, words which do not agree with one another. But the things that a man knows because he has seen them, the things he considers while he walks on the trails and while he sits by the fires, these things are not many, but they are sound. Then when a man is lonely he puts words to these things and the words become a song, and the song stays as it was said, in the memories of those who hear it."

—Albanian shepherd in the mountains of Thethi, 1921.
Told to Rose Wilder Land in *Peaks of Shala*.

1

Tank

Despite the code name Tank and the cover name Major S.S. Kendall—and despite the fact that he was a *civilian*—Dale McAdoo led the first American OSS Secret Intelligence mission into Albania on November 18, 1943.[1]

His landing place was a deep, water-level cave called Seaview on the desolate, wind-swept coast of Albania, a place uninhabited except for occasional herdsmen and, of course, German patrols. The cave was at the elbow end of the Karaburun Peninsula, which juts out into the Adriatic Sea like a thumbs-up. It was one of many caves that dotted the shoreline. The Karaburun was also deserted, but there were a series of German guns there dug into the mountains that faced the sea and sky waiting for an Allied invasion in force that would never come. The Germans did not know that. But they did know that the Allies were fighting their way up the boot of Italy just across the water. Anything was possible.

The Karaburun ran from the German-occupied island of Sazan off the coast of Vlora down to the Llogara Pass in the south. Crossing from Italy by boat at night, as McAdoo did, the mountains loomed black and ominous. There were German mines everywhere.

The Americans were far from the first foreigners to sail along the uncharted coast of ancient Albania, or to set foot on the timeworn land. The Albanians were descended from the Illyrians who first populated the land thousands of years earlier. Their language, stemming from the Indo-European, was among the oldest still-spoken tongues in the world. The ancient Greeks had sailed along the coast and used the same caves, carving their thoughts into the stones. The Romans conquered the Illyrians and made Albania a province. Caesar and Pompey fought over the Roman Empire along the coast at Durrës and later at Pharsalus in 48 B.C.

ITALY AND THE BALKANS

George Castrioti, known as Skanderbeg, Albania's national hero, fought off the Turks of the Ottoman Empire for twenty-five years before he was overwhelmed and died of a fever in 1468. Born in the mountain fortress of Kruja in Albania, Skanderbeg was raised as a Muslim and a janissary in the Ottoman army. Although a highly successful military leader for the Turks, Skanderbeg deserted and returned to his Roman Catholic roots in Kruja to lead the Albanian resistance against his former lords. When he died he had been named a Champion of Christendom by Pope Nicholas V and celebrated by other popes for warding off the Turks from further conquests in the west.

Following Skanderbeg's death, thousands of his Albanian Roman Catholic followers sought sanctuary in Italy, settling in scores of villages in the south and Sicily. They were known as *arbëreshë*, Italians of Albanian descent. They continued their Albanian customs and language for hundreds of years.

The Turks of the Ottoman Empire came into Albania and stayed for five hundred years, cutting the small country away from its natural European neighbors and turning it into a Muslim enclave, at least on the surface. Albanians have never been known to take religion, any religion, seriously. Roman Catholicism and Greek Orthodoxy survived in a sea of Islam, at least until the Communists arrived and abolished all religions outright. *The religion of Albania is Albania* is a common phrase used by Albanians to describe religion in their country. What the Turks did succeed in doing was to hold Albania back from European political, cultural, religious and material development that the rest of Western Europe experienced. The Ottoman Empire invaded, took over an undeveloped country, and made sure it stayed undeveloped for hundreds of years.

Albania, with the assent of the Great Powers, declared its shaky independence from the remnants of the sick Ottoman Empire in 1912. A provisional government was set up in Vlora, but the country was unable to defend itself from itself, let alone from foreign enemies. The Great Powers named German Prince William of Wied, an idle army officer, as head of state of the New Kingdom of Albania. Wied, along with his family, arrived in Durrës on March 7, 1914, just after he posed for a full-length portrait in London that was featured in the *Illustrated London News*. Prince Wied, after six baffling months of trying to bring order to a country enmeshed in conspiracy and anarchy, and with the outbreak of World War I on hand, quit Albania and went home to Germany. It is perhaps not an understatement to say that the prince probably found war in the trenches in France preferable to peace in Albania. He never returned.

Although Albania was technically neutral during the 1914–1918 war, it was either invaded or occupied by troops from Serbia, Greece, Italy, Austria and France. It emerged as an independent country at the end of the war, thanks to President Woodrow Wilson, but its size had shrunk to its present borders. It had a brief fling with democracy in 1924 when Fan Noli, a left-leaning Orthodox bishop, headed the government. The Harvard-educated Noli left Albania for the United States after he was overthrown by Amhed Zog in 1924. Zog named himself king in 1928 and ruled until he too fled after the Italian invasion on April 7, 1939.

Although Albanian governments may have changed from time to time, and princes, presidents and kings came and went, little changed for the majority of the Albanian people. They simply remained the poorest people in Europe. In their wake the Turks left illiteracy, hunger and poverty.

With McAdoo on this mission of the Office of Strategic Services (OSS) were Pvt. Don Orahood, an OSS radio operator, and Ismail Carapizzi, an Albanian guide and interpreter, who lived in Italy. The Allies had freed Carapizzi, 40, a Communist, from an Italian prison after he had served

five years of a life sentence. He had been put behind bars for his role in a plot designed to assassinate Italian dictator Benito Mussolini. Carapizzi, who was from Vlora (called Valona by the Italians), was earlier forced to flee Albania as a result of his Communist Party activities. He was a man of various abilities. Fluent in Serbian, French and Italian, Carapizzi worked in Bari as a carpenter. In that capacity he built a podium for an event that was to feature Mussolini. The Italian carabinieri arrested Carapizzi after it was discovered that the podium contained enough explosives to kill not only Mussolini, but also everyone around him. His only regret was that the bomb did not go off. Upon his release from prison he was recruited by the OSS.[2]

McAdoo and Carapizzi became close. Using paid Albanians and a few Germans as spies and sources, Carapizzi set up an effective intelligence system along the western region of Albania for the OSS. Carapizzi paid his informers in money supplied by McAdoo and the OSS. When he was murdered, McAdoo blamed himself for his death and never seemed to get over it.[3]

McAdoo, who was also fluent in Italian, had been studying art and opera in Italy before the war. He returned to the United States just before the war began and was recruited by the newly formed OSS. Obviously from a well-to-do family who could afford to have him study abroad, McAdoo also had an apartment in Manhattan. There he entertained his OSS friends with cocktails and his classical phonograph records.[4]

One of those friends was Max Corvo, an OSS agent of Italian heritage who was charged with recruiting anti–Fascist leaders in New York for eventual help in Allied operations in Sicily and Italy. "Dale McAdoo participated in some of the meetings because he was acquainted with some of those who had left Italy in the late 1930s as a result of the 1938 anti–Jewish laws promulgated by Mussolini after he consolidated his alliance with Hitler," Corvo wrote. "McAdoo should have played a more important role in the work of the Italian section, but essentially he loved to conduct highly philosophical discussions over cocktails and was primarily a student of events. He was a civilian and wanted to retain his civilian status."[5]

"That's why McAdoo and Tony [British actor and SOE Major Anthony Quayle] got along so beautifully," said OSS Lt. Nick Kukich, who lived with both men in the caves at Seaview. "They both loved to talk, tell stories and drink."[6] The SOE was the Special Operations Executive, Britain's wartime agency charged with sabotage and stirring resistance in enemy-occupied territory.

Seaview was where McAdoo, Orahood and Carapizzi landed on that dark night after heading out from Bari hours before on a British MTB (motor torpedo boat). The site was one of a series of well-hidden caves that faced the sea. The caves, which had served as safe haven for pirates and smugglers for centuries, were carved deeply in the steep cliffs. They were difficult to find and difficult to get to even when found, either by land or sea.

The mountains came down to the sea in most places and the caves were embedded into the bottom of the mountains. The closest road was

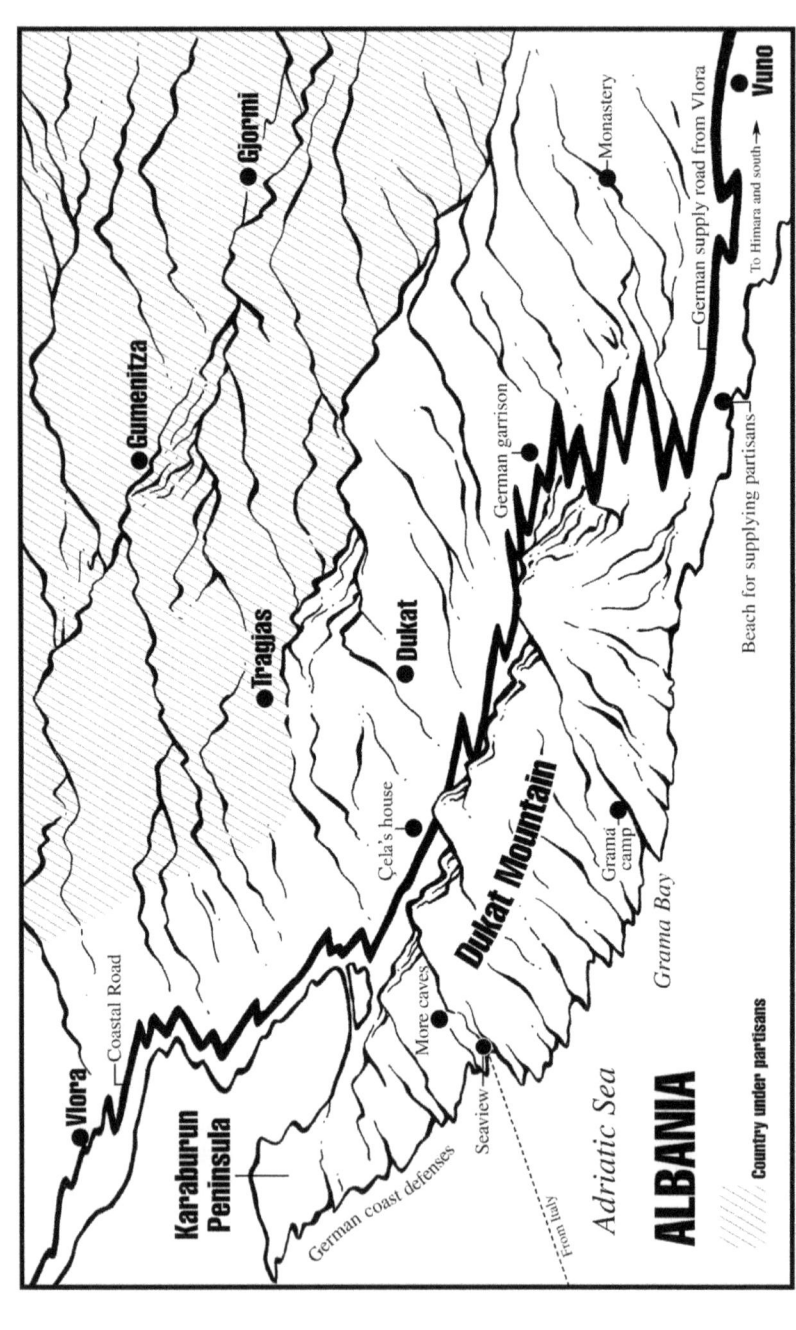

the inland coastal road that ran from Saranda in the south to Vlora in the north. The Germans used the road to transport troops and material to and from Greece. It took six to eight hours of tough mountain climbing to get to caves from the road. Frequently herdsmen—the few hardy souls who lived near the barren and remote region—would bring their grazing sheep and goats to the higher caves for shelter during severe weather. Named Seaview by the British, the Albanians called the main cave the "Cave of the She Bears," although no one seemed to know why.

Further up the coast toward the island of Sazan was another cave called Shpella e Haxhi Alië—the Cave of Haxhi Alia, a 14th-century Albanian pirate. Albanian legend had it that Haxhi Alia preyed on ships from Italy and the Ottoman Empire from his headquarters at the caves and used many of the deeper caves to store his booty. Although this cave would have been ideal for the Allies, it proved to be too close to the German garrison at Sazan.

Waiting for them at the cave this night was British SOE Major Gerry Field, who had been initially charged with setting up the base at Seaview. He held a lantern. The ship stopped well away from the shoreline and the rocks. The men rowed directly into the cave after leaving the MTB even though there was a small sandy strip of beach to the right of the cave. They did not see it in the dark. The cave was of such height that the men could all stand on a slab of granite by the side of the mouth of the cave. To the right were entrances into the deeper recesses of the cave.

Major Field had become disillusioned with the Albanians and his assignment and would be evacuated after wounding himself with a hand grenade.[7] He had been fishing with it. Reginald Hibbert wrote, "He [Field] was living in desperately hard circumstances in a cave, cold and very short of food, in an area devastated by German drives against the Partisans [Communists] and by mutual fighting between Partisans and Ballists [pro German Balli Kombëtar]. Field had become so allergic to both Partisans and Ballists that he would not allow Albanians near him and lived in his poverty surrounded by Italian soldiers who hoped to escape to Italy."[8]

Major Field was not the only British officer who was driven half mad by the Albanians, or held them in contempt. The ever-class-conscious Major Quayle had disdain for them as well. In his report on his return from Seaview to Italy he wrote: "In the village [Dukat] and valley lives a quite illiterate shepherd population with a sprinkling of educated leaders. In the mountains live shepherds only. I cannot adequately describe the ignorance, avariciousness, decadence, and lack of patriotism and, in short, utter baseness of these people. They are the legatees of long years of inbreeding, lack of education and foreign—particularly Turkish—occupation. We are robbed, swindled, cheated and chiseled on every occasion. The shepherds have no sense of patriotism. To them we are the same as the Germans—someone to make money out of. The only difference is that they are afraid of the Germans. They would give us away without any hesitation if threatened by the Huns, yet it is impossible to find a hiding place in this mountain which they will not know about within 30 minutes."[9]

Neither the Americans, nor the British landing ahead of them, had any initial understanding about the complicated military and political situation that faced them in Albania. For one thing, the Germans made frequent use of the coastal road and had troops stationed in Vlora to the north, Saranda in the south, and Dukat and the Llogara Pass in between. In addition, the Balli Kombëtar (National Front), the pro–German right-wing nationalist group that opposed the Communist Partisans, controlled the region. This meant that any attempt by the OSS to contact the Partisans had to go through territory controlled by the Ballists, Balli, or BK, as they were known, and the BK was now locked in a life and death civil war with the Partisans.

While some Balli members cooperated with the Allies out of conviction, most did so only for money. For pay they provided McAdoo and the British SOE with guides, guards and information, but they refused to attack the Germans. For the BK, the Communist Partisans were the real enemy, not the Germans. At stake was who would control the country once the Germans left.

It was somewhat ironic that Tank McAdoo should have been leading this American foray into German-occupied territory in the first place. His job, working out of Cairo, had been to seek out and recruit Albanian expatriates for the OSS, train them as radio operators, and infiltrate them back into their homeland. He had not been very successful.

McAdoo arrived in Cairo in June 1943, a month before the Allied invasion of Sicily on July 10. His job was to find Albanians willing to return to their country and fight. Although he scoured the region he had little to show for his efforts and he could only stand by and await the arrival of American OSS agents, including Americanized Albanian immigrants, who were being recruited and trained in the United States.

The Office of Strategic Services, the forerunner of the Central Intelligence Agency (CIA), was formed in June 1942, and William J. "Wild Bill" Donovan, a World War I Medal of Honor winner, became its first director. Among its various units were Special Operations (SO), which conducted guerrilla operations, Secret Intelligence (SI), which controlled agent operations and gathered information; and the Maritime Unit (MU), which, in the case of Albania, ran boats from Italy to the Albanian coast. Even upon its creation, it was forecast that the new, well-financed agency would have problems with the British. And so it did.

"The slow maturing of inter–Allied cooperation had several causes," the OSS reported. "British intelligence services had their own operations and plans to protect and feared that working too closely with the inexperienced Americans would jeopardize the safety of their operatives in occupied Europe. This British caution kept the Americans in the awkward status of junior partners for much of the war."[10]

The SOE—Special Operations Executive—was the agency of the British government, created in July 1940, that was charged with fomenting resistance in Europe and elsewhere. Its aim was to establish behind-the-lines guerrilla and subversive warfare.

OSS plans called for the establishment of an SI (Secret Intelligence) base in Albania by November 1943. However, realization of those plans appeared doubtful. McAdoo simply could not find any Albanian recruits in Egypt or in the region, and those American OSS recruits being trained as radio operators in the United States would not arrive in Cairo in time. In the end he would set up the OSS base himself.

The British, meanwhile, also operating out of Cairo, were regularly dropping members of its SOE into Albania, Yugoslavia and elsewhere in the Balkans. As a matter of fact, members of the SOE were already in Albania meeting with resistance leaders before the United States could even get into the Balkan intelligence business. By the time Tank McAdoo landed on the Albanian coast, fresh from the newly established OSS base in Bari, Italy, the British had already trained and attempted to lead the Albanian guerrillas into battle against the Italians and the newly arrived Germans.

The Albanian Section of the OSS left Cairo and set up headquarters in Bari, as did the British SOE. The base at Bari was established shortly after the Allies landed on the mainland in September and made their way up the boot of Italy. The OSS contingent in Bari came under the 2677th Regiment of the U.S. Army, which covered the Balkans. Harry T. Fultz, a combat veteran of World War I, and a civilian with a solid understanding of Albania, headed the Albanian Section.

Although they worked together most of the time, the roles of the SOE and the OSS in Albania were different. The SOE had the leading role in the country, where it was initially charged with arming and training any resistance group. Increasingly this came to mean the Communist Partisans, which turned out to be the only resistance group willing to fight the Germans. The BK and the Legaliteti, which was the third resistance group, ended up either collaborating with the Germans or sitting out the war waiting to see which side would win. The Legaliteti favored the return of King

Ahmed Zog. All three groups sought to take over the country once the Germans left. The difference was that the Communists were willing to fight with the Allies against the occupiers, when it served their interest. Still, they were willing to fight and die for their cause. Their cause was revolution and change. The BK and the Legaliteti wanted to protect the status quo. They were opposed to change. In the end the BK collaborated with the German occupiers in a quisling government, and fought with the Germans against the Partisans. The Legaliteti ended up fighting no one.

In one winter combat action, the BK attacked a British SOE group, seriously wounding and capturing the commanding general, Brigadier E.F. "Trotsky" Davies. The Albanians proudly turned Davies over to the Germans in Tirana. Davies spent the rest of the war in a German POW camp.

Not only did the British provide arms and ammunition (much of it American) and training to the Partisans, the British were also active in the fighting. The SOE blew up bridges, called in Allied air strikes and set up ambushes. The British sent in its combat-hardened Long Range Desert Group (LRDG), fresh from combat success in North Africa, to attack German formations. The SOE gathered intelligence as well, but it was its military activity that made life difficult for the Germans. While much of its time was spent training, arming and persuading the Partisan resistance groups to attack, the SOE wasted little time in attacking on its own. This was often done without the knowledge of Enver Hoxha, the Communist Partisan leader, which strained relations between the Partisans and the British.

The Secret Intelligence Unit of the OSS had the job of gathering intelligence and rescuing downed Allied airmen. These airmen were the crews who flew the long and dangerous bombing mission from Italy to the oil fields in Ploesti, Romania. Many times they were forced to bail out of shot-up planes over Yugoslavia or Albania on the way back to Italy. The OSS found them and brought them to the Albanian coast, where they were put on boats for Italy. The OSS did not engage in combat with the Germans unless forced to do so. Unlike SOE operations, there were no combat forays into Albania by Special Operations (SO) Units of the OSS. The only Special Operations mission by the OSS in Albania involved the rescue of a planeload of American nurses, medical technicians and crewmen who crash-landed in a remote area of Albania in 1943. Like other rescued Americans, these nurses and technicians also passed through Seaview.

The main concern of the OSS was to establish liaison with the resistance, gather information and report on the fighting and maneuvers of German divisions assigned to Albania. The Allies feared that these divisions could be sent to Italy as reinforcements.

The OSS had problems with the British from the start. Who would be in charge in Albania? Would it be the British, because of their experience, or the brash Americans, the newcomers? Kermit Roosevelt, the chief OSS historian, said it was early on decided that no Special Operations (SO) combat units would be sent into Albania. This would be left to the SOE, as would the problem of supply. Five OSS Secret Intelligence (SI) units were sent to Albania, however, the first being the mission headed by McAdoo. All were eventually attached to the Communist Partisans since they ended up doing the fighting and controlled most of the country.

The United States and the British, in effect, decided to support the Communists even though it was understood that Communist Party leader Enver Hoxha worshiped Joseph Stalin and that the Communists would take over the country once the Germans left. This was not a policy that pleased many, but it was the only policy that made sense at the time, or so it seemed. The plan to throw Allied support behind the Communists was controversial among the British, and remained so for many years. It was hardly mentioned in the United States. Unlike the American debate that raged after the war over "Who lost China?" nobody seemed to care about "Who lost Albania?"

But before the battle over which resistance group the Allies were going to support was decided, the skirmish between the British and the Americans over who was in charge in Albania had to first be settled.

Roosevelt wrote: "The British SOE mission in Albania had refused to cooperate with OSS agents, unless they accepted British command and used British communications. The three men [in the McAdoo mission] therefore, with Communist FNC help [Fronti Nacional Çlirimtar, National Liberation Front] established themselves independently in a cave by the sea."[11] There the men, with the help of Carapizzi, "built up a network of agents and by January 1944 were radioing German battle order, economic information and intelligence on the strength of the rival guerrilla groups." Roosevelt was also critical of the support the British provided for the Americans in Albania. "Support of U.S. teams by the Balkan Air Force [British] was unreliable throughout."[12] The OSS sought to overcome this problem by dropping its own supplies to its teams in the field. These drops were mainly successful even though supplies were frequently stolen by the Partisans or by the British SOE, according to OSS agents.

Fultz, in an order to his men in Albania in April 1944, spelled out the relationship with the British. "Our dealings with the British must be as frank as we can make them even though at times we may assume that they are not entirely frank with us. Our relationship must be such that it is obvious to the Albanians in particular that we are Allies and that we are working together. While they have had much more experience in the field than we have had I think we do not need to yield to them on that score at all. We can more than hold our own with them in communications, in the intelligence which we can send in."

Later in the same message Fultz added that the general order under which the OSS operated made it clear "that American SI is not under the command "of the British Special Operations Executive. We work with them, liaise with them and in some instances they are expected to work for us but we are not responsible to them."[13]

Albania and the Balkans during this period in time came under the British sphere of influence. The United States clearly was the junior partner. Early on in the war British Prime Minister Winston Churchill persuaded President Roosevelt that the British should maintain the upper hand in Albania and the Balkans and that the newly formed OSS should be subservient to the SOE. Although OSS Chief William Donovan agreed to the policy, he later had a change of mind. After all, it was the U.S. that was supplying the most resources in men and materiel to the war effort. In the end the OSS in Albania kept its independence from the British, using its own radio communications to relay back to OSS headquarters its own information. Frequently the OSS and the SOE worked together. At other times they competed with each other. Often Enver Hoxha played one group off against the other.

One key difference in the approach of the OSS and the SOE was language. As strange as it may seem, no one in the British SOE in Albania could speak Albanian. Although several British officers picked up a smattering of the language by the end of the war, none could speak it fluently. Nor did the British seek out any Albanians living in Great Britain or elsewhere who could join their forces in Albania. Some Albanian leaders could speak English, having learned it at the American Vocational School. Others could speak Italian, French, Greek, Serbian or German. But by and large, the English officers were at a disadvantage and had to rely on Albanian interpreters. Even if they had an interpreter, their words, in the highly charged political atmosphere of Albania, were often misinterpreted with serious consequences. Although he was fluent in French, Hoxha insisted on speaking Albanian whenever he met with the British SOE and the American OSS.

The OSS, in contrast to the British, made an effort to seek out and enlist Albanian immigrants in the United States who could speak Albanian and could serve as interpreters and radio operators. In addition, the OSS had something of a secret weapon when it came to dealing with Enver Hoxha and the Partisan leaders. This was Captain Thomas E. Stefan of Laconia, New Hampshire. Stefan, born in the United States of Albanian immigrant parents, was fluent in Albanian and would prove—to the chagrin of the British—to be a valuable asset to the OSS.

But in the beginning Albania was strictly a British show.

In April 1943, Maj. Billy McLean, Captain David Smiley and Lieutenant Garry Duffy, all members of the SOE, walked uninvited into Albania from Greece, where they had landed by parachute. They carried with them machine guns and bags of gold. Their mission was to meet up with leaders of any guerrilla groups willing to fight the Italians or Germans.[14]

What the members of the first British SOE mission unexpectedly found was a rudimentary, untrained volunteer Communist army stashed away in the rugged hills of Southern Albania. In June, McLean and Smiley traveled north to Labinot, near Elbasan, to meet with Enver Hoxha, the leader of this new Communist army. Hoxha, ever suspicious of foreigners, did not welcome his British visitors warmly.

The Communist Party in Albania was formed in November 1941 following the Italian invasion of Albania. The world shrugged as Italian dictator Benito Mussolini, the new Roman emperor, directed his forces to overrun the country on April 7, 1939. It was Good Friday. King Amhed Zog, the self-appointed Albanian monarch, shamelessly fled the country with his wife, his newborn son, his bodyguard and all the treasure he could take with him. He decided to watch the fighting in his country from a distance. Zog and his party settled in London for the duration of the war. He never came back.

By the close of 1941, Enver Hoxha, a long-time admirer of Joseph Stalin, headed the Albanian Communist Party. He and his fellow Communists organized resistance groups in the hills—as did other anti–Italian groups—and began to harass the Italian occupiers. It was at this point that Hoxha called for a conference of all Albanian resistance leaders in order to unite and form a common front against the Italians. The meeting, which attracted Albanians intent on opposing the Italian occupation, was dominated by Hoxha and the Communists. Out of this conference, held in the village of Peza, just southwest of Tirana, in September 1942, came the creation of the Fronti Nacional Çlirimtar (FNC). sometimes referred to as the Lëvizja Nacional Çlirimtar (LNC). In either case it was the National Liberation Movement. Headed by Hoxha, the LNC became the temporary umbrella group of the resistance movement.

Meanwhile, leading Albanian right-wingers, establishment politicians and conservative tribal chiefs from the north, met several months after the creation of the LNC to form their own organization, the Balli Kombëtar (National Front). These Albanians, nationalists all, hoped to serve as a political-counter movement to the Communist-dominated LNC. At about this time the third resistance group, the Legaliteti or Zogist Party, was set up. It was made up of northern tribal leaders and headed by Abas Kupi, an illiterate tribal leader and friend of Zog who had led a brief delaying action against the Italian invasion at the port of Durrës. Unlike the BK, Abas Kupi wanted King Zog to return to power. Hoxha simply wanted Zog dead.

Although they were all nationalists, the two groups—the BK and Legaliteti on one side—and Hoxha and the Communists on the other—differed both geographically and politically. Albania is divided into two parts separated by the Shkumbini River. The Communists tended to come from south of the river. They were Tosks and spoke the Tosk dialect of Albanian. The leaders were generally better educated and worldlier, living close to Greece and having studied abroad.

Their religion, if they had one, was Eastern Orthodox or Islam. They believed in Communism. They wanted to create a socialist state, like the Soviet Union. They were Reds.

The Balli or BK was made up of Tirana businessmen, landowners, intellectuals and some conservative tribal leaders. The Legaliteti were all men of the mountains of northern Albania, men who lived in tribal settings and who were fiercely independent. The men of the Legaliteti were Ghegs, as were some of the BK, and spoke a harsher sounding version of the Albanian language. They were Roman Catholic, family oriented, tribal and conservative. Both groups hated and feared the Communists, as well they should have. Enver Hoxha was a shrewd organizer who never wavered from his goal of dominating the resistance. Hoxha knew that the center of Albania, which contained the capital Tirana, was, like the Albanian soul, up for grabs. And he was willing to fight for it.

An OSS report of the fighting at the time noted Partisan activity:

"During the first nine months of 1943 the Partisans were very active against the Axis (Italians and Germans), containing about five Italian divisions and later two and a half German divisions, attacking convoys, liberating whole areas, capturing several small towns, and driving the Axis into the larger towns and on to the main roads. The Balli, although numerically as strong as the LNC, were unable to develop their organization so rapidly and started losing influence."[15]

The Italian occupation of Albania in 1939 would be the beginning of Mussolini's inevitable downfall. Mussolini, intent on showing Hitler that he too could play the role of conqueror, invaded Greece from Albania in October 1940 and was soundly defeated. The underestimated Greek Army mauled Mussolini's soldiers and chased the Italians back into Albania, where Albanian resistance groups waited. Early guerrilla attacks on the

Italians increased after Mussolini's armies were thrown out of Greece in 1941. Mussolini was only saved from further embarrassment when Hitler invaded and conquered both Yugoslavia and Greece in April 1941.

At that fateful June 1943 meeting of the British with Hoxha and fellow LNC leaders Baba Faja, a Bektashi leader, and Myslim Peza, a resistance leader, in Labinot, McLean told the Communist leaders that the British would airdrop weapons, explosives, food, clothing and boots to his newly formed 1st Partisan Brigade. To Hoxha's disgust, MacLean also informed him that Allied supplies would also be provided to the BK and Abas Kupi, who, the British understood at the time, were also resisting the occupation.

Hoxha, 35 years old in 1943, took an immediate dislike to McLean. The SOE officer, Hoxha wrote years later, "seemed quite young, no more than 30 years of age, slim, not short, rather tall, with very regular features, and a cold, intelligent clean shaven face. He was fair-haired, with intelligent blue eyes, with the look of a savage cat about them."[16]

Hoxha, who hated the British, flew into a rage, according to his memoirs, disgusted that the British would provide supplies to his Albanian enemies. The BK, Hoxha told McLean, "do not fight the Italians, but are organizing for war against us. The only 'war' they wage is against the roast chickens and lambs which they steal from the suffering peasants."[17]

"In general," wrote Julian Amery, who served in Albania with the SOE, "they [McLean and Smiley] found the leaders of the LNC often slow to co-operate and always suspicious of British intentions. Indeed, every time McLean gave support to the Balli Kombëtar in their operations against the Italians he found himself accused by Enver Hoja [sic] of deliberately seeking to strengthen reactionary elements in Albania. Nor could he escape coming to the conclusion that the Communist leaders were more interested in eliminating their rivals and seizing political power after the war than in the immediate task of killing Italians."[18]

Still, the Partisans did fight and kill Italians and Germans and they would have continued to fight them even if the British were not on hand to provide supplies and help in training. Often the British officers, coming from a totally different military culture—and having different war plans—disparaged the fighting ability of the Partisans. Both Smiley and Kemp wrote about their disgust when Gen. Mehmet Shehu prematurely pulled his 1st Partisan Brigade away from an ambush of Germans that they had set up on a road outside of Korcë. However, there was more to it than that, as Smiley would later note. "At the time we attributed this fiasco to rank cowardice. In fairness to Shehu, however, who was a brave man, and to the Partisans themselves, we did not then know that Shehu had received a directive ordering him not to fight the Germans or Italians, but to preserve his brigade in readiness for fights with their political opponents that lay ahead."[19]

Kemp saw it the same way: "We reached Panarit the following afternoon, where we found McLean and Smiley, very despondent over the failure of the Brigade to put up a fight after all the training and armament it had received. I tried to comfort them by pointing out that a month's training was hardly enough to turn a rabble of peasants and artisans into disciplined soldiers who could be expected to stand up to shelling; that by trying to fight 'brigade actions' the Partisans were only sacrificing their natural advantages of mobility and knowledge of the country, in order to meet the enemy on his own ground where his superior training and armament were bound to tell; finally that they would do better for the moment to confine themselves to small, carefully planned 'bullying' actions, dispersing whenever the enemy concentrated against them.

"There was, of course, one point that was not yet apparent to me: Enver Hoxha and Mehmet Shehu were not building up their military formations in order to fight Germans or Italians, but in order to gain control of Albania for themselves by force; they were not going to risk serious losses in operations which to them were only of secondary importance."[20]

Hoxha saw things differently. To him the Allies—particularly the British—were in Albania to thwart his plans and to support the reactionaries. To him the Anglo-Americans were capitalists who opposed Communism and were determined to dictate to the Albanian people who would run the country after the war. Hoxha was not only a true-believing Communist, he was an ardent nationalist as well. In addition, Hoxha bitterly resented it when the SOE conducted its own operations against the Germans without his knowledge and without any apparent concern about German retaliation. The innocent civilian hostages taken and killed by the Germans were not British; they were Albanians. The villages razed and torched were not British villages; they were Albanian villages.

"Wherever they went, especially when they carried out 'actions,' when they blew up bridges or roads, they carelessly left behind them such things as cigarette packets, meat tins and so on, branded Made in England, so that the occupiers [Germans] would understand that the authors were British and pursue them," Hoxha later wrote. The British, he said, would leave "quite unconcerned that villages were burnt and reprisals carried out against the population in the zones where they operated."[21]

Enver Hoxha and his Communist Partisans had different goals than the British and, later, the Americans. The Allies had a war against the Germans to win in Europe. Hoxha also had a war against the Germans to fight. But he also had a civil war against the BK and the Legaliteti to wage at the same time. Hoxha wanted to fight his war on his terms, and not the terms of the British or the Americans. Hoxha did not and would not fight for the British—if he could help it—even though the British were there advising him, training his troops, dropping him arms—and taking casualities.

An OSS agent, touring southern Albania in August 1944, filed this report on the Partisans: "The Albanian Partisan is by nature a fierce, unafraid fellow. The feeling of each man is this: 'Let the Allies supply us and we will clear the Germans out of our land. Give us heavy weapons to combat their heavy weapons and we ask no more. This is our battle. We want no Allied troops. We know how to fight the enemy.'"[22]

The British found that they had stepped into the middle of a chaotic three-sided civil war they could not prevent or control, as well as a war against the Germans. The weapons they supplied the three groups of guerillas to fight the Italians and Germans were regularly used by the three to fight one another.

In July and August another six British SOE officers, along with radio operators and NCOs with paramilitary training, were parachuted in to McLean and Smiley at their headquarters in Shtyllë in Southern Albania. Among these officers were Major Field, who was sent to the Albanian coast and the Seaview base, and Majors Bill Tilman and Peter Kemp, both of whom would write books about their Albanian experience, as would Smiley.

By mid–August 1943 the Communist Party of Albania (CPA) paraded its first organized military unit—the 800-member 1st Brigade—largely equipped and trained by the British. Its commander was Mehmet Shehu, a Communist who had fought in Spain, who would become the leading military figure in the war in Albania. Enver Hoxha, of course, would emerge as the CPA political leader as well as the commander in chief of the armed forces.

Peter Kemp vividly described the 1st Brigade, now armed with weapons captured from the Germans and Italians in North Africa, in his memoirs. "The men were of every age from fifteen to sixty. Against a background of peasant misery or artisan squalor the contrast of this free life under arms in the mountains made a strong emotional appeal to each of them. They seemed fit, cheerful and enthusiastic; sitting around their campfires under the stars they would sing of their courage and endurance, the skill of their officers and the wisdom of their leaders. There were some girls among them, who carried rifles and dressed like the men and whose functions, we were repeatedly assured, were strictly confined to cooking, nursing and fighting. Dress varied from town or peasant clothes to uniforms captured from the Italians and British battle-dresses issued by Smiley. Officers, who wore no other insignia, were saluted with clenched fist and the Partisan slogan 'Vdekje Fashizmit! Liri Popullit!' ('Death to Fascism! Freedom to the people!')."[23]

Tilman, a free-spirited mountain climber in civilian life, was impressed by the rude and strict living conditions of the Partisans. "For immorality, theft, looting, or even failing to put into the common pool what had been captured from the enemy, the penalty was death. On one occasion five boys of Shepr who had found and sold some drugs, which had been picked up near the dropping ground long after they had been dropped, were sentenced to be shot. Only their youth and strenuous pleading of every family in the village saved them. And one afternoon, just before I left, three men were tried in Shepr, two for immorality and one for stealing cigarette papers from a comrade. The British officer who happened to arrive that day to relieve me had to step over their bodies lying in a lane by the church where they had been shot."[24]

The Communist-led Partisans had attacked and fought many small-scale guerrilla battles with the Italian army of occupation before the British arrived. The British added supplies and savvy. Smiley described one such battle as he, separated from McNeil en route to Partisan headquarters, came across a group of partisans planning to attack a battalion of Italians in Leskovik, near the Greek border. While holding the Italians in their barracks with constant fire, the Partisans were able to launch three successful ambushes on Italian relief columns.

"I had a fine ringside seat of the ambush carried out on the Italian column from Korcë. As soon as the convoy rounded a bend they were halted by a roadblock made from rocks and boulders rolled onto the road; a murderous fire was opened on them from all sides, and I could see the Italians leaping out of their lorries to try to take cover, and several were hit and fell. The Partisans captured much equipment, and four machine guns and thirteen prisoners, whom they shot out of hand."[25]

The Italians, forced back into Albania by the Greeks, faced increasing hit-and-run attacks from various newly formed Albanian guerrilla bands. The Italians retaliated by burning villages and killing thousands of innocent peasants. Many non-combatants—men, women and children—were forced to flee into the mountains where they suffered from hunger and cold. This brutal Italian policy of retaliation, however, served mainly to swell the ranks of the guerrillas.

While Hoxha and the Partisans frequently blamed the British for bringing about German or Italian retribution, the Partisans caused much of the retribution themselves. The village of Borova just inside the Greek border in southern Albania was an example. The Partisans in early July 1943 attacked a column of Germans headed toward Greece in Barmash, a village just south of Ersekë. Many Germans were killed. A second German convoy then descended on the nearby village of Borova seeking retribution. The Germans killed the entire population and burned the village down. A total of 106 men, women, children and "cradle babies" were murdered in retaliation.[26]

America's need for information about the enemy in Albania grew increasingly acute when, following the Allied invasion of mainland Italy on September 8, 1943, the Italians surrendered and dropped out of the war.

The Italian government abandoned its army of occupation in Albania—some seven to eight divisions—and thousands of Italian soldiers were left to fend for themselves. The Albanian Partisans sought to capture and strip Italian soldiers of their weapons while various British officers worked to persuade Italian commanders to surrender their forces to them. The Germans, meanwhile, seeking to fill the void, moved troops in immediately to take over towns and villages that had been garrisoned by the Italians. These troops, from the 1st Mountain Division, the 297th Infantry Division and the Division Group Steyrer (composed of security battalions), poured into Albania from Greece and Yugoslavia in August and September 1943. The Germans from Greece occupied the southern half of Albania while the troops from Yugoslavia occupied the north.

Caught between the Partisans and the Germans, many Italian soldiers suffered greatly.

"Many Italians were led off into German captivity, many others drifted into a sort of serfdom in Albanian villages, many starved, all were demoralized," wrote Reginald Hibbert. "Only a small number, not more than 1,500, joined the Partisans and were formed into a battalion named after the Italian Communist Antonio Gramsci."[27] An untold number of Italians made their way to the Albanian coast, some ended up at the caves at Seaview, where they sought boat passage across the Adriatic Sea to Italy. One of these was Italian Gen. Adolfo Infante, former commander of the Pinerolo Division, who shared a cave with McAdoo and Marine Corps Sgt. Nick Kukich for weeks before he could be evacuated. Gen. Infante, later a military police commander in Rome, awarded Kukich with the Knight's Cross of the Order of the Crown medal for his wartime assistance.[28]

The British SOE and American OSS officers stationed at Seaview fed and housed the Italians with supplies sent in from Bari on OSS boats. They would then load as many Italians as they could on board for the ship's return to Italy. At other times the Italians were captured by roaming German patrols and forced to fight for the Germans, or were sent to Germany as slave labor. Still others drowned attempting to row out to the ships, or died of starvation or exposure, or both, in the unkind mountains of Albania. Several Italians died at Seaview and were buried in graves dug out of the hard, rocky soil.[29]

The OSS estimated that there were some 20,000 Italian soldiers set adrift in Albania, while some 1500 to 3,000 joined the Partisan army. Those were the fortunate ones. "However, the large majority of these soldiers who entered with Mussolini's invading army are wandering helpless all over Albania. They are to be found working in the fields, in mills, on roads and in cities, or starving in camps located near all the larger cities of the country. Most of the Italians look like scarecrows. They are dressed in what they can get—often with trousers having a hundred patches, with no shoes ... all are emaciated and a considerable number have grown too weak to work."[30]

Major Anthony Quayle, upon relieving Major Field at Seaview, described what he saw this way: "The plight of thousands of Italian soldiers in Albania was extreme.... The worst off were those who had hoped to join the Partisans; they had been relieved of their coats, uniforms, boots, weapons and ammunition; then they had been turned out into the mountains with a farewell burst of machine-gun fire. The Italians had been the oppressors for years, and the Partisans were not slow to take revenge. Even those who had merely run away were soon in great distress; they were treated by the peasants with contempt. Some were harnessed together like mules and for a daily handful of maize bread forced to drag the clumsy wooden ploughs. While they could stand, they were fed; when they were too feeble to work, they were turned loose to fend for themselves. Many of them died where they fell, beside the mountain tracks. How the survivors found their way to Seaview I do not know, but they did—some wounded, all with malaria."[31]

The Germans, meanwhile, launched a propaganda effort to persuade the Italians to surrender to them. They distributed leaflets printed in both Italian and German warning of dire consequences if the Italians fell into the hands of the Partisans. Italian soldiers and civilians were also urged by the Germans to turn themselves in for reparation back to Italy. "According to superior order," one leaflet issued in Italian and Albanian by the quisling mayor of the Vlora area said, "it is made known to all Italians living in the city or area of Vlora, who desire to return to their Fatherland, without reserve of fear to apply to the German Command of Vlora at the entrance of the right stairway of this Command."[32] Very few did, and those who did were whisked off to uncertain fates in Germany.

It was not as though Albania or neighboring Yugoslavia were major fields of battle for the Americans or the British during World War II. They were not. Although thousands of Italians, Germans and resistance fighters were killed during fierce guerrilla fighting, there were no major Allied set piece battles in either country. By August 1944 the OSS had only sixty agents in Yugoslavia assigned to either Communist leader Joseph Broz Tito or Nationalist Gen. Draza Mihailovic. In Greece there were fifteen OSS officers and one hundred and sixty enlisted men. In Albania the OSS had four SI teams—five officers and around 25 enlisted men—in the country, and these were assigned mainly to Enver Hoxha's Partisan Army. By the time the OSS arrived in Albania, Italy was out of the war and the BK was already fighting side by side with the Germans against the Partisans throughout most of the country. At first the OSS could operate along the Seaview coast with paid Balli members, but this only lasted until a German offensive forced them to leave the base for good. By this time the BK had already joined arms with the Germans.

What neither the British nor the Americans appreciated at the time was that in September 1943, a civil war in Albania had already broken out. Following the Italian decision to drop out of the war, the BK agreed to collaborate with the Germans. That left Abas Kupi's Legaliteti Party as the only anti–Communist resistance group left still perhaps willing to fight the Germans. The problem was that Kupi did not want to fight the Germans. Kupi wanted arms dropped to him before he would agree to attack the Germans. The British government wanted him to attack the Germans before it supplied him with arms. Both McLean and Smiley, with Kupi in the mountains of North Albania, pleaded with their government to support Kupi, the only hope left as an alternative to a Communist takeover of Albania. The British government, in a decision that is still debated, chose to support Enver Hoxha and his Communists over Kupi on the grounds that the Communist Partisans were the only group willing to fight the Germans. The United States followed the British lead.

By the time McAdoo arrived at Seaview on that cold November night, the man he wanted to see—British SOE Brigadier "Trotsky" Davies—was attempting to determine who the British should be supporting in the confusing and changing murky political and military situation. It was Davies' job as a senior officer to cut through the confusion. Davies was a determined, dogged individual, who operated under difficult circumstances. He met with leaders of all the Albanian factions. He did not like Enver Hoxha very much, nor did he trust him. But Hoxha had an organization, he had a cause, he had enthusiastic volunteers and he was fighting and killing Germans. To Davies, in the end, it became clear just whom the British should be supporting. It was Enver Hoxha and the Communists.

No sooner did he radio his decision to British headquarters than he ran into a Balli ambush in the cold December mountains of Biza and was captured. His recommendation was discarded. The nasty civil war would rage on and the British would inadvertently prolong it by continuing to support the BK. The British would eventually come around and support the Communists, but by then it was clear that Enver Hoxha was going to win anyway. He would not need the British. Hoxha would hate the British for the rest of his life.

Gen. Davies, after being treated for his wounds in a German hospital in Tirana, was flown to Belgrade and a prisoner of war camp several weeks later. Davies later wrote: "We had turned right-handed and were passing over the Abas Kupi country now. He had made no use of the four plane-loads of arms I had given him in November, although he had promised to attack the Germans as soon as we gave him arms. The sorties were arranged to try him out and take him at his word. He had said that if we gave him money he knew where to put his hand on ten thousand rifles [men], but we had not believed him—large quantities of arms do not remain unused in the Balkans. He was a genial old fox, but, in my opinion, he had no intention of fighting and weakening his side, and intended to sit on the fence until he was forced off it by events, hoping the Partisans would weaken themselves against the Germans to a point where he could defeat them. He would produce every excuse to avoid a fight. I had no faith in the Zogists or the Balli attacking the Germans. There was no danger of the Partisans collaborating with the Boche, and they would fight when it suited them to fight, though not nearly as often as they should have done.... I sighed to think what we could have achieved had the genuine will been there to fight to free Albania. There were too many political groups, too many people ready to let others do the fighting—everyone looking to the postwar political position. What they never seemed to realize was that if they failed to get experience fighting now they would be beaten by more experienced forces later. The Partisans were bound to come out on top."[33]

With Davies gone, McLean and Smiley, both strong anti–Communists, continued to seek support for Kupi. But Kupi became irrelevant as the Partisans marched toward victory. Once a proud tribal leader in the mountains of northern Albania, Kupi was abandoned by the British on a deserted Albanian beach up by Shëngjin in northern Albania where he had sought to escape the advancing Partisans.

Stranded by the British, Kupi and his small group commandeered a fishing boat and set sail for Italy just before the Partisans could capture him, put him on trial and shoot him, as they did with other political leaders who opposed them. Kupi was adrift for seven days before the British rescued him.

Tank McAdoo had no idea of any of this, or of the fact that Davies had been wounded and captured. He was never to make the trip inland anyway because a German offensive in the Dukat region kept him pinned down at Seaview and—perhaps more importantly—his main Albanian agent, and his friend, Ismail Carapizzi was murdered.

2

Nick

Nick Kukich had three goals in mind when he joined the U.S. Marine Corps in 1940. The first was to escape from the coal mines of Ohio. The second was to get away from the Depression. The third, and most important of the three, was to help provide for his hardworking but aging parents. He would do all three.

The Marines paid Nick $30 a month, every month. He got three meals a day, a place to sleep and a chance to see the world. Of that dollar-a-day wage, Nick sent $26 home each month to Stevo and Sima Kukich of Dilles Bottom, Ohio, a small mining town that had gone bust during the Depression. The other $4 Nick kept for himself.

Kukich was born in that company mining town of Serbian immigrant parents in 1916. His father worked in the mines along with other immigrant miners from Serbia, Russia, Croatia and Czechoslovakia. He went to high school in Dilles Bottom but did not get to finish. He quit after the first year to go work in the mines. The work was hard but the money was good—as long as the work lasted. The mines shut down in 1939 and Nick, after a stint in the Civilian Conservation Corps—President Franklin D. Roosevelt's job-providing workforce for unemployed young men—joined the Marines.

After boot camp in Parris Island, South Carolina, Nick was shipped to Puerto Rico. When World War II broke out he was sent to the Marine Naval Air Station in Quantico, Virginia. He was a gunnery sergeant in charge of base security when the base commander, a former FBI agent, discovered that Nick was fluent in Serbian. He recommended Nick to the OSS, which at the time was in search of men who could speak foreign languages. Kukich was six feet tall, weighed some 180 pounds and was a squared-away Marine. He was accepted by the OSS and went through a six-week course in intelligence gathering, small arms, explosives, hand-to-hand combat, survival skills, Morse code and radio transmission.

In October 1943 he was on a U.S. Army troopship with other fellow Marines headed for North Africa. One of these Marines on board the ship was Captain John Hamilton, the *nom de guerre* of Hollywood actor Sterling Hayden. Hayden, 27, was a strikingly handsome and charismatic man who was already famous, having starred in two 1941 Hollywood movies and married Hollywood star actress Madeleine Carroll, the leading lady in both of them.

The movies were *Virginia* and *Bahama Passage*, both romantic films released in 1941. Everyone saw the films because back in the pre-television thirties and forties everyone went to the movies. British actress Madeleine Carroll was beautiful and famous, and movie fans across the country were familiar with the rags-to-riches story of how Sterling Hayden had been "discovered" working on the Boston waterfront as a sailor and fisherman and turned into a Hollywood leading man. And he had married Madeleine Carroll just before joining the war effort and shipping overseas.

Sterling Hayden was born in Montclair, New Jersey in 1916, the same year as Kukich. He spent his boyhood summers in Gloucester, Massachusetts, where he learned to love the sea. His parents sent him to the exclusive Browne and Nichols School in Cambridge. There he captained the rowing crew that raced along the Charles River. His schooling was cut short because of financial difficulties and Hayden decided that his future lay at sea. He would become a seaman. He worked on fishing boats out of Gloucester that fished off George's Banks. He also twice sailed around the world and participated in sailing races.

Typical of what the Boston newspaper wrote about him then was a story in the *Boston Post*, October 8, 1938, on the eve of a Gloucester boat race. "Neat seamanship may decide the victor of the fishermen's races, but in masculine pulchritude, Sterling W. Hayden, 22, tall, blond, lithe and a born sea-rover wins by 100 fathoms over fellow members of the *Gertrude L. Thebaud* and those aboard the champion *Bluenose*. Good sailor and the looks of a movie idol—a rare combination aboard a fishing schooner where hard work and ruggedness is the keynote.... Hayden stands straight as a ramrod and is 6 feet 5 inches tall. His deeply tanned face sharply offsets his bright blond hair—the color of honey. He weighs close to 200 pounds and is without a surplus ounce of flesh on his muscular frame. Gleaming teeth and his ready smile complete the picture which caused more than a few of the scores of women who viewed both schooners at the Fish Pier yesterday to inquire as to his identity."

Hayden quickly became a legend among Boston newspapermen. He was well known along the Boston waterfront and in the port of Gloucester in the late thirties for his sailing prowess, his good looks, and his ability to drink with the best the waterfront had to offer, and this included newspaper reporters and photographers. Boston newspapermen who worked for the *Boston Traveler*, the *Boston Post*, the *Boston Herald*, and the *Boston Globe*, as well as the Associated Press, continued to run stories and pictures of Hayden when he participated in sailboat races or joined a crew for an around-the-world voyage.

The waterfront in the thirties was a major beat for the Boston newspapers. The papers covered the arrival and departure of luxury liners, cargo ships, schooners and yachts, as well as the men who sailed them. In the era before national and international air travel, the waterfront was big news.

Hayden at one point lived on T Wharf, one of many wharves that jutted out into Boston Harbor, in a loft owned by Lawrence O'Toole, a Boston artist and drinking buddy. There they hosted many parties for newspapermen, visiting seamen, stockbrokers, businessmen, unemployed freeloaders and any women that might be on hand.

It was at the loft that Hayden announced in November 1938 that he had been hired to sail a brig from Gloucester to Tahiti and needed to round out a crew. O'Toole was the first to volunteer. Art Hansen, a photographer for the *Boston Traveler*, was the second, announcing that he would take a leave of absence to make the voyage. The crew was rounded out when Tom Horgan of the Associated Press did a story on the adventure. Volunteers made their way to the wharf.

Both the *Boston Herald* and the *Boston Globe* ran stories about the adventure the day Hayden and his eleven-man crew set sail on November 23, 1938. The *Herald* story, that began on page one of the paper, said the ship left the pier "amid the cheers of 100 well-wishers. Capt. Sterling Hayden, 22, taking his first command, peered out from his altitude of 6 feet 4 and found a head wind facing him." The *Globe* story, which ran inside the paper, said, "Youngest and biggest of the ship's company is her skipper, Sterling Hayden, 22. A blond giant, who stands 6 feet 4 without his sea boots." Not to be outdone, the *Herald* two days later ran a laudatory editorial about the voyage and the skipper—"a salt-hardened lad of 22" who was leading eleven "ill-advised young men." "The sea can be not only a hard and brutal master, but a dull and boring one as well," the editorial said. "There is no money in its service, as any sailor will tell you. It means loneliness, laziness, lovelessness. But always—just beyond the eternal horizon—there lies a vision or an experience worth a king's ransom. Eleven visionary young men, without question. But what young man wouldn't be with them?"

Upon his return the *Boston Herald* ran still another editorial praising the men who made the voyage.

It was these young men, Hayden's friends and sailing companions, who persuaded Hayden to seek out Hollywood and the movies. These were the same men who, after all, had been the ones who promoted him as a potential movie star in the stories they wrote about him. Charlie Dixon, a retired *Boston Globe* photographer, was the brother of the late Jack Dixon, a well-known photographer for the *Boston American* and a friend of Hayden's. Charlie Dixon was on hand with a group at the T Wharf apartment when, after many drinks, the subject of Hollywood came up. "Sterling, you're a handsome bastard. You ought to be in the movies," Jack Dixon told Hayden, not for the first time.

Under O'Toole's direction, they wrote some twenty letters to Hollywood figures, making sure the letters contained pictures and stories about Hayden, pictures they had taken and stories they had written. The letters urged Hollywood film directors "to take a look at this Viking and sign him up before anybody else does," according to Hayden's 1963 autobiography *Wanderer*. Charlie Dixon, in a 2005 interview, said Tom Horgan of the AP even called Hollywood gossip columnist Louella Parsons, whom he knew, and asked her to use her considerable influence on Hayden's behalf. One of the letters found its way to movie director Edward W. Griffiths, who was about to make the film *Virginia*. Griffiths gave Hayden a screen test in New York and hired him. Overnight Hayden became a star.

But there was not much "Hollywood" about Hayden, nor would there ever be. He was an independent, rugged, hard-drinking free spirit of a man. Hollywood billed him as "the most beautiful man in the movies." Women gravitated toward him, as did men. Yet he hated Hollywood even though the movies paid him lavishly. He often "quit" Hollywood to rejoin his sailing buddies in Boston or in Gloucester. One time, according to Charlie Dixon, Hayden drove his Cadillac all the way from Hollywood to the Boston waterfront because he missed his friends. When he got there Hayden ripped off the California license plates on the Cadillac and threw the plates into Boston Harbor, vowing never to return to Hollywood.

After joining the Marines in 1942, partially to impress his new wife, Hayden found that he could not take the life of a Marine Corps enlisted man. After boot camp he went to officers' school. Hayden found the rigid discipline abhorrent. He also came to hate the celebrity status that went with his new fame as a movie star. He changed his name to John Hamilton and he pulled strings and won a place in the newly formed OSS.

Two months after disembarking from the troopship, Hayden was stationed at a sea base just south of Bari. There dozens of Italian MAS (Motorbarca Armata Svan) torpedo boats and fishing schooners were tied up to the docks. All had been confiscated by the Americans and the British and were being refitted and manned with new crews, mainly Serbian Communist Partisans. Their job was to smuggle men, arms and ammunition across the Adriatic Sea to Yugoslavia and Albania.

Two months after he left the troopship, Gunnery Sgt. Nick Kukich, 27, nickname Cooky, code name Galba, was aboard one of those Italian fishing vessels, renamed *Sea Maid*, headed toward the dark coast of Albania. The ship was one of many Italian boats, both military and commercial, that had been refitted by the Allies and immediately put to use. Once on board Nick found that he was sailing with yet another actor. This was SOE Major Anthony Quayle. Quayle, 30, had joined the British Army after giving up the leading role in *Henry V*, a role he had taken from Laurence Olivier in the Old Vic Tour in 1939. Quayle was an established Shakespearean actor by the time war broke out in Europe. He would not begin to make films until after the war.

The *Sea Maid* was a sixty-foot diesel engine fishing boat armed with two light machine guns. It was loaded with food and ammunition for the men at Seaview as well as the personal gear of the men it was escorting to shore. It had a crew of four, all dressed as Italian fishermen, and it flew the Italian flag. Quayle was to take over from the wounded British SOE Major Gerry Field after making sure that Field was safely transferred to the boat for the trip back to Bari and medical attention. Other than that Quayle's orders were vague. "I was to take over Field's job. Exactly what the job was there was no time to explain," Quayle later wrote. "I would have to find out when I got there. 'Do the best you can,' I was told. 'Send out all the intelligence you can, and make yourself a bloody nuisance to the Germans. But whatever you do, keep open the base at Seaview. It is vital.' That is all the briefing I got."[1]

Nick Kukich's job was clear. Among the conflicting roles of the SOE, MI5 (British counterintelligence) and the OSS, Kukich's assignment was to set up radio communications, gather and relay enemy intelligence, and help with the rescue of downed American airmen, including twenty-six American nurses and medical technicians, and a crew of four, whose plane had crash-landed in Albania in November. Word had it that they had been rescued by the Communist Partisans and were headed toward the coast. He had his orders and, as the first U.S. Marine to set foot on Albanian soil, he would carry them out. He dressed in a U.S. Army uniform but he wore proudly the insignia of the Marines. On his left upper arm he wore a patch of the American flag. He carried an M1 .30 carbine strapped to his back and had a .45 handgun taped to his right leg. Around his waist was a money belt stuffed with British sovereigns and French napoleons. These gold coins would be used to pay agents and buy intelligence.

The boat bounced around over rough waters. Quayle noted: "On the last day of 1943, there was a heavy swell at sea and the *Sea Maid* rolled and plunged like a pig. I was not sick but was so wretched that if an E-Boat [swift, well-armed German surface ship] had come up out of the darkness and attacked, I would have been glad to die."[2]

"It was a rough trip," Nick Kukich said. He felt that Quayle, whom he had just met, did not make for the best of traveling companions. Quayle was, after all, a British officer, aloof and snobbish. Kukich thought Quayle to be some sort of English aristocrat and he, after all, was a coal miner. "Quayle kept to himself. He was reserved. I knew he was an actor but I did not know much more than that. He was no Sterling Hayden. He worried about German planes spotting us. I suggested that if we were spotted we could put out the fishing nets and make out as though we were fishing. But we got there all right. It was New Year's Eve."[3]

It was the group's third attempt to make a landing. The first time the crew was forced to turn back because of German submarine activity. The second attempt failed when the crew could not make contact with Seaview. This time the landing was a success.

Crewmen from the anchored *Sea Maid* rowed Quayle and Kukich ashore along with Nick's radio and supplies. They found Tank McAdoo, Orahood, Carapizzi and a reception party around a bonfire on the small beach at the base of the cliffs beside Seaview. Field was lying on a stretcher near the fire under a blanket, being looked after by several Italians. The Italians waded into the water and unloaded the supplies. They lifted Field and put him in the dinghy. The crewmen pushed off and headed back to the *Sea Maid* with Field. He was the first to be put aboard the *Sea Maid* for the journey home.

Quayle did not like Seaview, the adjacent caves or the base. There were dozens of "scarecrows"—hungry Italian soldiers—sitting around the entrances of the caves. Inside the damp caves were filled with fleas, lice and dung left from the animals kept there by shepherds. Scorpions and other crawling things scattered. A pack of wolves had recently killed one of the party's mules. There were empty ammunition boxes in the main cave piled on top of one another that served as table and chairs. A few rifles hung from pegs while several Thompson submachine guns were placed against the walls. What looked to be a pile of dirty laundry or rags was a bed. The place smelled.

Ragged Italian soldiers followed Quayle and Kukich around, asking to be taken to the *Sea Maid*. McAdoo had the job of picking the Italians

Top: The cave at Seaview on the Karaburun Peninsula (author's photograph). *Bottom:* Inside Seaview. Left to right: Nick Kukich, Dale McAdoo, Albanian OSS agent Hodo Meto, and Italian General Adolfo Infante (courtesy Nick Kukich).

who were taken to the boat. Those who did not get to go shouted and cursed, but there was nothing they could do but wait for the next boat.

Tank McAdoo, Carapizzi, plus two other Albanian agents had already set up a network of paid spies and informers. The two Albanian spies were Xhelil Çela and Hodo Meto. Çela's family owned a farm just over the Dukati Mountains from Seaview close to the coastal road. Meto, a teacher, also had roots in the Dukati region. Both spoke Italian and English. The network of informers they established ran from the village of Dukat along the coastal road up to Vlora on the coast, and even into the capital of Tirana. Carapizzi and Çela had more than a dozen Albanian agents in the field collecting information about the Germans and the collaborationist Balli government that the Germans had set up in Tirana, Vlora and elsewhere in the country.

The agents collected Albanian-language newspapers published by the Germans and the quisling Albanian government, as well as leaflets and propaganda put out by German headquarters. The agents monitored the disintegration of the Italian Army and the subsequent arrival and stationing of German troops. They provided information about Allied bombing and strafing attacks and—not infrequently—the strafing of innocent civilians along the roads. Carapizzi and Çela gathered these reports and brought them to McAdoo at Seaview. Information that was not immediately radioed to Bari was stored in pouches and sent to Bari when a supply boat arrived. The same boat carried rescued Allied airmen and Italian soldiers back to Italy.

It was from such documents that the men at Seaview eventually learned of the capture of Gen. Davies. A German leaflet picked up weeks after his capture gave them the story, at least the German version of it. Davies, the Albanian language leaflet said, "was harried into fighting in the Martanesh region during German operations there." The Martanesh region, a Partisan stronghold east of Tirana, was where Davies had his headquarters in a village called Biza. The Germans, the leaflet said, were "assisted by the brave men of Aziz Biçaku's" squad. Biçaku was a Balli commander. "After bitter fighting lasting many hours, the General was gravely wounded by Biçaku and together with his entourage were captured and handed over to German troops. A part of his staff fell into German hands on 25 December 1943. With this the English command in Albania was wiped out."[4]

This German offensive shattered Enver Hoxha's headquarters in the region. It was a major setback for the Communists. The Germans and the Balli had nearly captured Hoxha, who had been with Davies the day before, as well. Hoxha had been in the region for the inauguration of the

2nd Partisan Brigade. "The Partisans were ill-clothed, ill-shod and poorly fed, but their weapons, although diverse, were well cared for and they had with them an Italian unit with four mountain guns."[5] Hoxha repeatedly berated the British for not sending him enough supplies.

Davies several times tried to persuade Hoxha to escape the German December offensive by heading south. By the time Hoxha, Davies and their staffs began the journey south, it was too late. The Shkumbini River flooded and could not be crossed. Also, a bridge Hoxha planned to use for the crossing had been blown up by Smiley. This simply served to add fuel to Hoxha's burning hatred of the British.

The group retreated back into the unforgiving Çermenikë Mountains. The weather turned bitterly cold. Hoxha suggested that the British and Partisans split into two groups for easier feeding until he could figure out a way to escape the German offensive. Hoxha refused to heed Davies' recommendations that a smaller party attempt the move south.

Their situation worsened. The two leaders finally decided that it would be safer if their two groups split up. The day after Hoxha parted company with Davies, the general and his staff were attacked near the mountain village of Kostenjë by a force of some 200 Balli soldiers led by several German officers. The British attempted to escape into nearby woods but Davies was hit by gunfire, twice in the stomach and once in the leg. An Italian colonel who had been traveling with them was shot in the neck. The British made their way to a peasant's hut where the Balli surrounded them. Davies surrendered. Aziz Biçaku and the Balli had captured themselves a British general. The following day a German patrol took Davies and those captured with him down from the mountain to a waiting ambulance. Standing there with his BK squad was Biçaku, the man who had captured them. Davies said, "He stood there laughing with the Germans beside my stretcher before I was lifted up into the ambulance."[6] It was a major propaganda victory for the Balli and the Germans. It was a major embarrassment for the British.

Lt. Col. Arthur Nichols, Davies' chief of staff, managed to escape the ambush but died several days later from frostbite and gangrene. After enduring several days of exposure in the cold mountains, Nichols had made his way to a doctor in Tirana, but by then it was too late. Thus, in one stroke, the Germans and their Balli allies had put the two top British commanders in Albania out of action.

Hoxha and his staff fled deeper into the mountains. The effectiveness of the German offensive appeared to have caught Hoxha by surprise. The Germans and the Balli shattered his newly inaugurated 2nd Partisan Brigade and nearly put an end to the entire Partisan movement as well. It certainly ended, for the time being at least, any serious Partisan activity in central and northern Albania. Hoxha, in his later memoirs, painted a grim picture of his suffering Partisans. The image of his ragged, frozen and hungry troops leaving bloodstained footprints in the snow stayed with Hoxha for many years.

Reginald Hibbert, who served in Albania with the SOE, wrote about the event: "It looks as though Enver Hoxha must have lived a fugitive life in Çermenikë for most of January until rescued towards the end of the month by Mehmet Shehu's northward thrust, and that this thrust or march by at least two battalions of the 1st Brigade was a memorable exploit by the Partisan army's core unit."[7]

Hoxha was later to rewrite Partisan history and downplay the "long march" by Shehu that saved him from potential capture, making it appear that it was all part of his plan to break out by himself with his own forces and meet up with Shehu. "But at the beginning of 1944 the LNC had been shattered and dispersed as a political and military force north of the River Shkumbini. Action switched to the south."[8]

It was in the south that the Partisans began to rebuild their strength. And while they did, they were aided by information that came in to Seaview from its OSS agents in the field. In a February 1944 message, typical of the sort of information that came in, Carapizzi's spies noted the defense fortifications at the Tirana Airport. "Three AA machine guns in extreme North-West corner of field, among ruins and rubbish of what is thought to be the most recent Allied bombing. About twenty-five meters in from the Tirana-Durazzo Road, and about seventy meters from the right of East edge of the airport, an AA gun; twelve meters away is a quadrangular underground shelter, apparently for gasoline."[9]

The Allies bombed Tirana Airport several times, causing many civilian casualties. Allied planes also strafed Albanian roads used by civilians. Not only did the Balli government complain about the apparently indiscriminate bombing and strafing, so did the Partisans.

The Tirana newspaper *Bashkimi i Kombit* (*The Union of the Nation*), the official newspaper of the pro–German government, bitterly complained about the killing of innocent civilians. In its April 27, 1944 edition, sent to the OSS, the paper accused the Allies of killing Tirana schoolchildren. "It is also true that on other occasions your aviators have taken the lives of innocent workmen and villagers, flying low over the roads of Durrës, Kavaja, Valona, Shkodra and other cities, proving to the world that you do not specialize only in killing children. In this unfortunate Tirana, you Gentlemen have appeared conspicuously on market day, when the villagers come to town to purchase a kilo of salt or one lek worth of pepper. Their corpses, together with the corpses of horses and donkeys, were left on the streets and gutters, while you Gentlemen flew back to your bases, naturally to get a refreshing drink of whiskey, having completed your high mission, and reported the happiness you brought to the unfortunate people."

The article went on: "Never in history has this small nation of ours destroyed your homes or killed your women, children and unborn children. Not a single Albanian has dropped bombs on your city, but many Albanians have died and are dying for your war aims, Gentlemen."

On May 14 the paper accused the Allies of strafing buses carrying civilians as well as private cars along Albania roads. "Bravo: You have hunted military objectives: you have killed 10 unarmed and unprotected Albanians. This is not becoming great Allied warriors. This terror is not the least bit honorable, but releases on your heads all the bitter curses of Albanian mothers, wives and sisters whom you are bereaving."[10]

The Albanian complaints did not fall on deaf ears. Hardly had the newspaper published its charges when the OSS denied them. The OSS accused the "quislings" of the central Albanian government and the Germans of having troops on the vehicles and of attempting to "disguise these facts."[11]

But the charges were serious enough for Philip Adams, chief of the Albanian Desk in the State Department, to get involved. Adams, an old hand at the State Department, and an expert on Albania, expressed his concern about the "needless slaughter" of Albanian civilians to Fultz in a July 19, 1944 letter. Adams, a descendant of John Quincy Adams, with some foresight, wrote: "Let us not forget that the weakening of the minimum privileges and exemptions enjoyed by civilians may some day be a source of desolation to our own countrymen here in America, for the time is surely coming, when our own 'isolation,' (already a theoretic immunity) shall have ceased to exist owing to man's inventiveness."

Adams told the story of one of Mussolini's pilots who, "after dropping bombs on undefended Ethiopian villages, reported that he never had so much real sport in his whole life. In my opinion that's a state of mind to be avoided, even when retaliation in kind is unavoidable. I have hoped that our participation in this sector will emphasize the ideals for which America is fighting. If our men are true to those ideals the prestige of our country will not suffer in their hands, and we will enjoy the good will of all dissident groups there. I should be grievously disappointed if there is any loss or deterioration in the representative American character that we, one and all, are charged with."[12]

Even the die-hard Partisans realized the Allied destruction of their country and the killing of innocent civilians was harming them. After all, it was their country, and they would soon be running it. In a statement issued in June 1944 the Partisans attempted to put the bombing and strafing by the Allies in perspective. The destruction was the fault of the Germans, just as the Allies said it was. "Yesterday's bombing of Tirana by Allied planes, although they had specific targets, left a great number of Albanian victims," the statement said. "No one can say that it is in the interest of the Allies to inflict casualties or to harm the people who are fighting against the German invaders. But it is only natural that by attacking military objectives, which are in the hands of the invaders, the criminals of the people are in danger, also the civilian houses surrounding the targets. They are in danger because the Allies cannot allow the Hitlerite Germany to fortify positions and to hold aerodromes and depots in a strategic place such as Albania."[13]

Enver Hoxha, in his memoirs written and published years later, still bristled over the Allied bombings of Tirana. He accused the Allies—mainly the British—of "killing and wounding hundreds of residents and causing incalculable damage."[14]

The gathering of intelligence functioned well even as the situation for the McAdoo, Kukich and Quayle grew precarious. Agents in the field, once established, made the information available to whoever was working in the caves. If the caves were abandoned, as they were from time to time, arrangements were made for agents to place the information in pouches. The pouches were hidden in pre-arranged dropping-off points along the coast where they were picked up by the OSS agents and then taken to Bari.

One of these alternative dropping-off points was a second base set up by Quayle that was further south from Seaview. It was located at Grama Bay. To get there by land from Seaview took six to eight hours hiking over rugged terrain. Going by small boat took one hour. Because life at Seaview was so tense as a result of constant German patrols, Grama Bay or Sea Elephant, as it was called, served as an escape hatch. The bay, which was hidden from sight from the sea, was guarded by two rising cliffs that contained the narrow inlet. Once inside the inlet, the bay opened up and led to a pristine beach that was some eighty yards wide. The beach was surrounded on three sides by granite and marble cliffs upon which ancient Greek and Roman mariners and others had carved their names and their thoughts. Ancient sailors had dug handholds into the marble so they could climb the sides of the cliffs and make their carvings at even higher elevations. The water was deep close to the beach, which meant that supply ships could come in closer than at rocky Seaview.

Quayle described it this way: "A day's march south, towards Vuno but well inside Ballist country, I found the perfect bay—well-protected but

Looking out from the beach of Grama Bay, south of Seaview. The Allies moved here from Seaview following a German offensive. On the sides of the cliffs are carved ancient Illyrian and Greek inscriptions (author's photograph).

much bigger than Seaview. The entrance was three times wider and there was a good depth of water almost to the beach. The place was called Grama Bay. I recalled that *gramos* was Greek for 'a letter,' and there was some Ancient Greek lettering carved in a rock face near the sea—probably chiseled out centuries ago by sailors heading north into the Adriatic hoping to propitiate the gods of sea and wind."

After the base at Grama Bay was set up, the operatives of the OSS and SOE alternated between the two, depending on German activity. Many of the men preferred living at Grama Bay. Unlike Seaview, the men lived in the open in tents at Grama Bay and not in caves. When the weather was fair, and there were no Germans about, the atmosphere took on something of a holiday. Men swam in the clean, clear blue waters of the bay, or sunned themselves on the beach. Others marveled at the ancient inscriptions or picked up white ping pong ball–like stones along the shore, like sailors had no doubt done there many times during many centuries past. Skimming flat stones across the bay became a pastime.

The intelligence relayed to Bari indicated that the German Army in 1944 increasingly relied on foreign troops to fill its ranks. One report read:

"While all of the soldiers participating in the movement of troops along the Saranda-Valona road are in German uniforms, it is believed that the majority of the men are Armenians. A German NCO in charge of the detail guarding the Dukati section of the highway during this movement stated that all of the German troops originally in Greece and Albania are being moved to France and Italy, and that their places are being taken by other troops, such as Armenians, Rumanians and Bulgarians." Still other reports had the foreign troops surrendering to the partisans rather than fight for the Germans.

The mining of the beaches along Durrës, where the Germans feared an Allied landing in force, was contained in another intelligence report filed by an agent. "It is reported that 25,000 mines have been sown in this area. In the same area barbed wire defenses have been erected, and it is forbidden for anyone to enter this zone."[15]

The city of Vlora, like Durrës further north, was an important city for the Germans because of its commanding position along the coast. Vlora was also covered well by the agents that Carapizzi and Çela had enlisted. A sampling of reports showed constant Allied activity there. "The automobile of the Mayor of Valona (Vlora) was strafed near Scrofotina at 1700 hours on 13 May. The car was loaded with 18 tins of oil. While no one was killed or wounded in this attack, the oil was lost and the tires of the car were ruined."

During a raid five days later Allied planes "strafed the vehicle of the Harbor Master of Valona (Vlora), a German major, in the vicinity of the alcohol factory at Krionero. The German major was wounded in the forehead and his chauffeur was hit in the left arm. In the confusion caused by the strafing, two Communist prisoners who were being taken by the Germans for labor at Krionero, escaped. This escape caused a sensation because the prisoners are considered very dangerous.

"On the same day, in the course of bombing the oil pumping station at Scrofotina some damage was done to the barracks nearby and to the station. Two gypsies were killed.

"At the bridge over the Fojussa River no damage was done by the aircraft. However, beyond the bridge in the direction of Fieri, thirty solders were killed at Levan."[16]

While McAdoo and Kukich concentrated on gathering and sending intelligence, Quayle tried unsuccessfully to get the Balli, which controlled Dukat and the region, to agree to fight the Germans. Simultaneously he conducted forays through Balli-controlled territory to meet with Partisans who, unlike the Balli, were attacking the Germans whenever they could. Complicating matters still more was the fact that the Partisans and the Balli were fighting each other. And neither side trusted Quayle or the British.

The Allies were committed to providing arms and supplies to groups willing to fight the Germans. Quayle, Kukich and the others at Seaview could see that this increasingly meant the Communist Partisans. The problem facing the Allies in southern Albania was that in order to get substantial supplies inland to the Partisans the supplies had to come by boat to Seaview or Grama Bay or elsewhere along the coast. Then the supplies had to be carried by mule inland through Balli-controlled territory. The only alternative was to drop supplies by air. But the demand for Allied planes elsewhere, and the weather, made even limited drops difficult.

The sea was the only answer. The Balli controlled the coastal regions, however, and they would not let the supplies go through, or would confiscate them for their own use. Adding to Allied difficulties was the fact that the Allies at Seaview depended on the Balli for guards and early warning against German patrols.

Quayle wrote of a meeting he had with Balli leaders in the village of Dukat where he attempted to get them to fight the Germans. "They appreciated they were not helping the Allies with sabotage and ambushes, but they felt they were making a very real contribution by protecting Seaview, and concealing our presence from the Germans."[17]

The Balli, in addition, also cooperated in the rescue and evacuation of thirty Americans whose Dakota C-53 crash-landed in Albania on November 8, 1943. Aboard the plane were thirteen army flight nurses, thirteen army male medics, and a crew of four. It had been on its way to pick up and treat American wounded. The plane, originally headed for Bari from Catania, Sicily, hit a storm and ended up over Albania where it was apparently hit by German anti-aircraft fire over an air field in Lushnjë. The pilot managed to land the damaged plane on a dry lakebed near a remote village, between Elbsan and Berat, called Çestie. No sooner had the plane hit the ground than a contingent of Partisans on horseback appeared and rescued passengers and the crew.

The Partisans helped provide food and shelter for the Americans for days as they traveled from village to village in southern Albania, keeping a step ahead of the Germans. The trip took on aspects of a propaganda tour for the Partisans as they displayed the American "allies" to peasants in various villages. Eventually the Americans were turned over to the British SOE and, after more days of grueling travel and several German-dodging adventures, were escorted to the coast by SOE Lt. Gavan B. Duffy.

But the Americans still had to cross the dividing line between Partisan controlled territory and Balli territory, a crossing that was made even more difficult because of sporadic fighting between the Partisans and the Germans in the area. Capt. Lloyd G. Smith, a Special Operations officer in the OSS, was dispatched from Bari to meet the American party. Smith met up with Lt. Duffy and the Americans (minus three nurses who were holed up in Berat) in January. The delicate transfer of the Americans from the Partisans to the Balli was successful and, after a night spent in Dukat, the nurses were taken to Xhelil Çela's rambling home along the coastal road. There, after resting and obtaining fresh mules from Çela, the group made its way over the mountain to Seaview and to rescue by ship. They had been on the road for sixty days.[18]

Capt. Smith returned to Albania a month later to help evacuate the other three nurses who were hiding with a friendly family in Berat. He enlisted the help McAdoo, Quayle and Kukich. Together they enlisted the services of Hodo Meto and Xhelil Çela, both of whom had solid contacts in Berat. With well-spent pieces of gold the pair of Albanians were able to buy forged Albanian documents and clothes for the nurses. Smith also sent a letter to Midhat Frasheri, head of the collaborationist Albanian government, threatening reprisals if the nurses were harmed or inhibited from leaving Berat.

Once again an American party had to get through Partisan lines to get to the Balli-controlled coast. They again used Çela's safe house as a gathering point before climbing the mountains to Seaview. "The nurses were given the most comfortable cave to recuperate from their very tiring hike," Capt. Smith reported.[19]

Sometimes the Balli "protection" could turn deadly, even toward someone as seasoned in the ways of Albanian espionage, politics and life as Carapizzi. Carapizzi proved invaluable to both the Americans and the British. He was a lifelong Communist who wore the Partisan insignia on his cap, apparently to irritate other Albanians who were Balli, although he would remove it whenever he left the caves. He also had an American army uniform that he kept stored at Çela's house, changing into it whenever he crossed over the mountain to get to the caves. Despite his politics he was able to move through Balli lines in order to get to Vlora and Tirana where he picked up information about the Germans.

What kind of Communist was Carapizzi? Quayle, in his thinly-disguised 1945 novel about his World War II Albanian experience, *Eight Hours From England*, described a scene with Carapizzi (he used Carapizzi's real name) when he asked him about the Communist Partisans. "The agent's shrewd face broke into a smile when we asked him the question.

"'Partigani,' he repeated, laughing. He made a derogatory gesture with his hand. 'God damn!' he said with emphasis. They were the only two words of English that he knew and they made him laugh afresh.

"We told him to be serious, and he made an effort to stop laughing. 'But *they* are not serious,' he protested.

"'How do you mean?' I asked.

"'Major,' he said, 'for thirty years I have been a Communist, hein? For thirty years I have worked for the party. I tried to kill Mussolini, hein? Well, I tell you—of these Partisans I am ashamed. What are they...? Boys, irresponsible boys. What do they know of Communism...? Nothing. What do they do...? They make piggeries.' He was serious now, almost ridiculously serious. 'I am a Communist—yes.' He leaned forward, and with his finger tapped the machine-gun case. 'But I am not a terrorist.'

"'And are they?'

"The gesture he made in reply was eloquent."[20]

Kukich, who worked closely with him, said that Carapizzi had the "street smarts" needed to get along with anybody, although he tended to get careless at times. "He was certainly fearless, but he was also reckless."

He recalled that Carapizzi on several occasions sought permission to visit his mother in Vlora during one of his intelligence gathering missions. Kukich denied it, fearing that Carapizzi would get captured and then tortured for information. Nevertheless, Carapizzi would travel in disguise to his old neighborhood in hopes of seeing his mother from a distance.

"He came back one day and said that a friend told him that his mother had spotted him on the street in Vlora," Kukich recalled. "Carapizzi said his friend told him that his mother commented: 'He walks just like my son. But that can't be my son. My son is in jail in Italy.' I always felt bad, especially after he was killed, that I told him he couldn't see his mother."[21]

Kukich thought highly of Carapizzi. In a January 27, 1944 pouch-delivered letter to Fultz, which arrived in Bari only after Carapizzi had been killed, Kukich had nothing but praise for their top Albanian agent. "We need more men like Ismail," Kukich wrote. "I would go through hell and high water with him and the major [Tank McAdoo]. They're both really tops." Kukich added: "Ismail is getting a little careless. The major and I have called him on it and we explained it to him to be more careful in the future. He had a good one pulled on him by a guard in Tirana. While riding in a car this guard stops the car and asks Ismail for his pass. He pulls his pass out [and] hands it over to the guard. The guard replies, 'You read it to me. I can't read.'"[22]

The letter was written on the morning of the day that Carapizzi left Seaview for what turned out to be his last mission. Carapizzi had persuaded McAdoo that he needed to buy a car, an old Italian make that would get him from the coastal road by Dukat up to Vlora and Tirana. When not in use, he could hide the car in the barn at Çela's farm. The farm was about a mile from the road. Walking and hitching rides simply took too much time. It was also dangerous. McAdoo agreed.

McAdoo called a meeting at the main cave and dug out thirty British gold sovereigns from his cache of gold that he kept hidden there. The money was only for the car. Anything left over would go to an agent in Vlora. Carapizzi claimed he had cultivated a German officer and he wanted to give him money. So far Carapizzi had only given him American cigarettes, which he had readily taken without asking questions. Both Kukich and Quayle were at the meeting and witnessed McAdoo hand the gold sovereigns to Carapizzi. Carapizzi put the gold in a leather money belt he wore around his waist. Also at the meeting was a young Albanian from Dukat named Mysli Kali. Kali, 20, was one of the Balli guards paid by the Allies. His job this day was to accompany Carapizzi on the hike to Vlora, where the car was waiting, and protect him from robbers. Kukich did not like seeing McAdoo count out the gold sovereigns in front of the young Albanian guard. But there was nothing he could do about it.

The next morning Mysli Kali came back to Seaview alone. He said that he and Carapizzi had been ambushed and that Carapizzi had been killed. Carapizzi had been shot while he had been able to escape, Kali said. After hiding among rocks in the mountains for the night, Kali came back to make his report.

Led by Çela, the men found Carapizzi's naked body the next morning on a trail on the side of the mountain. He had been shot in the back and stabbed. One of the bullet holes was in the palm of his hand, which indicated that he had turned in a futile attempt to stop a shot with his hand. His clothes and shoes were gone, as well as the gold.

"I don't know how Carapizzi could have allowed the guard to get behind him," Kukich said. "He was much too savvy for that. I blamed Tank for giving him that money in front of the guard. He never should have done that."

The following day the men of Dukat came to Seaview and told McAdoo, Quayle and the others that an unrepentant Kali had been arrested. An eyewitness had come forward and refuted Kali's story. He said he had seen Kali shoot Carapizzi. They said they put Kali on trial in the village, found him guilty and sentenced him to death.

Quayle wrote: "That night the commander of the village guard, who was to carry out the execution, received a deputation from the family of the murderer—who numbered, what with uncles, brothers, cousins, nephews, some thirty men. These stated that if Mysli were not immediately released they would inform the Germans of the whereabouts of the British [and Americans] and of Dukat's relations with us. There is not the slightest doubt that this threat would have been put into effect. The village, therefore, shrugged its shoulders, released Mysli, and apologized to us, pointing out their helplessness."[23]

Xhelil Çela, who had translated for the villagers, was embarrassed over the decision of his Balli friends and neighbors to release Kali. "Where do you stand in all of this?" Quayle asked him when they returned to the caves. "'Major Queel,' he answered after a pause. 'Once I was very strong Ballist. Then one day I see men of my party shoulder to shoulder with Germans, fighting against other Albanians—against Partisans. I took the Ballist emblem from my hat and threw it on the ground. Since that day, I am nothing. Not Ballist. Not Communist. Only against Germans. And now I am in great troubles.' I glanced at the man's fierce profile as he gazed out to sea. He had spoken from his heart."[24]

Tank McAdoo was crushed by Carapizzi's murder, holding himself responsible. He had hired Mysli Kali. He had counted out the gold in front of the young man. McAdoo and Quayle contacted Skender Muço, the regional Balli commander and complained about Kali's release, but nothing was done. "Tank McAdoo never got over it," Kukich said. "He blamed himself for the murder. He took it very hard. I tried to console him. Nothing was the same for Tank after that. He became a different person."

In a hand written letter to Fultz dated January 29, 1944, two days after Carapizzi had been killed, Tank McAdoo had nothing but praise for him. "His thinking was nearly invariably sound," he wrote. "His lack of bitterness, after five dreadful years of prison, was remarkable. As far as I could judge, his loyalty to me and to 'Mr. Fooltz,' as he pronounced it, was complete. His courage and daring were amazing. He was one damn fine little guy, and his death has moved me more than I can describe."

In the same note, McAdoo recommended that in the future Allied agents work either with the Partisans or with the Balli, but not with both, as they had been trying to do. He said that he, as well as Quayle and Field before him, "are considered by the BK to be Partisans, and are considered by the Partisans to be BKs. I know this sounds monstrously stupid; so be it: the Albania of January, 1944, is politically absurd and monstrously stupid."

He said that his proposal was "the only way we can possibly deal with Albania. In Albania, I am afraid that the BK would rather see Germans win than to have the LNC [Communists] come into power. If the same is not true of the Communists, it's only because the Germans wouldn't accept the LNC as collaborators."[25]

Nothing was the same for Carapizzi's mother, either. Months later, after the fighting was over in the region, she traveled to Tirana to look for her son. She went to the OSS mission that was housed in the U.S consulate. Kukich cabled Fultz on December 6, 1944: "Mother of Ismail inquired about his death. She requests information on where he was killed, by whom and the place of burial. She only heard about his death three weeks ago ... told her that Myrto Kalo [sic] of Dukakti killed Ismail. Mother also asks if anything is being done to capture the killer."[26] The mother got no answer.

Still, the work of gathering intelligence had to go on. Although the Allies could work to avoid German patrols and keep gathering intelligence—as long as they remained few in number—the problem of what to do with the Italians grew as more and more continued to arrive at Seaview and Grama Bay seeking a way home. The Allies could not adequately house, feed or clothe them. They hardly had food for themselves. Most of the Italians were worse off than the poorest Albanian. And what struck Kukich and the others was the pathetic condition of the young men. They were eighteen, nineteen or twenty years old, but they looked much older with their sunken, unshaved faces and thin bodies. Many had malaria. The Italians arrived at the coast without weapons and dressed in rags. They had thrown their weapons away, or had lost them. Many had been disarmed by the Partisans. Even if rearmed they would not fight anyway. They were out of the war.

McAdoo put some of the Italians to work as cooks. Others cleaned the camp or tended the mules that were so necessary in order to carry their radio and equipment. Some of the Italians killed the weaker and older mules for food. Some fetched water from distant springs, or washed clothes. One of the Italian soldiers, a singer in civilian life, even sang some of the arias from Italian operas that McAdoo liked so much. Another was a wounded Italian doctor who treated the other wounded even as he treated himself. The Italians also unloaded the boats that came in with supplies and then loaded themselves onto the empty boats for passage home.

Tank McAdoo seemed a different person after Carapizzi was killed. To Kukich the change was obvious—his heart did not seem to be in the job anymore. He was a civilian anyway and not a soldier. They kept their camp rituals intact, however, especially when the camp was made empty when the most recent batch of Italians had been evacuated. McAdoo, Quayle and Kukich made their beds in the "officers" cave and lit candles and listened to the wind howl off the sea and the Adriatic crash against the cliffs. Quayle came up with a bottle of Scotch.

The three of them drank as Quayle and McAdoo discussed opera and the stage. "Tony and Tank knew a lot about both. After a while Tony would begin to recite Shakespeare. He knew all the plays. He knew all the parts in all the plays, all the roles—Macbeth, Hamlet, King Lear, Henry V. I think his favorite was *Hamlet*. He would play all of the characters. He would recite one part and then another as though he were performing on stage. He would do them all. It made the hair on my neck stand up. He had a great voice. It was wonderful to listen to him. He would go on all night, until the morning hours."[27]

Then Tank McAdoo surprisingly left on one of the supply ships and went back to Italy. In his February 18, 1944 report, after leaving Albania for Bari four days earlier, McAdoo wrote of Carapizzi: "Of my original party, the Albanian member proved to be an outstandingly capable worker of great courage and intelligence. In the two months that he worked with me before his death, he had developed greatly in accuracy of reporting, and at all times considered his primary job that of getting intelligence material for us."

McAdoo said that he intended to meet with Gen. Davies (who had already been captured) as soon as he had established his network of agents in western Albania. This was accomplished and the first intelligence reports began coming in at the end of January 1944. "On the 27th of January, however, the Albanian member of my party was murdered, and from his killing originated a chain of events of an emergency nature which, combined with the extensive Hun operations throughout southern Albania, demanded that we remain in the Valona [Vlora] area. It is hoped and believed that soon after my return to Albania we shall be able to establish our American base in the North."[28] Tank McAdoo did not return to Albania. Davies was captured. Nichols was dead. The base was never established.

A month after Carapizzi's death the Partisans ambushed a Balli truck along the coastal road near Dukat. They killed one member of the Balli and captured several others. One of the prisoners was Mysli Kali, who carried documents (but no gold) belonging to Carapizzi. Kali was again put on trial, this time by the 5th Partisan Brigade.

According to Quayle, when the second trial took place, a Partisan who had infiltrated the camp at Seaview testified that Carapizzi "was a renegade Communist and deserved to be killed" because he worked for the Americans. "Whoever murdered him was therefore rendering the 'party' a great service, and if anything should be praised for his action. Mysli

Kali was therefore released, and is still in Dukat in enjoyment of his life and our gold."29*

Kukich, who later would have a good, working relationship with Enver Hoxha, came to believe that Hoxha ordered the killing of Carapizzi. "I believe Hoxha had him executed. Hoxha did not like it that he was working for us, the Americans, and that he could get along with the Balli and the Germans. What kind of a Communist was that? But that was Carapizzi's job, to get along, to get information. Hoxha wanted to disrupt that work. So he had him killed."

Although their work ensured that they would spend a lot of time together, Kukich and Quayle—with McAdoo gone—often found themselves in disagreement. Kukich chafed at being ordered around by Quayle. Quayle frequently aggravated the situation by excluding Kukich, an enlisted man, from meetings he held with high-ranking Balli or Partisan officials. Kukich, in retaliation, stopped providing Quayle with intelligence gathered from Carapizzi and Çela, intelligence he routinely sent to OSS headquarters in Bari. After all, there was no written rule that he had to share anything with Quayle.

"Quayle would hardly talk to me when there was another officer around," Nick said. "He preferred to talk to officers. I was a sergeant. He didn't want me sleeping in the cave he shared with Tank. It was for officers. Because of Tank I had slept there anyway. Tony did not like it. We were not one group. We lacked togetherness. He treated me badly so I withheld information from him. Then he blew his stack. I told him, 'When you stop treating me badly, I'll share intelligence. I am a representative of the OSS and the American government and I expect to be treated as such. I expect to be treated equally.' After that we got along, like Eisenhower and Montgomery."

Things between the two remained smooth for a while, but Kukich had another run-in with Quayle over the rescue from the Germans of a group of Italians that had made their way to the coast. Quayle threatened to have Nick court-martialed over it.

---

* In October 2004 I interviewed Hodo Qepi in Dukat, a peasant farmer in his 80s. His brother Haxhi Qepi had worked for the Allied Mission and had been executed by the Communists after the war. Hodo said that the people of Dukat never put Kali on trial for killing Ismail Carapizzi, but was a lie they told the British and Americans. "They could not put him on trial because his father ran the village," he said. He said, "The Communists rewarded him for the killing by making him a brigade commander. He was very influential with the Communists as was his family. He ran all the farming communes in Dukat after the war. He was working with a young man one day in the early Sixties and the young man went for a swim in the pond. He went under. Kali went in to save him and they both drowned." Hodo Qepi chuckled at the memory, obviously pleased. "It took God a while but he took care of Mysli Kali."

The incident cost sixty Italian soldiers their freedom, and possibly their lives. It also contributed to Quayle's bitterness against the captain of the rescue ship—fellow actor Sterling Hayden, the American Marine Corps skipper. It also deepened the animosity between Quayle and Kukich.

In his 1990 autobiography *A Time to Speak*, Quayle implies—but never openly states—that it was Hayden's fault that the Italians were captured by the Germans because Hayden refused to take them on board his ship.

Hayden, or Hamilton, as he was known, crossed the Adriatic many times with supplies for the Partisans in Yugoslavia and Albania. An experienced seaman, Hayden knew the sea. A swashbuckling, hard-living extrovert, Hayden was a popular figure among the soldiers of the OSS in Bari. He was good company in a Bari bar. He was better company at sea. He was a good seaman, respected by the men who sailed with him, who were mainly Serbian Communist Partisans. During his trips to the island of Vis on the Dalmatian Coast of Yugoslavia, or to Seaview or Grama Bay in Albania, Hayden dropped off arms, ammunition and agents, and brought back rescued American airmen and Italian soldiers. He was known to be an admirer of Tito.

Quayle wrote of the night when he rowed out to meet a hundred-foot trawler that had dropped anchor outside the entrance of Grama Bay. He urged the crew to bring the trawler in closer to the shore so that the unloading of supplies would be easier. "The reply was drunken laughter and a torrent of words that I took to be Serbian. Next moment a heavy ammunition box was dropped on my head, followed by another, then another till the flimsy boat was in danger of sinking."

Quayle and his Italian helpers rowed back and forth unloading the supplies. Becoming tired, he scribbled "a furious note" to the captain of the ship pleading with him to bring his boat in closer to the shore. "Half an hour later I made out a heavy wooden tender heading for the beach—one man rowing, another sitting in the stern. She ran easily up on the beach, and out of the stern rose the figure of an enormous man, a man built on the scale of the Trojan War.

"An American voice called out, 'Well—what's all the trouble?'"

Quayle explained that it was safe to bring the trawler in closer, making the unloading easier. "'I am the captain of this ship,' he replied, 'and I do not think it is safe. Therefore, I shall remain outside. What's more, in another twenty minutes, I shall up-anchor and sail.'

"'But there are still a dozen of Italians waiting to get on board.'

"'That's your business. If they get on board in time, I'll take them. If not—not.'

"He turned, climbed back into the tender, and rowed away. We struggled on till we heard the trawler's engine come alive, then the rattle of her anchor chain being winched aboard. Most of the Italians collapsed on the beach in despair; some tried to swim out to the ship. Three were drowned."

Quayle, who implied that Hayden was to blame for the death of the Italians, later added that he had to leave another sixty Italians behind because of the sudden appearance of a German patrol that chased them out of Seaview before they could be rescued. He also implied that some of the sixty were among those refused passage by the American skipper.

Hiding out from the Germans in a shepherd's hut with Kukich and others on February 29, 1944, Quayle said he looked out the window with his field glasses and "picked up a sight I had dreaded—our sixty Italians being marched along the road toward Valona [Vlora] under guard."

Weeks later in Italy, after having recovered from jaundice and malaria, Quayle returned to duty. "My first day back in Bari, I walked into the HQ mess and saw, lunching there, a man I was unlikely to forget—a tall, handsome man with the head of an ancient hero. It was the American captain who would not bring his trawler into Grama Bay.

"I turned to the mess sergeant. 'That big man over there, at the long table. Who is he?'

"The sergeant was surprised by my ignorance. 'Don't you know, sir? That's Sterling Hayden, the movie star.'

"I turned and left the room. I had no desire for further acquaintance with Mr. Hayden."[30]

Hayden had a different version of the event, or a different version of the event described by Quayle. In his autobiography *Wanderer*, Hayden (without mentioning Quayle) wrote briefly about an incident where he was to pick up some Italians. "Like the night I took the converted fishing boat and ran her across to Albania, where thirty Italians were holed up in a deep cave. They had been on the march for over a year, hiding out in the mountains of Greece, trying desperately to make their way to Italy. That was the night an E-Boat went by off-shore as we lay in the cove. I had agreed to carry the Italians back to Otranto, but I reckoned without my pilot Ivosevitch. He took a Thompson machine gun ashore with the rubber boat, and then I heard the firing. He came back on board alone. 'We go!' he had cried. All the Italians were dead. I didn't know what to say to this man whose wife had been raped to death."[31]

Kukich, who admired Hayden—even if he thought him somewhat eccentric—said Hayden's description of the killing of the Italians was either a figment of Hayden's fertile imagination, or that the killing happened elsewhere, perhaps along the coast of Yugoslavia. "It did not happen where we were. It could not have happened. We would have known. There were no bodies."

He said that what Quayle did was take two incidents—his confrontation with Hayden, where three Italians did drown, and the capture of the sixty Italians, and roll them into one narrative.

"I was not there at Grama Bay when he had that run-in with Hayden, although I heard about it later. But I was there when we were trying to get those sixty Italians rescued. It was a different incident. And we were at Grama Bay, not Seaview.

"We had the Italians there. I saw this Italian ship coming in. I went to signal it to show we were there and ready. Quayle told me not to signal. He said it was a German destroyer and we would give away our position. I told him, 'No way is that a German destroyer. It's an Italian ship. I knew because I had studied the charts. I knew it was an Italian ship used by us [the OSS]. I went to signal. Quayle ordered me to stop. 'If you signal I'll have your court-martialed,' he said. I argued with him but it was no use."

"The following night the Germans chased us out of there. Everybody scattered. The next morning I looked out the window of the house we were staying at in Dukat. I could see in the morning fog the sixty Italians being marched along the road with Germans guarding them. I told Quayle. He looked out the window and then he looked at me. He felt guilty. It never should have happened, but it did."[32]

Slowly they made their way back to Seaview. The caves were ransacked and deserted. The radio was smashed and useless. All the Italians were gone. The mules were gone. There was no one to fetch water. There was no one to cook. There was no one to sing.

3

Hudson

Lt. Jim Hudson was crushed when Harry T. Fultz, civilian head of the Albanian Desk, Company B, 2677th Regiment, OSS, Provisional, assigned him his code name. It was "Bill."

Considering that he was to replace a man with the code name of Tank, Hudson, newly arrived at OSS headquarters in Bari from Cairo, expected something more romantic and warlike than just plain Bill. He had been recruited by the OSS in Cairo for its Special Intelligence (SI) unit, and he wanted to see some action. After SI training he was flown to Italy. It was early February 1944. The Allies had earlier moved up the boot of Italy, freeing Bari. It was where OSS headquarters and Fultz were located.

Hudson entered Fultz's office and handed him his orders. After looking them over Fultz said, "You can't use your own name here. What do you want to be called?" Before Hudson could respond with a name of his own choosing, Fultz said, "We'll call you Bill."

"What kind of a spy name was that?" Hudson wondered. "What a plain, ordinary name, worse even than Jim," Hudson wrote in "Tales of War," his electronic memoir.

Hudson was what was called a "gung-ho" officer. He was highly motivated, aggressive and action oriented. Although he spoke no foreign language, he was the kind of officer who made you speak the language he spoke. Hudson was commissioned a 2nd lieutenant in 1939 after four years in the Reserve Officer Training Corps (ROTC) at Gettysburg College in Pennsylvania. Although given a deferment because of his employment as a research chemist, Hudson was readmitted into the army following the December 7, 1941 Japanese attack on Pearl Harbor.

Fultz, 56, a combat veteran of World War I, had been recruited by the OSS in 1943. At the time he was director of special education for the state of Illinois. Fultz had gone to Albania in 1922 as director of the new American Vocational School in Tirana, a school sponsored by the Junior American Red Cross. There fortunate Albanian boys and young men could learn modern vocational skills and farming techniques as well as English. It was an unusual school for backward Albania, attracting boys from the peasantry and from mountain clans. Many of the boys were the first of their families to go to school, any school. There the young students learned the rudiments of a technology that had been absent in Albania. Once up and running, the school became the sole source of Tirana's electricity for four years; provided the city with ice in the summer an dairy products all year round; introduced improved methods of husbandry as well as modern growing techniques for fruits, vegetable and grains; provided farmers with a mechanical means of threshing; maintained one of the few printing presses in the country; and constructed sixteen buildings in Tirana, including the American Legation building. Fultz ran the school until it was nationalized by the Zog government in 1933. He then returned to the United States.[1]

Fultz was recruited by the OSS in 1943. He was an expert on Albania and he knew many of the Albanians involved in the fighting over their country. They had been his students. Fultz's OSS code name was Gates, but because of his age, the men of the OSS affectionately referred to him as Plak, the Albanian word for old man. His job was to run the organization that sent agents into Albania and to collect and interpret the intelligence they brought back.

Fultz was convinced that it was incumbent upon the Allies to supply the Partisans, and only the Partisans, because they were the only resistance group fighting the Germans. He resented British policy of withholding arms from the Communists because the Communists were engaged in a civil war with the Ballists. The British wanted to teach Hoxha and the Partisans a lesson. This only helped the Germans, Fultz argued, because the BK refused to fight the Germans but agreed to collaborate with them against the Partisans.

Fultz, in a February 22, 1944 memo to Philip Adams in Washington, said the Germans needed five divisions to occupy Albania. But because the BK and the pro–Zogists refused to fight, the Germans were able to reduce their forces by fifty per cent. "Perhaps the divisions that are not in Albania are today over at the Anzio bridgehead killing Americans and British while we try to figure out ways to teach recalcitrant Partisans 'a sharp lesson,'" Fultz said. The Allies had landed at Anzio on January 22. In February the Germans launched a strong counteroffensive that threatened to throw the Allies back into the sea.

"The only resistance to the Germans is coming from the Partisans,"

Fultz said, despite their lack of supplies. A pair of American airmen witnessed a unit of Partisans in retreat from a German offensive in December in the villages of Kuç and Gelemi, Fultz wrote. "They heard a British Officer make insinuating remarks about the retreat and lack of fighting qualities [of the Partisans] knowing very well that those against whom he directed his remarks were down to their last few rounds of ammunition while 100 miles away in Italy there was an abundance [of supplies] if any one really wanted to make a determined effort to get it where it was needed." Somewhat prophetically, Fultz added: "We should not be surprised if later we find that these people have no love for the Allies; for either the British or ourselves."[2]

Like Sgt. Nick Kukich and Maj. Anthony Quayle before him, it too would take Hudson three attempts to land on the coast of Albania. The first time was aboard the Italian fishing trawler renamed *Yankee*, piloted by Capt. John Hamilton—Sterling Hayden—on March 14. "Hamilton was much more reassuring than the boat," Hudson wrote. "He had broad shoulders, a neck like a Brahman bull, and a shock of blond hair ruffled in the most orderly fashion." Despite his good looks and physical presence, Hayden could not bring the ship to shore. A storm forced the party back to port. The next attempt failed as well.

Sterling Hayden then left to visit his actress wife Madeleine Carroll, who had arrived in Italy with the Red Cross to work with the wounded at a hospital in Foggia. "Madeleine's coming to Italy to entertain the troops, but I've got to get to Foggia to see her before those sex-starved generals get to her," Hayden told Hudson. "I wouldn't trust them as far as I could throw the *Yankee*."[3]

On the third try, this time with the trawler piloted by a Yugoslavian skipper, the ship made it to Seaview. Accompanying Hudson, 26, on the trip was OSS Lt. Thomas E. Stefan, 27, code name Art. Of the OSS group, Stefan was the only American-born agent who spoke Albanian. His assignment was to go from Seaview across Balli and German lines and hook up with Communist Partisan leader Enver Hoxha, then headquartered in Odriçan, a tiny village hidden in the remote mountains of southern Albania.

By the time Hudson's party arrived at Seaview, Nick Kukich had been the sole Special Intelligence OSS agent in Albania for over a month, from February 14, when Tank left, to the March 20 arrival of Hudson. Hudson, upon meeting Kukich on the pebble beach by Seaview, described him this way: "One towered well over six feet. His unkempt hair grew uninhibited and slid off the top of his head, surrounded his ears and almost buried his mouth. It was a bush any man would have been proud of."[4]

One of Kukich's duties was the help evacuate Major Quayle, who had come down with malaria. On March 28 Kukich cabled Fultz and Maj. Eliot Watrous of the SOE in Bari regarding the evacuation of the ailing Quayle. "Delay is endangering the whole mission as Seaview is in a bad situation. I must discuss with you events as soon as possible since they are moving rapidly. Everything depends on you. Please do all you can." On April 2 Kukich cabled: "Will stand by as arranged by your message. Quayle's condition is very poor. It was reported by the shepherds that on the night of the 31st a ship was standing off Sea Elephant [Grama Bay, which was the other base]. We suggest you get new navigator and lookout," Kukich cabled sarcastically, since they were at Seaview and not Sea Elephant (Grama Bay), which was further down the coast. Kukich included a short message from Hudson. "For Gates from Bill: In Valona there are 500 Germans and 1000 Armenians."[5]

Kukich thought he and Tank McAdoo had set up a pretty good intelligence network with Xhelil Çela, Hodo Meto and Carapizzi. It ran from Dukat up along the coast to Vlora and Durrës and then inland to Tirana. They had agents in the field reporting to them at Seaview on a regular basis. But Hudson had bigger ideas. He wanted to expand the network to include the cities of Elbasan, Fieri, Berat and Scutari (Shkodra) up in northern Albania, more than doubling the area under surveillance—and doubling the OSS commitment.

Kukich, still only a sergeant and outranked by Hudson, a first lieutenant, had his doubts. In a pouch-delivered letter to Fultz dated March 29, 1944—only eight days after Hudson had arrived at Seaview—he wrote, "Bill is a nice chap but he can't handle people like Tank did. He is learning fast and I'm doing all I can in helping him. He has a few faults which we all have and I'm sure we are on the right track. He has nice plans but it will be a big job in carrying them out. We have a nice system set up now only if Jerry doesn't interfere. This mt. [mountain] is getting hot and the Jerries [Germans] know that we are in this area."[6]

Just as Hudson was about to put his plans into effect, the Germans launched an offensive in the area in an attempt to ferret out the Allied agents they knew were operating in the region. Stefan left Seaview in early April and went inland. Hudson, Kukich and several British officers fled the caves and headed over the Dukati Mountains seeking refuge.

Many loyal shepherds, farmers and residents of Dukat, who provided an early warning system as well as food and shelter, protected the group. Others, in fear of the Germans, turned them away.

The village of Dukat, strategically located along the coastal road between Vlora in the north and Saranda in the south, was made up of two types of people. On one hand were young hotheads who were tied into the Balli Kombëtar. These young men wanted to stand up to the Communist Partisans and work with the Germans in the hope of defeating the Communists and take over their country. They were not friendly toward the British or Americans. The older men of Dukat tended to side with the Allies. They were more cautious. They could see that the Allies would win the war. Once the war was won then they could deal with the Communists. Certainly, in the final analysis, the Americans and the British would not allow the Communists to seize power—or so they thought. Still others were conflicted and chose to do nothing. Some feared Partisan retribution if they helped the Germans; others were afraid of German reprisals if they helped the Allies. Some Albanians, mainly poor shepherds, simply wanted to survive. They did so by pilfering supplies that the Allies stored in the caves.

The people of Dukat—subsistence farmers who worked small patches of rocky soil and tended herds of sheep and goats—were well aware of the destruction caused by war in southern Albania. They had seen neighboring villagers killed, homes burned and livestock stolen, killed or run off. It was estimated by the OSS that by late 1943 and early 1944, one third of southern Albania had been burned by the Italians, one third by the Germans and only one third was left still to destroy. Dukat was part of the latter one third and the residents wanted it kept that way. Still, some Balli residents of the Dukat, despite the danger, worked for the Allies as guards and lookouts and spies. Many Albanians looked kindly upon the Americans. Not only were there thousands of Albanian immigrants living in the United States—mainly in the Boston and New England area—but also they sent money back to relatives in Albania. Albanians also had a warm spot in their hearts for President Woodrow Wilson, whom they credited for defending Albanian territorial integrity at the Paris Peace Conference in 1919.

Hardly had the Allies abandoned Seaview—leaving to actually protect its location from the Germans—when the Germans launched an offensive against Dukat April 3 and against the neighboring village of Tragjas a week later. German troops from the 1st Mountain Division occupied Dukat in an effort to locate the Allied mission. The Germans, newly arrived from the Russian front, had their numbers reinforced by drafting foreigners into their ranks, including many Armenians. They arrested suspected Allied sympathizers in Dukat for questioning, confiscated weapons, and invaded and destroyed homes in an effort to track down American and British agents.

On April 8 Hudson and Kukich, hiding in the hills above the neighboring village of Tragjas, watched from safety as German troops, along with Ballist collaborators, invaded the village and forced residents from their homes. Ironically, Lt. Stefan, along with his two radio operators—who were also on the run from the same Germans—watched the same action in Tragjas from a different hiding post in the mountains, unaware that his fellow OSS men were in the vicinity.

The village, just north and inland from Dukat, was considered to be strongly pro–Partisan. As the OSS agents remained concealed, the Germans emptied the homes of men, women and children and then burned the homes down that they had not burned on previous raids. The lucky few villagers who were able to escape fled into the mountains.[7]

Although Hudson and Kukich and their party were armed with M-1 rifles, Thompson submachine guns, carbines and .45 automatics, their firepower and numbers were too puny to have any influence on the action that took place below them. They could do nothing but watch.

Hudson later described observing the Germans through binoculars burn the village and chase the villagers into the mountains. "It was surreal. There was not a sound of outcry. Not a scream of terror. Not a plea of mercy, for the distance was too great to hear anything but the report of guns.... They were helpless to intervene."[8]

While hiding out in shepherd huts in the hills, Kukich was still able to send reports back to Bari by radio, however, and Hudson had the pouch system of reports functioning. Besides the problem of the Germans searching for them, the Allies still attracted the company of roaming Italian soldiers seeking food, shelter and a way back to Italy, which made the matter of their concealment even more difficult.

The day following the action at Tragjas, Hudson decided to split the party in two so that one would survive if the other group were captured. The people of Dukat, intent on appeasing the Germans, were anxious that the Allies leave the area because it was felt that the Germans would punish the villagers if any American or British agents were captured. Hudson and Kukich, along with their Albanian guides and Italian newcomers, hiked deeper into the woods. The Germans kept the pressure on, however, sending some six hundred troops north from Himara and another two hundred south from Vlora in an effort to trap the Allies.

"The worst news came on 22 April," Hudson wrote in his June 5, 1944 OSS report. "A messenger from Dukati told us that the Germans had shot two shepherds in the sweep near Seaview and took several prisoners. They felt sure that some of these would talk for they all knew we were in the vicinity. The prisoners were taken to Valona [Vlora] where the Gestapo (German secret police) could work on them."

The group headed north into a swamp area just south of Vlora. "Three Germans sauntered passed [sic] within ten feet of us. One of our guides was about to run but Galba [Kukich] pulled a .45 and stuck it in his face. He stopped," Hudson reported. The group stayed in "this muddy hell" for three days, the only comfort being "the sight of Allied planes roaring overhead to attack targets in the vicinity."

When the Germans left, Hudson and his party made their way back to the makeshift camp they had built near Dukat among shepherds' huts. The Germans, finding no Allies, had gone. But the camp had been trashed and all their supplies stolen by shepherds and a former guard from Dukat. When Hudson and Kukich demanded that the elders of Dukat force the thieves to return the supplies, the elders countered with a demand of their own that bordered on extortion. The elders said that the German occupation of their village—which was precipitated by the presence of Americans in the area—had caused six hundred gold sovereigns' worth of destruction and it was incumbent upon the Allies to pay for the damage.

Hudson and Kukich said that they had no authority to approve such a payment. During a stormy meeting with the elders in the center of Dukat, the village elders threatened that if the payment were not made in two weeks—or by May 30—they would reveal their whereabouts to the Germans. This ultimatum infuriated the Americans. Kukich immediately radioed Fultz for instructions. Hudson sent the following cable to Fultz on May 18: "Dukati has issued an ultimatum to the Allied Missions to the effect that they make payment for damages done by the Germans by May 30th. The American Mission included in this. If payment is not made our position will be precarious."[9]

Fultz thought the people of Dukat were engaged in outright blackmail. This, coupled with information that still another offensive against the Allies was in the works, persuaded Fultz to pull out his OSS agents and shut Seaview down, at least for the time being. In a May 20 memorandum to Washington, Fultz wrote that the Dukat claim for damages "is unwarranted and should not be paid and that both American and British personnel should be withdrawn at the earliest possible time."

"While the base has yielded reasonably good results from an intelligence point of view it has had a varied history. It has been raided by Germans during the last week in February and the personnel were obliged to shift from one location in the area to another to avoid detection and capture. During the month from the middle of February to the middle of March our men were constantly on the move but in spite of that, except for a period of ten days, maintained daily w/t (radio) contact. Since that time the Germans have sent frequent patrols into the area and during the period from April 17, 1944 to May 4, 1944 they sent in a strong force of some five hundred men in a determined effort to comb the area and pickup members of the Allied Missions there. While there were some extremely narrow escapes both our own personnel and that of the British evaded capture."

Fultz said his decision was based on the fact that "a. the area in which the base operates is too well known and because of continued German activity has become too restricted for personnel to work effectively; b. while the base has contributed much in the way for Albanian intelligence we are no longer justified in keeping men working there in almost constant jeopardy; c. the current demands of the local population if yielded to now will be repeated and stepped up without any added assurance of protection from frequent German attempts to roundup personnel of this mission."

Another OSS commander in Bari summed up the situation in Dukat this way: "The way in which the Albanians attempted to force this issue led the British and American authorities to the conclusion that this was a form of blackmail and that if the funds were not forthcoming, the Allied personnel might be turned over to the enemy. It was also felt that if the funds were paid in this instance the Albanians might consider this a profitable source of revenue and repeat the process, or even sell out to the Germans for a higher price." And while the agents would be pulled out and the site closed down, the possibility remained that the OSS would return at some later date.[10]

Although Hudson went along with Fultz's order, he later had serious misgivings about abandoning the people of Dukat. The villagers were angry when they learned that Seaview would be shut down. Hudson said he talked to the people in order to placate their fears. "I still have the original notes that I scribbled on a piece of paper of that speech. In essence, I called for their patriotism and reminded them of the rewards the Allies would give them after the war. How wrong I was in my prognostication," Hudson said years later.

"We allowed our friends to die. I recoil to this day from my words that turned out to be such lies. I was convinced that we would be generous to our friends, but we were selfish. We only cared for our own safety and used them to win the war. Morals were meaningless. How could we expect more from Dukati? Fultz had already sent us a radio message, a copy of which I still possess, to evacuate the country, for OSS feared we would be captured, compromised or killed if Dukati did not get the reparations they asked for. OSS was not about to pay them anything. The OSS position was that the middle of a war is no time to negotiate, but on retrospection, I am not sure that we were right."

Hudson added: "There is no doubt that we had profited much by the protection the entire village gave the Americans and the British. Frankly, with a hostile Dukati, Seaview and our infiltrations and evacuations from the beach just below, would have been untenable." The villagers "not only allowed us the safe use of that beach, but often helped us carry supplies over the mountain to the Partisans, even though the two groups hated each other. It was a strange case of mutual dependency yet differing widely in their political views of the future. To maintain that trichotomy, the Allies, Dukati and Communist Partisans, the people in Dukati had the most to lose. They were totally under the control of the Germans, and could be readily located, since their family and farms were located on the main coastal road."

Hudson said the men of the village would argue with each other and complain about the injustice of helping the Allies without any compensation. "That was not completely true, for a few of the men did get paid for borrowing their donkeys for carrying supplies, and similar acts, but the bulk of the people got no monetary benefit, and they risked the very lives of their families and the cruelty they knew the Germans could commit if they suspected anything. They endured several cross-examinations by the Gestapo without cracking. A remarkable fact. They did deserve Allied recognition and compensation." But they did not get either.[11]

On the night of May 25 Hudson and Kukich rowed out to a waiting Italian trawler, climbed aboard and left for Bari. Seaview, for the time being, was closed. Kukich had been in Albania for five months. In July he received a battlefield promotion from gunnery sergeant to second lieutenant. Hudson, in Albania for two months, was made a captain. Both then took parachute training.

Since the need for OSS intelligence persisted, Hudson was not idle for long. On July 25, 1944, Hudson, along with PFC Kostas "Gus" Routsis, an Albanian-American radio operator, and Albanians Xhilil Çela and Xhevit Hamid, left Brindisi for the Albanian coast aboard an Italian MAS boat. Both Çela and Hamid had been very helpful to the Allies. The OSS idea was to reestablish contact with agents in the field while avoiding villagers from Dukat as well as members of the Balli. Rather than taking up residence at Seaview as they did before, this time the OSS would stay for just several days. Hudson would rehire Albanian agents or hire new ones and set up secret drop-off points along the coast for the pouches that would be hidden there and picked up by the OSS and brought to Bari. The mission was to be at least one of five quick hit-and-run missions Hudson would undertake over the next several months.

Routsis, 18, was a naturalized American who had been born in Frashtan, Albania, a Greek-speaking village in southern Albania. He and his older brother George had migrated to the United States with their parents just ten years earlier. They were reared in Middletown, Connecticut, where their father owned a restaurant. Both graduated from high school and could speak English, Albanian and Greek. Drafted into the army in 1943, the brothers volunteered for the OSS and radio school. Now both were in Albania—Gus with Hudson and George with Stefan. Later the bothers would be reunited at Hoxha's headquarters in Odriçan.

Çela and Hamid, who worked for Çela, had been evacuated from Seaview with Hudson and Kukich in May. Now they were returning to once again help the OSS gather information of vital importance about the Germans.

Fultz was extremely confident of Çela's usefulness. Çela, after all, had gone to the "Fultz School," as many Albanians called the American Vocational School. In a July 17 memo seeking security clearance and recommending that the OSS hire Çela, Fultz pointed out how helpful Çela had been during the initial Seaview operation. Çela, whose family owned a farm on the plains of Dukat along the coastal road, appeared to be a pro–Allied Albanian patriot concerned about the future of his country. Fultz said that Çela, "one of the local Albanians from an influential family was important in helping to maintain the base [Seaview] and in protecting members of the Allied Mission there. He has helped both British and Americans in innumerable ways offering his home as a sanctuary, providing food and lodging without cost; arranging for the collecting of military intelligence for the Valona [Vlora] area; assisting in liaison between the Allied mission and the local population and in many ways to which Lt. Hudson and any others who have served in that difficult location can testify. In so far as we know he has done all of these things for the Allied cause without expecting or receiving pay either from ourselves or from the British," Fultz wrote. Fultz noted that Çela and Hamid had come out of Albania with Hudson and Kukich.

He added: "Since coming to Italy he has been with the British LRDG [Long Range Desert Group] and has returned to the Seaview area with them on three different occasions in helping to work out a raid on the Albanian coast which was conducted with complete success on the night of 29 June 1944 at which time a concrete protected lookout station in Valona [Vlora] was completely leveled and prisoners were taken. Chela [sic] has wanted for some time to work entirely with Americans. He speaks English well and is well-educated in terms of education in that country.... In addition to what Chela might do for us in this area he has so well-proven himself that he could of great value for other areas as well."[12]

When Hudson and his men arrived at the lowest cave at Seaview, which was at sea level, and the supplies were unloaded, Routsis found that his radio did not work. Hudson instructed Routsis to remain at the cave and attempt to repair the radio, while he, Xhilil Çela and Xhevit Hamid went inland over the Dukati Mountains to meet with a group of Albanian agents at Çela's home, where his brother Agim awaited them.

Before he left, Hudson told Routsis to stay alert, watch for German patrols and guard their supplies. Routsis, although he was born in Albania, did not like being left alone in a strange place. "Their departure changed the whole atmosphere in the cave," he said. "I became conscious and frightened as the waves produced all kinds of weird noises, smashing against this isolate fortress. Reflections of the sun on the water danced and quivered on the ceiling of the cave. Never was there a still moment. There were swallows flying by during the day and bats at night."[13]

Hudson and his two Albanian companions, meanwhile, climbed for six hours over the Dukati Mountains before reaching Çela's farmhouse. Agim was there with several other Albanians, some of whom Hudson recognized. They sat at a table drinking raki, the fiery Albanian home brew. After the traditional Albanian welcome and shots of raki, they got down to business. Hudson told the Albanians that the OSS needed to reestablish its network of operations and establish new contacts. It needed all the information it could get about German troop activity and the conditions in Albania. It needed information about visual sightings of troops and written documents of all kinds—German and Albanian newspapers, pamphlets, posters, and so on.

Xheles Seferi, whom the OSS had employed before, agreed to continue to cover the Tirana area where he would collect all the newspapers and periodicals published by the Albanian quisling government, the Germans and the Balli Kombëtar. Alim Hodo, a new man recommended by the others, was to work the Berat area. Nusret Llupa, code name "Pietro," and Tahir Hoxha, known as "X," were to continue to cover the active Vlora region. The main difference in the operations was that instead of reporting to the caves at Seaview, Agim Çela was to act as the central agent who would gather all of the information provided by the field agents. Agim would turn that information over to a courier who would then place the intelligence in pouches. The pouches would be placed in secret hiding places along the coast for retrieval by the OSS. The plan was solid, the men were trustworthy. After more raki, the changing hands of some gold sovereigns, and a round of handshakes and embraces, Hudson and his team headed back to the coast.[14]

Back at Seaview, Routsis had decided to go for a swim off of the rubber boat that had brought them in. It was moored in the lagoon just in front of the cave. No sooner was he in the water than he heard an explosion, and then another. The explosions sounded like hand grenades. Routsis tried to pull the boat into the cave and out of the way. He could not do it so he pulled it into the shade where it could not be seen. He heard another explosion, this time closer. "Oh, oh, now I'm in trouble," he thought. He climbed behind some rocks and checked his M-1 rifle and the .45 he carried on his side. He watched two figures approach. "I see this man stick his hands in a pouch and pull something out and throw it into the water. It was a grenade. They weren't Germans because they weren't dressed in military uniforms. They weren't Partisans—they'd be carrying weapons. They weren't members of the Balli Kombëtar—they too would be carrying weapons for protection. Plain, ordinary, common everyday fishermen was what they were."

Routsis got out from behind the rocks and approached the pair, a man and a woman. He leveled his rifle at them and they raised their arms. "I heard the woman say in Greek to the man, 'What are we going to do now? This German is going to kill us.' 'Relax,' I said in Greek. 'I am not a German. I'm an American from the American Army.' They understood my Greek. Their arms came down and they relaxed. 'Nothing is going to happen to you.' I took out a little black book I carried and made believe I took down their names and their village. I told them that I was sending the information back to Italy and that if anything happened to me, if they told the Germans I was here, we would bomb and destroy their village. They promised me again and again that they had no such intention and, in fact, were willing to help the Americans in every way possible to drive out the German barbarians. I let them go."[15]

Hudson was disturbed by Routsis' encounter with the Albanians, convinced that the Albanians would reveal their position to the Germans. The Germans would send a patrol by land or a boat by sea to investigate. They had to get out of there as soon as they could. Hudson and his men policed the area thoroughly to eliminate all signs that anyone had been there. At dusk they signaled for the boat. On July 29 the same Italian MAS boat that brought them in evacuated the party.

The intelligence from the coastal region of Albania that the OSS deemed so important began to flow again, as it had flowed before the OSS had been forced to vacate Seaview weeks earlier. But now they were able to function without the people of Dukat becoming aware of their presence. Their visits to the coast to pick up the pouches crammed with documents were made in stealth, quickly and quietly.

It did not take the people of Dukat long to notice that the Allied permanent base at Seaview had been abandoned. Many missed the money the

Americans and British paid those Dukatis who worked for them, money they sorely needed. The Germans became more aggressive. They launched a series of offensives against the Partisans, and they turned on Albanians they suspected of sympathizing with the Allies.

Hodo Meto, who had worked for the OSS at Seaview, was now unemployed. He wrote two letters to Fultz in August beseeching him to send the OSS back to Seaview. Hodo, who had learned English as a student at Fultz's American Vocational School, wrote that the villagers of Dukat had made a mistake in handing the Allies the ultimatum. "I never imagined the Germans were so much [sic] barbarians," he said in his letter to Fultz. As a result of that barbarism, he said, the people of Dukat "changed again the opinion of here [sic] keeping the Mission." If the Americans returned, he said, the people of Dukat would now rise up and fight the Germans. "We are ready to give our blood too, to fight against the Germans if you [supply] us with war material and when you Mr. F. judge that the time has come."[16]

Hodo Meto's plea for the people of Dukat came too late. After being occupied and terrorized by the Germans, the village was attacked and captured by the Partisans in September.

Pietro proved invaluable in Vlora. His reports, written in Italian, were packed with the type of information the Allies badly needed about the Germans and the collaborationist Albanians. Pietro earmarked his reports to Hudson, as did agent X and another agent known only as "Z." Pietro, undoubtedly, had a sense of humor, for he called one of his sub-agents in Vlora "Staff Sgt. Bill" or "Bill."

In one undated report, sent during the summer of 1944, Pietro reported: "Operations are in progress all over Albania except in the Elbasan area where they have already finished. Staff Sgt. Bill, interpreter for the office of German Secret Police, tells me that 2,000 Albanians guilty of Communism have been arrested.... Bill, the above mentioned told me that quite a few Communists had been killed in the Pogradec area."

In the same message Pietro told of an attempted Communist assassination on the life of Vizhdan Risilia, the quisling, German-appointed prefect (mayor) of Valona. "He always has four German guards in the house, three always around him. Of these the Communists wounded one German soldier. The prefect told me that two of the Communists were wounded but that none of them were captured."

Although he apparently associated with the prefect, Pietro did not have a high opinion of him. In his May report to the OSS, Pietro wrote, "The prefect of Valona is not a solid citizen (uomo serio). He is a bey. He received his secondary schooling in Austria and speaks German well. The

Germans used their influence to have him made prefect when they arrived here. He is closely connected with the Germans and is not esteemed highly by the population. He does not have a fine character. Once in a while, in order to curry favor with the people, he intervenes to lessen the terrorism and barbarism which the enemies inflict upon the population."

Pietro, like other Albanians, was concerned with civilian deaths as a result of American and British bombing and strafing. "From the bombardments so far effected by the British and American planes no damage is visible to German military objectives. Along the Fieri road, etc., within 20 days they destroyed 13 German automobiles and 4 private cars with their passengers. God only knows how many soldiers! Seven Albanians."

Also of concern to Pietro was the growing number of Armenians in the German Army, conscripted to fill the thinning ranks of the German military. "The Armenians are behaving very badly. Wherever they go, they steal and massacre the population."[17]

The Armenian troops, who were badly treated by the Germans, were not the only soldiers forced to steal. German troops also resorted to theft. Many of the Armenian soldiers had no shoes and were poorly clothed. The Germans distrusted them and discriminated against them, considering them to be "hopelessly inferior" to the German soldier. In a report on German troop morale in Vlora, Z reported that the "war-weary" Germans "were stealing sheep and goats in several places" for food or to obtain money.

It was apparent that the German Army, retreating from the Soviet Union following the mauling it received at the Battle of Stalingrad, was badly in need of replacements as the army retreated westward. In April 1944, Z reported on the nationality of German troops in southern Albania. "While all of the soldiers participating in the movement of troops along the Saranda-Valona road are in German uniforms, it is believed that the majority of the men are Armenians. A German NCO (sergeant) in charge of the detail guarding the Dukati section of the highway during this movement stated that all of the German troops originally in Greece and Albania are being moved to France and to Italy, and that their places are being taken by other troops, such as Armenians, Rumanians and Bulgarians."[18]

In a June report to the OSS, Z said that while some German soldiers were still confident, many feared that the war was lost, but they had no alternative but to fight on. "These, while they realize that Germany and the German Army will be defeated, are determined to fight to the end. This determination comes from the belief that they and their families will be ill-treated by the allies when and if they surrender. Constant German propaganda seems to foster this attitude."

Still, there were "incurable optimists" among the Germans, Z noted. "They are cocky and self-assured and have been taken in completely by the Nazi theory of German invincibility. They believe that the German Army has many secret weapons, and that these and the superior German organization and fighting ability will make an Allied invasion effort so costly that the Allies will sue for a negotiated peace."[19]

The Armenian troops with the Germans in Albania resembled in many ways what the defeated Italian troops were to the Partisans and the Allies. Sometime they were helpful; at other times they were a burden. Like the Italians, many of the Armenian soldiers surrendered or deserted and came over to the Partisan side. "Sources report that two hundred and fifty Armenians surrendered to the IVth Partisan Brigade on 12 May 1944. This action took place near Korcë," Z reported.

By the end of the summer 1944 the Partisans appeared to have the Germans, who were retreating from Greece and Albania anyway, on their heels. During the week of August 14–21, the Partisans launched several guerrilla raids on the Germans around the city of Fieri. "The enemy forces were routed with a loss of 20 Germans and an unspecified number of Ballists killed. Seventy Ballists were captured and released the following day," Z reported. Three Ballist commanders were killed and 135 Ballist soldiers deserted and joined the Partisans, Z said.[20]

Despite reports of surrender, the execution of prisoners by both the Partisans and the quisling Balli Kombëtar government in Tirana and Vlora were not uncommon. On April 3 the German command in Vlora, along with the Balli Kombëtar and the Regiment of Gendarmerie Kosova (Kosovar Albanians fighting for the Germans) jointly announced the execution by firing squad in the town center of five Communists. Those executed included a Moslem imam and a woman.[21]

The Partisans reacted in kind, of course, but they were not as meticulous as the Germans in keeping records. Often prisoners were buried in unmarked graves they were forced to dig before being shot. Other times, when propaganda warranted it, the Partisans announced an execution, as it did when it captured Lazar Fundo, a native of Korcë who renounced the Communist Party to join the Italian Fascists and later the Germans.[22]

There were times when the Partisans shot at the British. This happened following a British commando raid against German positions on the coastal village of Himarë in southern Albania in August. "When their officers remonstrated that the British were allies," the OSS report of the incident said, "a Partisan called Selim replied 'German or British, it is all the same to us,' and he kept on firing. Source invited an explanation and the Partisan said it was a mistake of judgment. Source asked whether Selim had been punished and the Albanian Partisan said 'No.'"[23]

Enver Hoxha may have disliked the Americans and hated the British, but his feelings did not greatly influence the emotions of other Communist Partisan groups fighting in the region, especially in neighboring Montenegro, where many Albanians lived. There Partisan groups under Tito welcomed American support.

An unidentified American OSS agent submitted the following report about a funeral held for an American flight sergeant who was killed on a combat mission over Montenegro in July 1944.

"Along about the middle of July 1944, I was notified by radio that 9 U.S. fliers had bailed out safely over Moykovac and that one flier was dead upon landing. The Partisan Brigade commander asked for instructions. He was told to send the fliers to Kolasin and bury the dead soldier at Moykovac.

"I went to Kolasin. Upon arrival I was informed by General P. Dapcevic, C.O. 2nd Partisan Army Corps, that the fliers were en route by horseback and that the body of a Sergeant was also being carried to Kolasin for burial with full military honors. I was also informed that a Lieut. was hurt and was being carried by hand stretcher bearers.

"The fliers arrived at Kolasin at 1600 and the body of Sergeant K. was taken to the hospital. A casket was ready and the local Partisan girls had made an American flag from parachute silk. This was draped on the casket and many wreaths were made from wild flowers and carried by the Partisans. We wrote out the inscriptions and they were copied in English. a) To an American Flier who died for his country. b) Sgt. K, an American Hero. c) (In Serbian) Our Comrade (Drug) who died for Liberty.

"At about 1700 hours the funeral parade started for the cemetery which is about 2 kilometers outside of town. The Partisan 2nd Corps band led, then came a platoon of armed soldiers (men and women) and then the casket. The Ptzn. Staff and Dr. Miljanic, the President of Montenegro. There were roughly two thousand people along the line of march all standing at attention.

"Three Orthodox Priests read the ceremony and then Dr. Miljanic made a short address in French. He is a beautiful speaker. In brief, he asked any Americans who were Comrades of the dead soldier to please let his relatives know that although he is sleeping a long way from his native land he is always going to be looked after by men, women and children who, too, have suffered losses by death in war. They will always honor and take care of this last resting place of an American Comrade who came so far to give his life for the cause of Freedom.

"The Priests sprinkled earth on the simple wooden box and the final volley was fired by a squad of Partisans.

"The cross on the grave at present is a wooden one. I will try to have a stone one made if possible and also some sort of identification tag made to mark it.

"The site of the cemetery is indeed beautiful. It nestles among the mountains three thousand feet up. The valley is green and the former flying companions of the dead Sergeant roar overhead almost daily on their way to the same kind of mission in which he took part before his death.

"This is all I can say. Everything was perfectly carried out with simple dignity and a very deep affection on the part of the people here to whom America and all the name stands for means so much."[24]

4

Tom

Thomas Eftim Stefan—"Tommy" to his friends—was all you would want a high school boy to be. He was a good student and all-around athlete at Laconia High School in Laconia, New Hampshire. He was not tall but he was muscular and rugged. He was handsome. He was built like a wrestler. The yearbook of his 1936 graduating class lists his accomplishments. He played football, baseball and basketball. He was on the tennis team. He was a member of the student council and the International Friendship Club and was on the National Honor Society. His ambition? "To enter the consular service or law."

Laconia is set in the beautiful lakes region of the Granite State, just north of Concord. Long before the advent of interstate highways, mass communications and a dominant tourism industry, Laconia was a small, barely accessible working-class mill town. Laconia had lumber mills, textile plants and shoe factories. It was also known as the place where railroad cars were built. Soon these railroad cars carried tourists to the region, tourists who needed hotels and boarding houses and restaurants. Immigrants, especially French Canadians, were attracted to the area in the early 1900s. There was work to be had and it was a good place to raise a family. There were snow-topped mountains, green woods and sparkling blue lakes, like Lake Winnipesauke, and there was time and space for hunting, hiking, fishing, sailing, swimming and skiing.

Among those immigrants who landed in Laconia were Eftim and Emma Stefan, Tom's parents. They came first to Boston from the Korcë region in southern Albania in the early 1900's. Korcë, close to the Greek border, was where many of the early Albanian immigrants came from. Then, seeking work and opportunity, and a place to raise a family, Eftim

4. Tom

and Emma headed north to Laconia. Laconia was away from the slums and tenements of the immigrant ghettoes of Boston. To men from Albania, the clean air, sunlight, mountains and open skies reminded them of their home country. Tom was born in Laconia on March 21, 1919. He was the oldest of four children. He had three sisters, Ethel, Dorothy and Mary.

Although Laconia was made up of many immigrant groups, being an immigrant from Albania was unusual because there were so few of them in the United States at the time, and most of them lived in Massachusetts. The Massachusetts 1930 census counted only 2,938 people listed as Albanian-born. Albanian church records and the records of fraternal organizations said there were 8,800 Albanians in Massachusetts, but the larger figure included American-born children of Albanian parents.[1] Often, because they were Eastern Orthodox in religion, and came from an area close to Greece, they were counted as Greek.

There is little doubt that Tom was his father's pride. Eftim Stefan came from a tradition that not only honored the birth of male children, but heaped additional honors on the birth of the first male child. Among those honors was the middle name of Eftim.

Even though hard economic times struck the country following the 1929 Wall Street stock market crash, the Stefan family appeared to have survived well enough to allow Tom to finish high school. His parents owned and operated a small grocery store in Laconia where the whole family worked. It appeared to have done well enough to support the family through a difficult economic era. Albanian immigrant families of the time were close-knit and supportive, as were many immigrant families of other ethnic groups newly arrived in America. Albanian was spoken at home so that Tom was well grounded in the language of his ancestors.

Normally Tom Stefan would have gone to work after graduation, as was the custom of the children of immigrants. They were expected to follow in the footsteps of their fathers—working in the family store, or restaurant, or shoe repair shop. The children of Albanian immigrants before World War II did not as a rule go to college.

But Tom Stefan wanted to make something of himself. He wanted to go to college. He wanted to become a lawyer. Although he was the son of Albanian immigrants, he was not brought up among other Albanians or their children living in the United States. He spoke Albanian at home, but he was brought up in a diverse community where there were no Albanians. His friends and classmates had names like Royce, Collins, Noyes and Booth. The parents of the children of Laconia might have been from French Canada, Poland, Italy, Greece, or Russia, but they were all Americans, just as Stefan was.

Tom Stefan was smart as well, being named to the National Honor Society in his senior year. After graduation Stefan enrolled at Marietta College in Marietta, Ohio. It was a long way from Laconia but Stefan seemed to have thrived at the small school. His college life at Marietta came to an end two years later in 1938, however, when his father died. Without financial help from home he was forced to leave school.

Stefan at 20 years of age returned to Laconia but he did not remain there very long. He was ambitious and opportunity in Laconia was limited. He wanted to go to law school but he did not have the money. In 1939 Stefan moved to Boston. Despite the scarcity of jobs as a result of the Depression, Stefan did get work as a shipping clerk in a men's clothing store. He later got another job in a restaurant that was run by several Albanians. There he could at least eat for nothing. He enrolled at Suffolk University Law School and took law classes at night. Suffolk University at the time was a small urban school that taught law to many working-class residents of Boston. Workingmen could work days and study law nights. It would take them much longer to finish law school and become lawyers, but if they persevered, it could be done

Boston before World War II was a blue-collar working-class city of immigrants. Although the Irish generally controlled its politics, the Yankee Brahmins still controlled the finances. Below these two dominant ethnic groups was everybody else—the Italians, Greeks, Poles, Russians, Lithuanians, Jews and the blacks. All had their places of worship, newspapers, fraternities, clubs and neighborhoods—the Yankees on Beacon Hill and the Back Bay, the Irish in South Boston, the Italians in the North End, and the Jews and blacks in Roxbury. Everybody else, including members of every new and poor immigrant group, lived crowded into cold-water tenement slums in the South End or the West End, which were the poorest sections of the city.

Stefan's job at the Arch Street Tavern in downtown Boston was as a menial busboy, a sort of assistant waiter. He set and cleared tables and brought customers water. He washed dishes and swept the floor. As noted in *The Albanian Struggle*, "In Boston hundreds of Albanians are employed as cooks, countermen, and bus boys. The Greeks before them had gone into this kind of work; and when an Albanian could find nothing else, he turned to a restaurant owned by prosperous Greeks or staffed by indigent ones. Many Albanians spoke Greek; moreover, they and the Greeks had in common their membership in the in the Orthodox faith. But the conditions of labor in Greek restaurants are no better, and often they are worse, than in other restaurants. The workers toil from 10 to 12 hours a day for a small weekly wage and their meals. They protest against long hours, complain of the long monotony of working with pots and pans. Since the Depression, many younger people, unable to find other employment, have had to seek restaurant jobs. They belong to the most discouraged and disillusioned sections of the Albanian population—the section that dares not think about its future."[2]

Stefan was an American, not an Albanian immigrant. The restaurant he worked at was run by Albanians, not Greeks, but the conditions were the same.

The restaurant, the Arch Street Tavern in downtown Boston, was also a drinking hangout frequented by newspaper reporters. The newsmen worked for the two Hearst-owned tabloids that were housed around the corner from the restaurant in Winthrop Square. The papers were the evening *Boston Record* and the morning *Boston American*. When the presses rolled the newspaper building shook and the rumbling of the presses could be heard around the square and in the tavern. Orange-painted newspaper delivery trucks lined the streets outside the building, constantly pulling in and out of loading docks, loading up with the latest editions, adding to the noise.

In between editions or assignments, reporters, photographers, editors and copy desk people ate and drank at the tavern and Stefan made friends with them. He listened to their stories and their talk about events, particularly talk about a pending war. He worked all day at the restaurant and he studied law at night. He did get to know some of the reporters, and he doubtlessly drank with them. But he was no Sterling Hayden. Despite the fact that both Hayden and Stefan were friends with newsmen from some of the same newspapers, there is no evidence that the two ever met at the time. Although nobody wrote about Stefan as they did Hayden, Stefan did have his cheering section at the Hearst publication. This was made clear later when the *Boston American* ran a story about Stefan's exploits following the fall of Tirana in November 1944.

All men of Stefan's age were aware of a potential war. He not only heard the talk about the war in Europe from the newspapermen, but the Albanians talked frequently about Italian dictator Benito Mussolini's invasion of Albania.

The Albanian presence in Boston and in Massachusetts may have been small in numbers before World War II, but Boston was the nerve center of the Albanian Diaspora in the United States. Ninety-five per cent of the Albanian population in Massachusetts belonged to the Orthodox faith. There were six Albanian Orthodox churches in the state, three in Boston and one each in Natick, Worcester and Southbridge. Each church was a focal point of social activity and political awareness. Bishop Fan Noli, who was prime minister of Albania for six months in 1924, was head of the Albanian Orthodox Church of North America with headquarters at St. George's Orthodox Church in South Boston.

The Albanians had several weekly newspapers published in Albanian and English. Two of them, *Dielli* (Sun) and *Bota* (People), were published in Boston. A third called *Liria* (Freedom) later joined the other two. There were still several other papers that came and went as economics or politics dictated. All were filled with news about Albania.

On December 7, 1941, the Japanese bombed Pearl Harbor. The United States declared war on Japan, and Germany and Italy, the other two members of the Axis, declared war on the United States. World War II had begun. Four months after that bombing, on April 10, 1942, Stefan left his job and his studies and enlisted in U.S. Army as a private. Following basic training at Fort Belvoir, Virginia, Stefan attended field artillery school. He was made an officer on January 14, 1943, and assigned to the 36th Infantry Division. Stefan then attended the army's military intelligence school at Camp Ritchie, Maryland, and upon graduation joined the OSS on August 18, 1943.

One of Stefan's first jobs for the OSS was to help recruit Albanian immigrants for the OSS. The OSS badly needed recruits who could speak foreign languages and it made a great effort to find them and persuade them to join the newly formed organization. In a war that stretched around the globe and included countries with many different languages, the OSS needed all the men it could get who could speak those languages. Albanian was one of those languages. The OSS also hired civilians like McAdoo and Fultz and, being an inter-service agency, welcomed into its ranks volunteers from all branches of service, like Marines Hayden and Kukich.

When Stefan had left Boston he had been a lowly bus boy. When he returned in an effort to seek out Albanian-speaking candidates for the OSS, he was an officer. One can only speculate on the impression he made when, dressed in his army uniform as an officer rather than as a bus boy and dishwasher, he visited his old restaurant.

Stefan appeared to have succeeded in his recruiting mission. Three months later, in November 1943, just after he was shipped overseas, Stefan was promoted to first lieutenant. The recommendation for his promotion read: "This officer has assisted the chief of his section in recruiting and training of qualified enlisted civilian personnel for an overseas mission of a secret nature, and has acted in an advisory capacity to the section chief on geographical and political matters, providing valuable information relative to the mission based on knowledge and research." In an attachment the OSS said Stefan "will be in charge of operational and intelligence activities in one of the Nazi-occupied Balkan states. [He] is thoroughly qualified to take charge of these field operations by linguistic and geographical knowledge and by training in intelligence work."[3]

Now Stefan, PFC Albert Tolie of St. Louis and Navy Seaman Angelo Metro of Boston, one of the men Stefan persuaded to join the OSS, were stuck in the mountains above the village of Tragjas, watching it burn. Tolie and Metro were Albanian-Americans trained as radio operators. The three had set out from Seaview in a foot of snow for the interior of Albania on April 3, 1944. Stefan's orders were for him to work his way through German lines, meet up with the British SOE in the area, and make contact with Enver Hoxha at his headquarters somewhere in the Korcë region of the country. Tolie had come from Korcë and knew the region. Stefan's parents had come from there as well. Metro was born in Boston.

Hardly had the three left the safety of the caves at Seaview, where they had arrived on March 20, and climbed and crossed the snowbound Dukati Mountains, than they ran into one of the patrols the Germans had launched in their effort to ferret out the Allies from their seacoast caves. "Unfortunately the time selected coincided with a period of intense German activity. The unit on the first night reached the village of Tragjas and intended to hole in there to wait for darkness to make the next stage of its journey. However it was routed out by news that the Germans were on the way to the village and barely had time to escape up the nearby mountains with personal kits and w/t (radio) equipment. All other stores and equipment including bedding was lost. An hour or so later it sat up on the mountain overlooking the village, watched the Germans come in with Ballists and burn the house where it had stopped for a part of the previous night."[4]

Stefan, Tolie and Metro—although on a separate mission—ended up in the same area of Tragjas as Hudson and Kukich, and both groups in different locations watched the Germans burn the pro–Partisan village and scatter the villagers. While Hudson, Kukich and their party went one way to escape from the Germans, Stefan and his two men went another.

Stefan, Tolie and Metro hid out from the Germans for several days, roaming the mountains in search of safety and food. The trio's knowledge of the Albanian language proved vital as they sought to avoid capture and meet up with Enver Hoxha at his headquarters. Although Stefan spoke Albanian well, he had learned his Albanian in the United States. Nevertheless, the Albanians they came across were greatly impressed when they came across an American officer who spoke their language, even if he did so with an accent. Tolie and Metro spoke Albanian like natives.

With the radio still intact, Stefan was able to send off two messages to Gates (Fultz) in Bari. The first, dated April 7, said: "I am four hours from Gomeniça. I have been on the run since leaving Galba [Kukich]. I have failed to locate the English mission. The Germans are in Gomeniça. Contact from the Central [Communist] Committee have reached us.... Situation is perilous here. I have no food or supplies." The second message was dated four days later, April 11. It read: "We are being surrounded by the Germans and we have no food or clothing. Only our radio is left. 15 reds are here. Part of Battalion P [Partisan] is dropping back. Will try to keep contact. Have been on the run for three days."[5]

Stefan made his way back down to Tragjas when it appeared that the Germans and their Balli allies had left. He found refuge in the Tragjas home of Hito Alimerko, the local head of the Communist Partisans. Alimerko housed Stefan and his two comrades for several days. His house, located away from the rest of the homes in the village, had not been burned. Stefan shared what little food he had with them. Alimerko's two sons Reuf and Pasho met Stefan and his two companions.

Interviewed in Tirana in October 2004, the brothers remembered that Stefan gave their father a Thompson submachine gun as well as a .45 caliber handgun. "He was grateful for my father's help," Reuf Alimerko said. Pasho recalled how impressed they were with Stefan. "He was an American of Albanian descent, an officer, and he was fighting the Germans over here. He was young and energetic and he spoke Albanian well." Their father, they said, spoke highly of Stefan the rest of his life, although they did not meet again. Hito Alimerko died in 1972.

After leaving Tragjas, Stefan came across several British SOE officers making their way toward the coast. Reginald Hibbert wrote, "When the German pressure was relaxed and it became possible to move back to the coast (Lt. Col. Norman) Wheeler encountered by chance Lt. Stefan, an American officer of the OSS who had landed with two others at the Seaview base in Balli Kombëtar territory on the coast nearer to Vlora and was trying to find his way to the Partisans. Wheeler has described the meeting as a poor man's Stanley and Livingstone."[6]

Stefan, in a later hand-written message, told Fultz that his when his group entered Tragjas after the Germans left, the village women told him that they recognized the Balli men from Dukat who had participated in the raid on their village. They were led by one Maliq Koshena, a Dukati Balli chief. This was the man, Stefan said, that the British had supplied with arms on the condition that they would not be used against the Communists. "My last day at Seaview I acted as interpreter for the British when they turned over arms to the people of Dukati on the condition that they would not be used against the Reds. Maliq Koshena promised faithfully, then look what happened.

"When I first arrived here I talked with several Bally [Balli] leaders, including Muço [Skender Muço, regional Balli Kombëtar leader] and they had me believing that the Reds were doing all this terrorizing and burning." Instead, Stefan found that the terror and burning was coming from both sides. "After this operation we got trapped in those same mts. with no food, clothing, or a roof to sleep under. We lived on corn bread and eggs, and I was feeding 20 to 25 people every meal, who had to leave their homes and were destitute. No wonder the gold went fast. Wheeler found us in this condition on the twentieth of April and he was dismayed at our living quarters."[7]

After being resupplied by airdrop, Stefan again set out to find Enver Hoxha. Stefan and his two radio operators hiked for several days through rugged mountain country in southern Albania in a general direction toward Korcë. The region was Hoxha's stronghold and Stefan found that the people were very supportive of Hoxha and helpful toward the newly arrived American soldiers.

The Communist Party movement in Albania generally began in the south before eventually spreading to the rest of the country. Many of the early Communist Party recruits were from the city of Korcë or from the region. The area also served as a training ground for recruits and a zone of safety for Hoxha and the Partisans. It was here that Hoxha found refuge following his escape from the Germans during the winter of 1943–1944. Partisans also made it a habit to retreat to these hills following guerrilla raids on German convoys. When German retaliatory patrols left the roads and chased the Partisans back into the mountains following an action, they often ran into well-placed ambushes.

Stefan arrived at Hoxha's headquarters at Odriçan in late April. Although there were several British SOE officers and men assigned to Hoxha headquarters, Stefan was the first American. Odriçan was a well hidden small village of some twenty houses. The village was ringed by guards. It was where Hoxha and his staff conducted their war against the Germans. The British had been there for some time, assigned to a small house well away from the house Hoxha used as his headquarters. Hoxha appears to have given Stefan a warm welcome, at least warmer than the ever-suspicious leader of the Partisans ever gave the British. This may have been due to the fact that Stefan was the first American soldier to come to his headquarters. More than likely Hoxha probably extended his hand in friendship to Stefan because Stefan's parents were from Albania. And not only could Stefan speak Albanian, he spoke in Hoxha's own Tosk dialect.

Hoxha was thirty-six years old at the time. He was six feet tall, which was taller than most Albanians. He some time ago had exchanged his Partisan makeshift outfit for the uniform of an officer. He was clean-shaven, as were most of the staff around him, and he was handsome. Stefan had just turned twenty-seven. At five feet, seven inches tall, he was shorter than Hoxha. His uniform was casual, as befitted a man who had marched for days over rugged Albanian mountain trails. On his left shoulder he wore a patch of the American flag, and it caught the attention of all the Partisans in the camp.

Hoxha many years later would disparage Stefan in his memoirs, as he disparaged most of the people who helped him in his climb to power. But during the time that Stefan was with him as the key liaison with the OSS and the United States, Hoxha thought enough of Stefan to take him into his confidence when, of course, it suited his purpose. Stefan, throughout the time he was with Hoxha in the field, appeared to have cultivated a close but professional relationship with the Communist leader. Sometimes, though, when he was frustrated by Hoxha, Stefan referred to him in sarcastic tones.

One of Stefan's first cables to Fultz after meeting with Hoxha was to ask for instructions on answering the many questions Hoxha brought up dealing with the intentions of the United States. Specifically Hoxha wanted to know what the United States would do for Albania in its battle against the Germans, and what it would give Albania in exchange for intelligence about the enemy.

Fultz, in a long reply, told Stefan that he should make it clear to Hoxha that the fighting in Albania was not an isolated war, but was part of the same coordinated war the Allies were fighting against the Germans.

Fultz, in an April 29, 1944 message to Stefan, wrote: "A good example of this coordination and of widespread reactions caused by any given action is that of the fighting in southern Italy last summer and autumn. While the Allies were fighting Axis troops in southern Italy, LNC and other Albanians were fighting Fascists [Italians] in Albania. Any troops held in Albania to hold that country could not be used in Italy against the Americans and the British and made our job that much more the easier. As a result of these combined efforts Italy collapsed and for the most part the Fascists were cleared out of Albania. Who cleared them out? Certainly not LNC and the Albanians alone. Except for American and British efforts in Italy the Fascists no doubt would still be in Albania and while the Nazis are there in their place we would still be one step less far along the road to the completion of the job. What are we offered in return for that?

"Eventually the Germans are going to clear out of Albania, partly though the efforts of the Albanians and party through American, British and Russian efforts, efforts which for the most part will be made not in Albania but away from Albania, fortunately for that country. Already the Germans there are jittery, not because of what is happening in Albania so much as it is because of what is happening on the Dniester River; in the air over Germany and France and because of what has happened and is happening in Italy. What are we offered for these efforts?"

Fultz went on: "I do not think the Albanians or we get anywhere if we think in terms of 'what am I offered' to do this and to do that, what am I offered for this isolated effort and that bit of action."

Then, after making no promises, Fultz hinted at membership for Albania in the United Nations as a reward. "If Albania wishes to become a member of the United Nations as many Albanians claim it does then it must see what it can contribute to the united effort of fighting Germans wherever they are to be found. If they start in with those easiest to find it will be the Germans in Albania."

Fultz told Stefan to specifically spell out to Hoxha that the Americans and the British agreed that the British would be responsible for combat operations, organizing resistance and delivering supplies. The Americans would be responsible for gathering intelligence. The intelligence was extremely important for the Allies, Fultz stressed. "If we can get out of the country quickly accurate, essential target information (troop concentrations, ammunition and fuel dumps, vehicle parks and convoys) planes that will be over a few of these can do more damage in half an hour or so of bombing and strafing than a brigade will do in a month of fighting. When Allied planes work closely with LNC or any other resistance group the Germans will be a bit more cautious in the way they chase them around." However, he told Stefan to warn Hoxha that "Americans are not to be played against [the] British."

Yet even though Fultz said the Americans came "bearing no gifts" for Hoxha and his Partisan army, he then urged Stefan to make sure the Albanians knew that the supplies delivered by the British were largely American supplies.

"However, although Britain actually brings the stuff in, all of these things are not British, for example the British battle dress. If any of the LNC wish to investigate personally let any of them wearing British battle dress lift the flap of the jacket and he will find a label indicating that it was made in Philadelphia Q. M. [quartermaster] Dept." he wrote.

Fultz said he did not want Stefan to barter for intelligence, or promise arms, ammunition and food in return for information. What the United States was promising, he said, was freedom for Albania and American friendship and gratitude. "Albania is going to need understanding friends in the days when final settlements are made," Fultz warned. "Americans are friends of Albania and I hope the Albanians do not want us to be ignorant and misunderstanding friends. Americans, when future decisions are made can help or hinder accordingly as they know more surely what has taken place during these years."[8]

Friendship, from Enver Hoxha's point of view, was fine. But guns were better. But if he took issue with what Stefan told him as a result of Fultz's message, there is no record of it. Hoxha, in dealing with the Allies at meetings in his headquarters at Odriçan or Helmës, rarely singled out the Americans for criticism. When he complained about the paucity of supplies coming in from the Allies for his Partisans, he usually blamed the British. He was convinced that the British were in a conspiracy with his enemies in Albania to prevent him and his Communists from coming to power. That is why, he thought, that the British continued to send supplies to Abas Kupi and to the Balli even though they would not fight the Germans. The Americans, as far as Hoxha was concerned, were being led by the nose by the British. But the Americans could be useful. So he befriended Stefan, and appeared to bring him into his inner circle, much to the resentment of the British.

This friendship was made clear when Hoxha invited Stefan to attend a four-day conference in late May in the town of Përmet in southern Albania. The town, once controlled by the Italians, had been attacked by the Partisans several times a year ago. It had been abandoned by the Italians upon the collapse of their government and was firmly under control of the Partisans.

Fultz was delighted by the invitation. He urged Stefan to get into a "close relationship with the local boys [Partisans]" but to "maintain a fairly independent position with respect to our cousins [the British]" as well as the Partisans.[9]

The meeting, called the Congress of Përmet, was a turning point in the war. Although the meeting was apparently designed to include representatives of all resistance groups, it was controlled by the Communists. Hoxha used the meeting to consolidate his control over the resistance and pave the way for his ascension to power once the war was over. Some 200 delegates from all parts of Albania met and elected an Anti-Fascist Committee of National Liberation with Hoxha at its head. The Congress also appointed Hoxha as supreme commander of the armed forces and gave him the rank of colonel-general, the highest rank it had. The Congress voted to reorganize the army and for the first time introduced official ranks. It newly named its army the National Liberation Army and appointed trusted Hoxha confidant Spiro Moisiu as chief of staff. The Congress voted to prohibit the return of King Zog and reserve to declare null and void all treaties signed under his regime.

Stefan, who had a ringside seat at the conference, was treated as something of a celebrity by the Albanian delegates. He was not only the first American soldier they met, he was of Albanian descent and he spoke the language easily. Since Stefan was the only Allied officer to attend the meeting, his reports to Bari were the only reports the Allies received about the event. The British had been upstaged, which did not displease Hoxha.

"The British were not too happy with Tom," Nick Kukich said. "They resented him because of his access to Hoxha." Kukich, who was introduced to Hoxha by Stefan after Kukich arrived at Partisan headquarters in July, said, "They (Hoxha and Stefan) seemed to get along pretty good. It seemed like Tom could go up and talk with Hoxha any time. In fact he never had to call him in advance. Tom had a good, strong personal relationship with Hoxha. Very strong."[10]

Some of that British resentment toward Stefan came out later in comments and books written by several of the British SOE officers and writers who ignored or diminished Stefan's accomplishments. British writer Jon Halliday noted that the first American OSS mission to Hoxha's headquarters arrived in May 1944. (It was April.) "It was headed by a very ineffectual figure, Tom Stefan, whom Hoxha treats with some disdain."[11]

Hibbert, who met Stefan in Albania, wrote that the British boycotted the Përmet meeting on the grounds that Hoxha would use the meeting to solidify his position at the expense of segments of the Balli Kombëtar and Abas Kupi, whom the British still hoped to get to fight the Germans. But it was already too late. The Balli had thrown in with the Germans and Kupi would not fight. British attempts to persuade Kupi to fight by sending in SOE officers and promising supplies at this point only served to fuel Hoxha's anti–British hatred. The civil war aspect of the Albanian World War II experience was just about over, and the Communists had won. Now the main goal was to rid the country of the Germans and arrest and execute all Albanian "traitors."

Hibbert also played down Stefan's role at Përmet. "American policy was unformed," Hibbert wrote, "and no U.S. mission had discovered Abas Kupi or other nationalist leadership candidates. As a result Lieutenant Stefan was able to go to Përmet and gratify the Partisans; and after the event it was possible to see that his presence had not committed the U.S. to anything."[12]

Hoxha did indeed treat Stefan with contempt in his memoirs—he called

Helmës, August 1944. Enver Hoxha (left) greets Captain Tom Stefan at his headquarters. Note American flag patch on Stefan's left shoulder (National Archives).

Stefan a "degenerate"—written some 40 years later, but in 1944 there is every indication that Hoxha welcomed Stefan to his headquarters with open arms. Stefan, after all, was the only officer, American or British, who could speak, read and write Albanian. He was the only American or British officer Hoxha could confer with in his native Tosk dialect. Rare photographs taken of the two show Hoxha and Stefan in friendly poses. The pictures, taken at Hoxha's headquarters in Helmës in 1944, show Stefan conferring with Hoxha and other Partisan leaders. Although there are other photographs of Hoxha with British or American officers, they are group poses that also include other Partisans. Stefan appears to have been the only Allied officer Hoxha posed for pictures with alone.

It was Stefan, not the British, who cabled the Allies back in Bari that the Congress had appointed Hoxha head of the reorganized armed forces and who listed all of the other military appointments made at the meeting. Stefan also informed the Allies that, although the Communists dominated the proceedings, they made up only a minority of the delegates in attendance. In addition, Stefan was the first to report back to Bari that Hoxha and the Albanian Communists were under the direct influence of

Helmës, August 1944. Left to right: Enver Hoxha, Captain Tom Stefan, Minister of Foreign Affairs Dr. Omer Nishani (National Archives).

Tito and the Yugoslav Communist Party.

"At Përmet amazing good planning and organization displayed," Stefan cabled back to Fultz in Bari on June 2. "I was very much impressed by the delegates from Scutari, Dibra, Tirana, and Mati. I conversed with 75 percent of the delegates personally and found that only about 5 percent were communists," Stefan said in the first of four cables sent that day, and the next day.

Hours later he sent a second cable. "Evidently the Communist Party is the guiding hand, and I have strong reason to believe that Hoxha and the others never made any decision without consulting a certain Kossovar named Ali Mali, who has been introduced to me as being a member of the Central Committee. I am sure he is Tito's representative and the man whom the Bally [Balli] call Dushanovich."

Ali Mali was Ali Duskanoviç, a veteran Yugoslav Communist who was Tito's emissary to the Përmet Congress.

In a third cable sent later the same day, Stefan reported: "Ali Mali remained in seclusion at the Congress. Before departing for my base, I went over the government with Hoxha. Ali entered from another room, and the rest of the talk, too lengthy to discuss, brought out certain facts leading to this conclusion. It was clearly shown that Zog, the British, Kupi, and Bally [Balli] occupy the same spot in Red Hearts. More in the next cable."

The next day, Stefan continued: "In the near future they intend to restrict movements of Allied officers from the Red into Bally [Balli] or Kupi territory. Their army is increasing daily and the political machine has a good foundation. To sum it all up, I should say that these people are going to play a heavy role in the government of the future because they are fighting for freedom and are prepared for great sacrifices and that Communism will continue to increase unless the Allies do some more propagandizing. The Red Army, Stalin and Tito are the Gods of the people in all areas we have visited so far."

Stefan on June 4 cabled Fultz again in order to emphasize Hoxha's insistence that the Allies—meaning the British—end their policy of conferring with Kupi or the Balli, or supplying them with arms. "The new Red policy is definite now that no Allied Mission will be allowed to cross into Bally [Balli] or Kupi areas. This is a touchy subject with the Red leader.... Please answer soonest before I speak to Hoxha, who will arrive here in two days."

Stefan knew that his information was important and that he was alone in obtaining it. The following day he again cabled Fultz. "Since I was the only Ally present at the Congress, could you announce information about it and the army over Bari radio? Reds are depending on us to do it."[13]

Hoxha remained convinced that the British were determined to thwart the Communist Partisan rise to power, and that was why the British continued to confer with the pro-Zogist Abas Kupi and other nationalist groups. It was as though the British maintained an "anybody but Hoxha" mentality, even though it was Hoxha's Partisans who were the only organized group fighting the Germans.

What Stefan's reports from the Përmet meeting showed is that Stefan was far from the "ineffectual" figure the British painted him as. He had Hoxha's ear and, among other things, was the first to report Tito's presence and influence on Hoxha at the meeting. Stefan, whether knowingly or not, was bound to infuriate the British when he cabled to OSS headquarters in Bari that Hoxha's deep hatred for the British equated them, in Hoxha's eyes, to the despised King Zog, the Balli and Kupi.

Stefan, the American novice, had beaten the experienced British at their own game and the British did not like it.

No sooner did the Congress of Përmet end than the Germans launched an offensive toward Përmet that scattered the Partisans. The Ger-

Helmës, August 1944. Left to right: Enver Hoxha, Captain Tom Stefan, Dr. Omer Nishani and Finance Minister Colonel Ramadan Çitaku (National Archives).

mans, in an effort to destroy the Partisans once and for all, burned villages like Panarit and Katundi and threatened Odriçan.

German Messerschmitt ME 110s roared over the mountaintops and strafed and bombed Partisan, British and American tents and houses in Odriçan in early June, causing havoc. Several Partisans were killed and more wounded. Angel, code name for Navy seaman Angelo Metro, witnessed one attack. Angel described the German air attack this way: "On the 5th of June, just as the sun was setting two German ME 110 appeared over the Korca Mountain top and came very low over our base and then over the British. The second time around one of the planes left and headed toward Berat while the other came in real low and fired a number of rounds. We all hit the deck as we didn't know what was going on. However, the next time around we watched the plane come in real low and strafed the British tents one after another. He came in about five different times firing bursts of machinegun fire and also in five different positions each time. At the same time Art [Stefan] was making his way up toward the British Mission and made a run for it when he saw the plane coming in. He lay out in the middle of an open field all the time the plane was firing bursts. He came running down to our base with his face all cut up and very shaken up."

Stefan filed his own handwritten report to Fultz on the attack and the "critical" situation in Albania on June 12, after he left the Odriçan region and made it to the relative safety of the coast. Stefan said, "This whole business started the third of June when I was strafed in the field while on my way to the British. I thought it was the end."

Stefan described how he and his British colleagues organized a run to the coast to escape the German offensive while Hoxha and his general staff remained confused. After being ordered by the British to bury their equipment in a pit—dug by Angel—Stefan, the British and their party, on mules borrowed from the British, headed for the village of Frasheri, four hours away. During the march Stefan could see smoke rise in the distance. The smoke was from his father's village of Stratobërdë, near Korcë. The Germans had set it afire, along with a string of other villages in their path.

"Heavy mortar and artillery fire could be heard behind us," Stefan reported. "The main party left at 4 A.M. for ODRICAN where LNC [Levizja Nacional Çlirimtare—National Liberation Movement] HQS were located. Palmer [British SOE Lt. Col. Alan] Palmer and I stayed to talk over the situation with General [Spiro] Moisiu and Colonel [Bedri] Spahiu, both of whom showed a lack of understanding of the situation.

"Much disgusted Palmer and I left for ODRICAN where we found General Hoxha and his staff entirely ignorant of the whole situation. He didn't even know where the hell his own troops were."

The Allies headed for the coast with the Germans hot on their heels. Stefan, his OSS radio operators and the British, reached the village of Borsh along the coast. It was close to Grama Bay and Seaview.

"The situation here is not good at all. Germans are making every effort to close the base. Partisans of the Sixth Brigade are holding off at SHEN VASIL in the south, and north of here just this side of HIMARA. On the other road the Huns are repairing the bridge at GJORMI and forces coming from VALONA have arrived at LEPENICA. Heavy forces are also concentrated at FIER.

"After discussing this situation it was obvious that we are in a helluva spot. Alan Palmer and I decided to stay in along with Lt. (C.L.D.) Newell and a radio operator. We plan to leave here immediately and join the 6th Brigade commander at KUCH. We are all heavily armed and will fight if we have to."[14]

Navy Seaman Metro, in a handwritten report to Fultz, which was co-signed by Tolie, told how he was ordered by a British officer to bury his radio equipment to keep it hidden from the Germans. In his June 14

Odriçan, September 1944. Enver Hoxha's second headquarters. Left to right: Koçi Xoxe, minister of the interior; Spiro Nako; Enver Hoxha; Dr. Omer Nishani; OSS Lt. Nick Kukich, OSS Lt. John O'Keefe, Hoxha's wife Nexhmije Hoxha; OSS Sgt. George Steffo (half hidden); and two unidentified Partisans. Xoxe was later executed and Nako "committed suicide" (National Archives).

report, written in long hand two days after he was evacuated, he pointed out that the Partisan commanders were not the only people confused by the German offensive. "When we got to Borsh the presence of more brass hats made things more complicated. Also amusing at times (was) when one officer gave someone an order, the next minute another officer would contradict the same order causing much confusion at times—as too many cooks spoil the soup. Here too life for an enlisted man was pretty tough. Well, it all adds up to the fact that an enlisted man has a pretty tough go of it when dealing with British majors and colonels. So much for that."[15]

The German June offensive was a major operation designed to clear the Partisans from the German main lines of communications that ran from Greece through Albania. This meant that the Germans needed the coastal road open for their motor traffic coming north from Greece. The German offensive shattered the 6th Partisan Brigade, which Stefan and Palmer had joined.

A report from an OSS agent who was an eyewitness to the German operation said the offensive began June 3 when elements of the German 1st Mountain Division attacked the Partisans near the village of Voskopojë in the Korcë region. "The Germans pillaged, ransacked and burned entire villages and crops ready for harvest. They killed women and children wantonly in almost every nook and corner of southern Albania.

"An example of German ruthlessness is provided by the town of VUNO, a place which had not been touched in previous operations. Here not a house was left standing. Two hundred eighty houses were burned out completely. Women and children driven into the mountains and attempting to hide were fired upon. All mules, sheep and goats were rounded up and carted off either toward VALONA or south along the coastal road to GREECE."

While the German 1st Mountain Division forced Hoxha, the Partisans and the Allies toward the coast, the Germans brought up the 104th Jaeger Division from Jannina in Greece and other troops down from Valona along the coastal road to trap the Partisans between the coastal road and the ocean. "Three battalions of Italians [who had joined the Germans], in addition to Austrians, Poles and Armenians moved south through VALONA along Valona-Himara Road to meet up with the 104th Jaegers coming from Greece. These troops were definitely identified by source as units of the 297th Infantry Division."

Allied planes supported the Partisans throughout the operation by bombing and strafing the Germans, but they could not halt the offensive. The Germans brought with them heavy artillery and mortars, along with prodigious amounts of ammunition, which they used to rake Partisan positions in the hills.

"The 6th Brigade, occupying the area around KUC, being attacked from the north, south and east by strong forces, continued to resist until they were virtually starved out. Exhausted and hungry the Brigade finally broke up into small units and took to the hills in all directions followed by the Germans. Source was with the 6th Brigade during the whole of this action and escaped with one of its units into the hills near BORSH."[16]

Partisan causalties were heavy in hand-to-hand fighting in the rugged terrain around the Kuc area as the Germans hounded and killed those Partisans who tried to escape north. The OSS estimated that the Germans killed ten Partisans for every German soldier killed or wounded. It estimated that some 2,000 Partisans were killed and an unknown number wounded. The offensive, which broke up Partisan formations and scattered the Partisans, was a heavy setback for Hoxha and he was happy to see the Germans end their attacks on June 14.

Stefan, in a second handwritten message to Fultz dated June 12, urged Fultz to debrief Metro and Tolie, who were evacuated from the coast that night with Stefan's messages. In his second message, Stefan, safe in his hiding place on the coast, complained to Fultz about the British stealing his intelligence, and about not having "the proper tools" to do his job right. Since his radio equipment had been buried, Stefan had to rely on the British to send his messages. Stefan wrote, "Although we have found our cousins [the British] very willing and cooperative, they have pulled a couple of fast ones on us. For example, there are several reports that have emanated from their base that were mine. It doesn't make much difference in the big picture because it all goes to the same place, but it makes a helluva difference to us in the field if Bari thinks we are getting info from the British. I dare say that this mission has given our cousins a helluva lot of good dope as the two boys will verify. But why talk about such small things at this time."

Stefan recommended promotions for "the two boys"—Angelo Metro and Albert Tolie. He also hinted that he was eligible for promotion to captain. "As for myself, the six months [in grade] are up and I suppose it is not [sic] in the laps of the gods. These are small things but they mean a heck of a lot to all of us." It was not the first time Stefan asked to be promoted to captain. In a handwritten note to Fultz dated May 4, Stefan reminded Fultz that "on June the 2nd I will have been in grade the necessary time for promotion to captain." He urged Fultz to speed up the necessary paperwork as had been done for others being promoted. "This means a lot to me, and I really appreciate it if you could do me the favor."[17]

If Stefan was looking for sympathy, a pat on the back, or a promotion from Fultz, he did not get it. Instead he got a message chiding him for allowing the British to bury his radio equipment and lead him scurrying to the coast. Clearly irritated with Stefan, Fultz told Stefan that he should have stayed with the Partisans instead of heading for the coast. "As one looks back over it now," Fultz in his reply said, "one might figure that you should have gone into the hills with the LNC group rather than to have headed toward the coast. I doubt if you would have had too much difficulty in evading the drive although I realize that his has been the most extensive sweep which has been made through there and the Boche probably were on your neck before you had much time to think things over and to plan differently from the way you did plan.

"In this one instance I have the feeling that the cousins may have had too much to say in determining the course which was followed. They have a tendency to do that sort of thing and as an aid to their moves they are clever at persuading people to bury w/t (radio) equipment and depend upon them for communication which they do not provide in anything like a satisfactory manner. They are also inclined to want to declare a state of emergency as a justification for their taking over and telling what should and what should not be done."[18]

Stefan seemed shaken by Fultz's response. Coming as it did from a man who was generally mild-mannered and respected by all around him, it apparently had an effect on Stefan. No sooner did he receive the message than Stefan did two things: he first compiled something of a manual for incoming OSS agents, and he sent Fultz an accompanying two-paragraph fawning letter seeking Fultz's advice.

Fultz liked Stefan's "manual" so much that he immediately had copies of it sent to other OSS agents in the field. The reason Fultz liked it was, apparently, that it cautioned incoming agents to not only be on guard when dealing with the Communist Partisans, but to be wary of British SOE agents as well, something he had already been preaching.

"Personnel should be very diplomatic in relations with BLOs (British Liaison Officers) and treat them as Allies. However, they should be wide awake in sharing their intelligence when the situation calls for it," Stefan wrote. "They should be informed that the BLOs will try to elicit what information we may have by stating that their function is supplying the Partisans; not gathering intelligence. This is not exactly true since their function is a dual one. It has been obvious to me that they also are concerned with sending in lengthy intelligence reports."

Stefan also cautioned OSS agents to be on guard against being drawn into the Communist Partisan practice of playing the Americans off against the British and vice versa, a subject he knew something about.

As far as the Communist Partisans were concerned, Stefan—who lived and fought with them, and who knew their language—had these comments and warning: "The Partisans are very honest and even slight evidence of a misdeed will result in the person concerned being shot.

"Our men should never report such things to higher authority unless absolutely sure.

"Partisans are very serious in their efforts, questions of sex or morality should never be raised in their presence.

"Reference should never be made to the fact that they sing communistic songs.

"Nothing should be said about Russia unless it is in praise for they hero worship that country.

"Try to impress upon our men that they are representative of America and should set an example of what we stand for."

In the accompanying July 4 letter to Fultz, Stefan wrote: "Just a few lines to ask a couple of questions which seem to bother me constantly. The first one is, am I getting the right type of intelligence that can be put to good use? And the second is: am I fulfilling your expectations as liaison officer to the Central Committee? I would appreciate your suggestions, criticisms and comments on the next drop. I'll do my best to carry out your orders to the letter. Let's have it."

Fultz replied on July 16 with the following: "All of us here consider that you have done very well indeed with a most difficult assignment." His basic advice to Stefan was simple: Be an American. "You will probably find that people there as well as elsewhere prefer that Americans be American. Your ability to speak the language should never be misunderstood. It merely gives you more and better equipment with which to try to analyze and to understand."[19]

It was good advice. Although Stefan was as close as anyone could get to Enver Hoxha, it was important for him to remember that they had different roles in life and that their countries had different roles in the world. Stefan understood that and he was able, most of the time, to deal with Hoxha on an even level while all others around the Albanian leader treated him like a god.

In the many exchanges of messages between Stefan and Fultz, Stefan frequently referred to Hoxha by the code name CINC—short for Commander in Chief of the Partisan army. However, when Stefan dictated his message to his radio operators, he pronounced Hoxha's code name as "Chink"—the derogatory American term for a Chinese person. Stefan's radio operators and the other Americans picked it up. "Tom came up with the name," Kostas "Gus" Routsis, one of Stefan's radio operators in Odriçan and Helmës, said. "He used it for Hoxha all the time. Yes, we all called Hoxha Chink. But never to his face."[20]

In between his cables about German formations, attacks on villages, ambushes and frequent Partisan requests for supplies, Stefan repeatedly complained about the British. Either the SOE officers were stealing personal supplies dropped in for the Americans, or they pilfered or hogged intelligence. In one sarcastic cable, Stefan asked: "Is it possible for us to have a special plane to drop us the same food which we have seen all the British missions [get]? This food bears American labels. We have to borrow food and depend on the British to get started."[21] In another cable Stefan complained that the British took credit on the BBC and Radio Bari for intelligence gathered by both the Americans and the British, claiming it as their own. This incident concerned a German atrocity. "It's the same old story," Stefan said in a handwritten report. "Everything American is called Allied, and everything British is called British." He added: "I hate like hell to think that I have to risk my life so that our cousins can get some dope to carry on their psychological warfare in that manner. In deference to the Americans it could be at least said that there are Americans in Albania.... Rest assured, I'll never hurl a bomb into this matter. BLO and Yank relations are still cordial. I'll be diplomatic but always suspicious of these babies."[22]

One incident Stefan did come across was the killing of two Ballists captured by the Partisans in late June in the village of Progonat. The two men returned to the village to evacuate their mothers and their wives. "On questioning they stated that they had led the Huns around these hills and returned thinking that the Germans were still in Progonat. Reds simply lined them up and shot them," Stefan reported. He noted that both men carried German stamped identification documents. "If this isn't proof of Bally [Balli] as an organization working with the Huns I'd like to know what else is needed. Can you wonder why the Partisans insist that Bally [Balli] be condemned as an organization."[23]

Outside of occasional forays along the Balli Kombëtar-controlled coast by Hudson to pick up intelligence, the OSS seemed totally committed to remain with and support Hoxha and his Communist Partisans. The Communists emerged as the only resistance group in Albania determined to fight the German occupiers. Even so, Hoxha was not an easy man to deal with. His intense hatred of the British was well known, and his dislike of the United States was only slightly tempered by his relationship with Stefan. He was suspicious of everyone.

On the eve of the start of an important conference with the Allies in Bari in August, Hoxha felt strong enough to assert himself with the Allies. He demanded official recognition of his "government" from the Allies. He demanded more supplies. His praised the Soviet Union, which had not lifted a finger to help the Partisans. He lauded Joe Stalin. Hoxha berated the British for their continued support of Abas Kupi in northern Albania. Hoxha now turned on the Americans as well. He insisted that he decide who the OSS sent into Albania. Ever wary, Hoxha suspected that the Albanian American OSS agents—as opposed to American-born agents—were sent to sabotage his efforts to take over Albania. If they were "real" Albanians, Hoxha said, they would be fighting in the Partisan army.

Hoxha's list of demands for the Allied conference in Bari included requests for financial assistance for a new Albanian government, for his Albanian National Liberation Army (ANLA), and for civilians who had been burned out of their homes. He demanded official recognition of a new provisional government, recognition of the ANLA as an Allied army, and acceptance of a military delegation to the Allied command in Italy.

The delegates chosen by Hoxha to attend the Bari conference were all trusted Communists and veteran Partisan fighters. They were Col. Bedri Spahiu, Lt. Col. Ramadan Çitaku and Major Frederick Nosi. They were accompanied by Stefan, who knew them all, and British Lt. Col. Alan Palmer. Nosi, who spoke English, was another graduate of Fultz's American Vocational School.

Before the delegation left for the coast in late July, Stefan was joined at Helmës, the alternate partisan headquarters, by newly-promoted 2nd Lt. Nick Kukich. Kukich, who took Stefan's place at Helmës during the conference, was joined by OSS Lt. John O'Keefe, who shortly parachuted in. All three—Stefan, Kukich and O'Keefe—would remain with the Partisans throughout the war and would be reunited in the capital following the battle of Tirana.

Hoxha was deadly serious about the Bari conference. He was a proud man and the conference would give him prestige he needed. He had a lot riding on its outcome, namely his future, the future of the Communist Party and the future of his country. He still had a lot to prove in the eyes of the Allies. He knew that. He also knew that the British behind his back held him up to ridicule. He would—with American help—be able to prove it, and that would give him more reason to distrust the SOE, and further wreck whatever was left of his relations with the British.

5

Nick, O'Keefe and Tom

Lt. Nick Kukich and Cpl. George Routsis, his Albanian-speaking radio operator, landed on the Albanian coast on the night of July 7, 1944. Since the Germans were thought to be still active around Seaview and Grama Bay, Kukich and Routsis landed further south, on the rocky beach below the village of Borsh.

Kukich and Routsis used extreme caution in working their way through the mountains and valleys as they headed toward Partisan headquarters in Helmës. Enver Hoxha alternated his headquarters from time to time between the villages of Helmës, in the mountains of southern Albania, and Odriçan, which was closer to the coast.

Roustis, older brother of Kostas "Gus" Routsis, who had accompanied Lt. Hudson in his first foray into Albania, knew the country fairly well. He and his brother had been born in the village of Frashton, a Greek minority village, south of the city of Gjirokastër.

It was Kukich's first trip back to Albania since he had been evacuated from the coast with Hudson in March. Although Hudson had returned several times to pick up pouches of intelligence, Kukich had remained in Italy. After a leave in Naples, and a quick course in parachute jumping—a skill that he never had to use—he was back in Albania, trudging through the rocky terrain like the foot soldier that he really was. It was a long, hard walk from the coast to Helmës that took almost a week. It was Kukich's first time in Partisan territory and he was shocked by the destruction they came across. Evidence of the German June offensive was everywhere. The men slept in gutted and abandoned farmhouses and barns or in deserted villages. The days were hot and the nights were cool.

When they arrived at Helmës, Kukich sent the following message to

5. Nick, O'Keefe and Tom

Fultz: "When I was at Seaview, at the time I didn't see the Partisan's side of this affair. I was with the Balli, and I didn't think that the Partisans suffered as much as was stated. Now that I am with the Partisans, I have seen what they have gone through.

"Their homes are burned and destroyed. Their children have suffered very much, going about bare-footed, with clothes made of blankets and Italian ground-sheets which they managed to get when the Italians capitulated. We clothed most of the Partisans in battle dress.

"I talked to a few men who were with the Fifth Brigade last winter, and they suffered the most. They had a lot of casualties from frost-bite and cold weather, resulting in the amputation of toes and, in a few cases of feet.

"The house Art [Stefan] stayed at was destroyed by Jerry [Germans]. Now the widow and her three small children sleep out in the open with only what clothes they wore when the house was burned. When a sortie comes in, we intend to give her a few blankets.

"In this same town, Helmës, Jerry—on his last operation—put an old lady, aged 65, in her house, locked the door and had her cremated alive. Balli men cooperated with Jerry, also used as guides on this ruthless operation. They killed everything in sight. Mules, horses and cows were shot and left out in the fields.

"I passed through twenty towns at least, and I found that all were burned and destroyed, that fruit trees were scorched from the fires of burning homes. They tried to burn the small wheat fields, but fortunately at the time the wheat wasn't ripe.

"We met women and children coming from the mountains, going in the direction of what was at one time 'home.' Most of them looked like survivors from a ship that had been sunk. One old lady stated that she had three of her grandchildren with her and all they had were some dried raisins which she rationed for ten days.

"We stopped at a spring near one town and started to eat our meal, which was plain corn bread. A small boy came up to us on legs that were hardly strong enough to carry his swollen under-nourished body. He thrust his small hand out toward us and looked at us with the most pitiful look I have ever seen on a human being. We gave him corn bread, which he immediately placed under what was at one time a shirt, and walked off into the nearby woods.

"In the town of Përmet the Partisans had tried to fight until it become hit-and-run because Jerry was very strong. The Partisans have returned now to reorganize. Their morale is very high, not only that of the men but that of women and children also. A person is always greeted with 'Vdekja Fashizmi' [Death to Fascism].

"An old lady remarked: 'the mountains shook, but we held fast.' Jerry used mortars on women and children when they ran for cover up into the mountains.

"Since I have been here with the Shtab [Hoxha's headquarters], I have seen a good many Balli prisoners. They are questioned and, if they haven't committed any crimes, they are released with the warning never again to fight the Partisans.

"The Shtab states that they haven't yet had a Balli prisoner fight them again after he had been released. Those Ballists here who have committed crimes are given a fair trial. If found guilty, they receive the sentence: 'pushkatim,' meaning the firing squad."[1]

Upon his arrival at Helmës, Stefan took Kukich and Routsis to a house they shared with the family who lived there, a mother and daughter. It was one of only a few homes in the village that had not been totally destroyed by the Germans in a previous attack. There was only one room in the house, which they all used. A hanging blanket separated the soldiers and their arms and radio equipment from the women. There was no running water or electricity, nor was there a toilet, Turkish or otherwise. The air in the mountains was fresh and clear, though, and nearby water rushed down cold mountain streams, bouncing off boulders and stones. Nights were pitch-black and thousands of stars were visible. Often, in the distance, the sounds of small arms fire and the thumping and crashing of mortars could be heard.

Stefan briefed Kukich and Routsis, warning them to be careful in what they said to both the Partisans and the British. Then he took Kukich to meet Hoxha.

"I was struck by Hoxha's appearance," Kukich said. "He was tall and good looking. He was a charming man, handsome enough to be a movie star. He could have been in the movies. He was always very well dressed in uniform. He could accept you and talk with you and smile. But then he could turn against you in an instant and go completely the other way. He could be ruthless."

Hoxha lived and worked in a plain, two-story house a stone's throw from the house where the OSS men lived. Although the British had a house also, most of the SOE men lived in tents quite some distance from the house Hoxha used. Hoxha had an office on the first floor while the living quarters were on the second floor. Although Hoxha's house was bigger than the rest of the houses in the small village, it too had no electricity or running water. Telephone lines had been set up among the various houses, however, and Hoxha could communicate by phone with his staff or with the Allied officers.

Hoxha sat at a makeshift desk when he conducted his meetings while those attending sat at a table that ran out from the desk. There was a map of Albania on the wall behind him. Guards were stationed on both sides of the map, like bookends. Although it was Albanian custom to offer guests raki, Hoxha never did. He frowned on drinking, for one thing. For another, he considered neither the British nor the Americans to be guests, since both had arrived in his country uninvited. Cigarettes were exchanged, however. Albanians loved to smoke and Hoxha was no exception. He relished the Lucky Strikes or Camel cigarettes the Americans passed around. He spoke Albanian at his meetings, although he used French when he thought the occasion called for it. His English interpreter usually was Fredrick Nosi, who had learned his English at Fultz's American Vocational School. Hoxha trusted him. Hoxha also had other interpreters, one of whom had lived in the United States and had been educated at Harvard. Unlike some other English speaking Albanians like Nosi, who talked as though delivering a newscast for the BBC, others were quite fluent in American English. With Stefan present, however, Hoxha needed no interpreter since Stefan served the purpose.

Stefan explained to Hoxha and his staff that Kukich would take his place while he attended the Bari conference and that he would continue the work that Stefan had been doing. "They seemed well pleased at first," Kukich said of Hoxha and his staff.[2]

But then things went downhill. As he did with Stefan on a prior occasion, Hoxha criticized Kukich for having worked with the hated Balli Kombëtar when he was at Seaview. "I told him that I was with them to get information about the Germans and that I had never fought with them against the Partisans. That was our mission, to get intelligence, and we did it," Kukich said. Hoxha seemed to relent. Hoxha had gone through the same routine with Stefan, whom he criticized for having spent time with Skënder Muço, a hated Balli Kombëtar leader, when Stefan was at Seaview. Hoxha had known because he had spies everywhere.

"After that was out of the way we got along," Kukich said. "As a matter of fact, I built up a good relationship with Hoxha. He called me Niko. He said to me 'You are one of us.' I wondered about that. What did he mean? He may not have liked Americans very much, but he hated the British, and he often pitted one off against the other. He was a very proud man. He told me he wanted to make sure the world knew that it was the Albanian Partisans who liberated Albania and not the Allies."[3]

Kukich was quick to make friends with as many Partisans as he could. One of his new friends was Partisan Col. Ramadan Çitaku, Hoxha's finance minister. Çitaku at the time was close to Hoxha and was one of the three delegates Hoxha sent to the Bari conference. Like Kukich, Çitaku spoke Serbian.

Kukich also became friendly with Ali Duskanoviç, the Serbian Communist Tito had sent to Albania to keep an eye on Hoxha. "He said the same thing to me. 'You are one of us,'" Kukich said. "And I said, 'Yeah, because my parents were born in Serbia, because I worked in the coal mines and all of that.' And he said 'No, because we know about you.' I wondered about that for a long time. Then, one night, I was listening to the BBC and they were talking about Communist organizations and they listed the International Workers Order as a Communist Party affiliate. Now I knew what Hoxha and Ali mean that I was one of them.

"Years before I was a baseball team manager in Pennsylvania. One day a guy comes up to me and says, 'If you have all your ball players sign up for the IWO we will buy you twenty uniforms.' That was a lot of money at that time. This was in 1934. And I says, 'What?' And he says, 'All you have to do is pay ten cents a month dues to the International Workers Order.' So we signed, and then forgot all about it. But then I knew. This is what Ali and Hoxha meant that I was 'one of them.' And that had a lot to do with Hoxha and my relationship with him."[4]

Kukich was in charge of the OSS contingent in Helmës after Stefan left for Bari. Although he had to deal with the British SOE, he tried to keep the British at arm's length. Like Stefan before him, Kukich suspected the British of stealing airdropped supplies that were meant for the OSS. Although the supplies were mostly American, the British were in charge of dropping them. Frequently the supplies landed in places other than the sites where the OSS had signaled for them to be dropped. British officers were then seen smoking Camels or Lucky Strikes, carrying new Thompson or Marlin submachine guns and eating Hershey candy bars.

The practice irritated Stefan and Kukich. Kukich carried his resentment toward the British from Seaview to Helmës. "They were arrogant, the British. They did not care about us. They looked down on us. We were the newcomers. They acted as though they could do nothing wrong. They took our sorties, our supplies, cigarettes, everything. The whole thing seemed to be a joke to them. I have to hand it to Tom, though. He gave it back to them. He could be as arrogant as they were."

Food was usually scarce at Helmës, so when Kukich planned to hold a dinner for Hoxha and his staff he decided to spend enough money to hold as fine a dinner as money could buy. When Major Marcus Lyon of the SOE, Kukich's British counterpart, heard about the dinner he decided that the British should hold one first. Kukich, on the advice of Fultz, deferred to the British. When Kukich told Hoxha that the British dinner would be held before his, the Albanian leader looked at him said, "Are you Americans lackeys to the British?" Kukich added, "I sent Hoxha's message to Fultz, but he did not reply."⁵

Usually each group ate with their own—the Americans with Americans, British with British and Albanians with Albanians. Hosting a dinner for a guest like Hoxha was considered an important and meaningful gesture. Often Dr. Omer Nishani, a physician and a party intellectual, visited Stefan, Kukich and Routsis in the evenings. They gave Nishani packages of Lucky Strike cigarettes or toothpaste. He in turn instructed them about the Albanian language or discussed Communist Party history and theory, or Albanian social mores. They taught him English and talked about the United States and democracy. Sometimes the Partisans put on plays in the center of the village, or gathered a fire and sang Communist songs. Other times the Partisans—those of who had gone to school—held classes and taught illiterate Albanian peasants how to read and write. Everyone used the clenched fist brought to the right ear as a salute and greeted one another, saying "Vdjeke Fashizmit"—Death to Fascism. The automatic reply was, "Liri Popullit"—Freedom to the people.

Hoxha and his staff usually held daily briefings for the officers of the SOE and OSS at his office. Hoxha always was well-groomed and immaculately dressed in a military uniform at the briefings, unlike the men he briefed. Out back he kept a well-bred riding horse obviously captured from the Italians or the Germans, since all Albanian horses were used for work. Hoxha usually began the briefings by chiding the British for failing to adequately provide him with supplies. "He would do this at just about every meeting," Kukich said. "You never knew when he was going to blow up. 'What are you doing for my army? What are you doing for my country?' he would demand of the British. 'Where are the mortars you promised? Where are the hand grenades? Do you count the grenades? Don't look at the Americans. You are the ones who are supposed to supply us with arms, not the Americans.'"

Following his outbursts Hoxha provided the Allied officers attending with information about the latest German formations, Partisan ambushes, Germans killed or captured, and possible future military actions. The British and Americans cabled the information back to their headquarters in Bari where it all ended up in the same place, Allied headquarters. Still, both the SOE and the OSS worked their own sources and sought additional intelligence in an effort to outdo each other. Here the British found themselves outmatched because of the ability of a half dozen or so Albanian American radio operators in Helmës who could speak Albanian, and who had relatives living in the region. These men were able to speak with them as well with the peasant farmers around Korcë. These farmers quickly learned to trust these young American soldiers who had been born in Albania and who now returned to help free their country.

When Kukich finally did hold his dinner for Hoxha and his staff, he did not spare expenses. He hired Hoxha's personal cook to roast a freshly killed lamb and a goat. The meat was served with potatoes, onions, cheese, bread and olives. He had plenty of raki on hand, as well as Scotch, wine and beer. The dinner was a success and Hoxha was appreciative.

What really drew Kukich closer to Hoxha had more to do with more than simply hosting a dinner for the Albanian leader; it had to do with providing Hoxha with information. Kukich was with Major Lyon in Lyon's tent drinking tea shortly after the dinner when Lyon went outside to relieve himself, leaving a notebook behind. "I then did something really uncalled for," Kukich said. "Still, I was trained in intelligence, and this was a way to help my friends." Ever suspicious of the British, Kukich flipped through the notebook and came across a reference to Hoxha and the three-member delegation that Hoxha had sent to the conference in Bari.

However, Lyon did not refer to Hoxha and the delegates by name in his notebook. Instead he referred to Hoxha as Goldilocks and Hoxha's three delegates as the Three Little Bears, Papa, Mama, and Baby Bears. Kukich made note of the reference. "I said to myself, 'This is just another example of the British playing with people.' It was a joke to them. Papa Bear, Mama Bear and Baby Bear. Hoxha was a joke to them. They looked down on Hoxha and the Albanian people. They mocked them," Kukich said.

Kukich met with Hoxha, with only Frederick Nosi present. He told the Albanian leader what he had learned. "Hoxha was furious," Kukich said. "His face flushed and turned red. 'Goldilocks and the Three Little Bears?' He slammed the table. 'They are making fun of us. They don't understand what we have been through,' he said. He was really mad. I had never seen him so mad. Then he got up from the table and hugged me. To Hoxha the information was big. 'You are one of us, Niko,' Hoxha said several times. I told him and Nosi that they must never tell the British how they got the information. 'You have to protect me. If the British find out I will be out of here in a minute.'"

Hoxha not only protected Kukich, but he took care of him by providing Kukich with intelligence twelve hours in advance of the British. "Lyon later came up to me and told me how angry Hoxha was with him and the British. He couldn't figure out why. I pretended I didn't know anything about it. I was so upset with the way the British treated Tom and me that I didn't care. We kept information from them, and I know they kept information from us," Kukich said.[6]

5. Nick, O'Keefe and Tom

Although they continued to have differences, the Allies worked together when the need arose.

When 1st Lt John H. O'Keefe parachuted into Albania July 26 to augment the OSS contingent in Helmes, he was greeted on the ground by Major Lyon.

O'Keefe, a native of Arkansas who went by code name Venol or Mazzini, had received his OSS training in Cairo and was transferred to Bari where he underwent parachute training. With O'Keefe on the jump from the C-47 that night were OSS Sgt. Vangel Kyrias and Salim Doda. Kyrias was an Albanian immigrant and an American citizen. He was fluent in English, having studied at the Fultz School. Doda was a former Albanian army officer who had served under King Zog. Doda had fought the Italians during the invasion. He was recruited by the OSS in Italy.

The OSS plan was for these men—called the Perry Unit—to meet with Hoxha and then travel north and join the Partisans for the assault on Tirana.

The men flew from Brindisi and jumped near the town of Leshnjë in southern Albania. Because the plane flew too high and its navigation was inaccurate, the jumpers landed far from their target. Some of their supplies scattered. When they gathered what supplies they could, they found that they were missing rifles, food and cigarettes. They met Major Lyon. With the British major was Cpl. George Routsis. Both had made the trip from Helmës to Leshnjë with mules to carry the supplies back. It was a four-hour march.

Kukich brought O'Keefe to meet Hoxha the next day. Hoxha at first greeted O'Keefe "warmly," but his attitude changed when he found out that Doda was an Albanian citizen. "We were immediately questioned as to the duties and intentions of the American unit and personnel involved." O'Keefe later reported. "Upon learning that Sali Doda was an Albanian citizen, General Hoxha objected to his becoming a member of the Perry Unit for the following reasons: that he wanted no Albanian to pose in American uniform in Albania; that he was needed as a soldier in the Partisan Army, due to his experience as a soldier and an officer. We had no choice but to agree to this."

O'Keefe, who planned to leave Helmës for Peza, southwest of Tirana, the following day to establish a liaison base with Partisan forces there, found that he could not leave because Hoxha also questioned Kyrias' citizenship. "On July 31, I was informed by Gen. Hoxha that he did not approve of Sgt. Kyrias as a member of the Perry unit on the grounds that he did not believe that Kyrias was an American citizen since he only left Albania in 1941," O'Keefe reported. "I attempted to explain that since Kyrias was a member of the American Armed Forces, the usual period of time was not required for citizenship. Gen. Hoxha apparently did not believe this as he demanded proof of citizenship."

Kyrias' citizenship papers were on file with his records in Bari and O'Keefe radioed to have Stefan bring them with him when he returned from the Bari conference.

"After Gen. Hoxha's ultimatum that Kyrias would not be permitted to leave without proof of citizenship, the usually warm attitude of the Partisans toward the Americans cooled considerably," O'Keefe wrote. "Many of the people there were not as friendly as they had been in the past. All Americans were instructed that they could not leave the area of Helmës without a pass. The exact reasons for this attitude are not known, but it is believed that the apparent dislike of the FNC toward Sgt. Kyrias is responsible for it. It was obvious that he was not trusted to any great extent by any of them."[7]

Hardly had he arrived than O'Keefe on July 28 cabled Fultz. "Perry mission welcome. Hoxha knows Salih [sic] is Albanian. He refuses to allow him go north with us. He must fight with Partisans or stay with Shtab and Nick. Give your advice soonest. Venol."

Three days later, Kukich cabled Fultz: "Gen. Hoxha states that no Albanian citizen will pose in American uniform in Albania. Afraid of getting involved with politics. Urgent need of men like Salim in Ptz Army for leadership. Explained our need of him. Hoxha then stated that Salim could stay with Shtab and Yank Mission but he can't go north with Perry."

Kukich cabled on Aug. 2: "Perry mission delayed until Nepos [Kyrias] proves he is American citizen. Shtab refuses to accept our word for this. They must see citizenship papers." O'Keefe cabled on August 3: "SHTAB does not trust Nepos. Feel that it is useless to go north with him. Strongly advise that he be evacuated in order to preserve American prestige."[8]

Fultz was not pleased. The men Hoxha objected to were the men that Fultz had trained and in whom he had great confidence. Doda was an experienced officer. Kyrias was a former pupil and a protégé. It was almost as though Hoxha were tweaking Fultz. Fultz, in a memo to Stefan, who was still at the conference in Bari, said that while he would try to comply with Hoxha's personnel demands "however unreasonable," Stefan should make tell Hoxha that his demands could be misinterpreted. "Certain kinds of decisions and actions on the part of the Cinc and his group, inevitably will be interpreted as anti–American or anti–Allied or both," Fultz wrote.

"While they may expect that no one will interfere with their right to make certain decisions and take certain actions, they must at the same time expect that there will be a hardening of attitude rather than a softening, which would come from understanding. Because of this careful consideration should be given to anything which provokes and adds to it [a hardening attitude]," Fultz said.

He added peevishly: "Unwise decisions and actions, or decisions and actions that appear to others to be unwise are not condoned necessarily by suffering and sacrifices which have been made. Other people have fought barefooted and ragged for their liberties. Having done so necessarily does not license one to be shortsighted or lack in critical self-analysis."[9]

While nothing was to be finalized regarding the OSS personnel at Helmës until Stefan's return, Hoxha remained dissatisfied. He did not like Fultz's response. He pulled Kukich aside one day and told him that he would not be pushed around. "I am the one who decides who stays and who goes," he told Kukich. "Nobody else. The Americans do not tell me what to do, the British do not tell me what to do. No one tells me what to do."[10] He seemed happiest when he created problems for the Allies in general and the British in particular. It seemed that Hoxha spent the entire month of August 1944—when Stefan was away in Bari—stirring up trouble for the Allies. His constant complaints about supplies were expected. What was not expected was the ratcheting up of his discontent as the month went by. It is possible, but unable to be proved, that Hoxha's increasingly unfriendly behavior was due to the fact that Stefan was not there to advise him otherwise.

Hoxha seemed intent on embarrassing the Allies with his openly obsequious behavior toward the Soviet Union. He also sought to challenge the British by threatening to capture SOE operatives who were still with Abas Kupi in the north.

When representatives of the Soviet Union arrived at Helmës on August 11, Hoxha acted as though the Russians had sent a division of combat-hardened troops rather than just two officers, a Major Ivanov and a Lt. Turin. O'Keefe said the two were given "an outstanding reception" even though they had arrived empty-handed. "We later learned in an interview with the Russians that their duties were primarily intelligence and they had no intentions of supplying the Partisans in any way."[11]

Kukich, in an August 19 message to Fultz, described the arrival of the two Russians this way: "They received an ovation which will never be forgotten by any of the Yanks here. The Ptz. began to fire every available weapon they had on hand for a period of two hours. Then at first we thought the war had ended."

Kukich said Major Lyon held a lunch for the two Russians the day after they arrived but failed to invite Enver Hoxha or the Shtab. Hoxha, needless to say, took this as another British insult. So when Kukich held an OSS lunch for the two Russians, not only did Hoxha attend, but he brought along his entire staff. Although no discussions of policy took place, Kukich did report that Dr. Nishani made some "smart" remarks to Major Lyon about Allied supplies, which were all American. Lyon replied, "Yes, even my uniform is American," Kukich reported.

Kukich said that the Russians, who spoke Serbian, were concerned that the Partisans did not have enough weapons, even though they were not supplying any. "He also said it was bad that prisoners were being shot," Kukich said.

Kukich also reported that Hoxha was so pleased with the lunch that he invited him back to his office and gave him several reports that he did not give to the British. Kukich, bonding with Hoxha, sent the reports off to Fultz right away.

One of Hoxha's aims throughout the war was to give the impression that the Partisan movement was made up of people with various political views, and not just Communists. This view seems to have rubbed off on Kukich. In his August 19 report to Fultz, Kukich added, "I have spoken to a good many of the Ptz. and my opinion is that they are not all reds [sic] as other people have stated. If a person salutes with a clenched fist it doesn't mean that he is a red. The clenched fist salute they state is one thing that has kept them united. In time they expect to do away with this salute and use the military salute. I have asked a few of your students what the percentage was here and it's nearly always about the same 6 to 7 percent [who are Communists]. Some of the Ptz. leaders are reds but the majority want a democratic government."[12]

Kukich's "lunch" for the Partisan leaders was not lunch in the traditional American sense. The Albanian lunch, which was the main meal of the day, was a four-hour affair where a heavy meal of lamb was served along with bread, rice pilaf, potatoes, cheese, olives, and salad. Guests drank homemade raki, Scotch if it was available, as well as wine and beer. Cigarettes were copiously consumed as the Albanians were heavy smokers. Although food was scare, enough gold pieces could secure almost anything. After the meal everyone took a nap.

While the arrival of the two Russian officers came as no surprise to the Allies, Hoxha's next move did. A week following the lunch, Hoxha called Kukich, Major Lyon and Russian Major Ivanov into his office. Hoxha insisted on the removal from Albania of three British officers who were with Hoxha's enemy Abas Kupi. The three were SOE Lt. Col Billy McLean, head of the British mission to Kupi, Major David Smiley and Major George Seymour.

In an August 26 message to Fultz, in which he quoted Hoxha directly,

5. Nick, O'Keefe and Tom 115

Kukich reported Hoxha saying: "It was made clear to [Lt. Col. Alan] Palmer and [Major Philip] Leake that we could not recognize any member of Allied missions who is in contact with Quislings. We have helped a number of these men out of enemy territory and a party continues to remain with Kupi, who is fighting with the Germans against us. These officers, McLean, Smiley and Seymour [who had already left the country] are organizing the reactionaries against us. Allied officers cannot and will not work with Quislings. These men are no longer considered Allies and we will give them five days to leave Albania or they may join other British to be evacuated. If these officers are not withdrawn within the period specified we shall send in Partisan patrols to capture them and they will be tried by a Partisan Military Court. This is no joke and we must defend ourselves." Kukich added: "This is the exact statement of Gen. Hoxha on the night of 25 August 1944."[13]

Hoxha's troubling threat came just as his delegation to Bari had secured three important concessions from the Allies. This agreement with the Allies called for the doubling of military supplies to be sent to the Partisans by air, the bringing out of Partisan wounded for treatment in Allied hospitals in Italy, and the acceptance of a permanent delegation of two Partisan officers to Allied headquarters in Bari.

Julian Amery, who had been with Kupi, wrote that Hoxha's statement simply outraged the British. "That Enver Hoja [sic] should thus have dared to impugn the good faith of British officers, let alone to threaten their arrest and trial, is eloquent of the hostility, or at least the contempt, which he felt for the British authorities." Amery said that although Hoxha, faced with the loss of support and supplies, relented and withdrew his allegations, he had still won a victory. The victory was in forcing the Allies to finally recognize that further support of Kupi could mean only more trouble for the Allies from Hoxha.[14]

Stefan met with Hoxha as soon as he returned to Helmës. Hoxha, having made his point, told Stefan that his remarks about the British were all a misunderstanding and that he had no intention of arresting the British officers. On September 2, Stefan cabled Fultz: "Hoxha says that never at any time had he harbored the intent to have McLean and Smiley stand trial before a Partisan military court. He further stated that he was motivated in making such a rash statement as a result of new documentary evidence that he will allow us to inspect. Quoting Hoxha, 'In view of my consistent effort to have the Kupi Mission withdraw with no result, I found it necessary to make a threatening gesture. No malice was intended.'"[15]

Hoxha's statement brought an end to the matter, at least for the time being. For him it was a victory. He had embarrassed the British, and he had wrested several important concessions from the Allies at the Bari conference. Goldilocks indeed.

When Stefan returned to Helmës he arrived with newly promoted Cpl. Kostas "Gus" Routsis, whose brother George was already there. This was Gus Routsis' second trip to Albania, having first landed with Hudson at Seaview in July.

Gus Routsis, who kept a handwritten journal of his experiences in Albania, said the first time their converted Italian fishing trawler approached the coast it had to turn back because of heavy German coastal artillery fire. The second time the men successfully landed on the coast at Himarë, just north of Borsh.

A British boat with supplies arrived at the beach at the same time and the Americans joined a contingent of Partisans and loaded the supplies onto mules for the trip inland to Helmës. Gus Routsis recorded that his group passed many graves of soldiers buried along the beach.

Stefan also had with him several other Albanian-born OSS radio operators. They were Sgt. George Steffo, Sgt. Spiro Thanas and Cpl. Milton Tassi. All were from the Greater Boston area and all could speak Albanian. They were all American citizens. Stefan brought with him the citizenship papers of Sgt. Kyrias that so concerned Enver Hoxha.

The arrival of the new men meant that Stefan infiltrated four more Albanian-born Americans into Albania, despite warnings from Hoxha that he did not want any more Albanian-born American OSS personnel in his country.

When they arrived at Helmës on Sept. 1, Stefan rushed off to see Hoxha, while Gus was reunited with his brother George as well as the rest of the American OSS unit.

After a week in Helmës the Americans were forced to relocate to Odriçan, a nine-hour march, when Hoxha shifted his headquarters there. Once there the Routsis brothers set up their radio in a house provided by the Partisans. The brothers operated the radio in shifts. In between radio operating duties, the men rescued downed Allied airmen and took them to the coast, where boats took them to Italy. The Routsis brothers, like some of the other Albanian-American soldiers, were also able to get to their native village of Frashtan. There they found that many of their cousins were missing—they had left to join the Partisans.[16]

Stefan met the two Russians in Odriçan. He cabled Fultz on September 6: "Following info based on confab with new mission. We [Russians] came to Albania because our Allies have failed to inform us about this country. Our mission is an intelligence mission. Russia is interested in erasing all fascist obstacles in Europe and that applies to Albania as well. They are very secretive about their radio which works only at night or evening. Powerful transmitter directly from charging engines, they have contact with both Moscow and Bari. Much info goes out every night, obviously not military. He has told me that Hoxha requested arms and was informed that [supplying arms] was not the function of this mission. He states that the partisan intelligence system is very poor. They live in a house close by and rarely go out except to visit Hoxha."[17]

It seemed that the issue of the Russian presence at Hoxha's headquarters, as well as Hoxha's determination to ban all Albanian-born Americans from serving with the OSS in Albania, dominated Stefan's time during most of September. On September 19, Stefan told Fultz in a cable that since the arrival of the two Russians, "every effort is being made to extol the deeds of Russian and the Red Army" at the expense of the United States and the Allies. "Certain members of the Shtab who are Red-minded are making an all-out effort through the use of clever propaganda to undermine the American sympathy which exists in Albania. The people are 100% anti–British and attempts are being made to tie us up with them while holding Russians out as a perfect example. Some effort must be made by declarations or otherwise at this time to convince these people that America is interested in her welfare—or is she?"[18]

Fultz seemed unconcerned about Hoxha's adulation of the Soviets. It was well known that Hoxha idolized Joseph Stalin and patterned his Albanian Communist Party after the Soviet model. Fultz believed that Hoxha placed Stalin on a pedestal partly to irk the Allies.

It was Hoxha's criticism of Albanian-born American OSS personnel that concerned Fultz. Stefan appeared to have worked out something of a compromise with Hoxha over the issue. Hoxha, after examining the citizenship papers of Sgt. Kyrias, allowed him to stay, but he insisted that Salim Doda be evacuated.

Stefan radioed Fultz on Sept. 13: "Shtab acting like an old woman. Accepts all men now here but in future will not accept anyone whom we have that was born in Albania. Hoxha says send only American-born."[19]

Fultz responded with two long messages. In the first, dated Sept. 14, Fultz wrote that he did not believe Hoxha would solve his problems by keeping "the politically itchy Alb-Americans" out of Albania, but that it was Hoxha's call and he would not contest it. Stefan cabled back: "The General has asked me to tell you that he has nothing against the Alb-Americans in general, but that in view of the situation which is now a political one he cannot afford to allow them to come in. He takes the position that most of the men we have are biased [against him]."[20]

His other message, dated the next day, brought Fultz out in his erudite best.

Sensing that the war in Albania was coming to an end, and that the Communist Partisans would win (which is reason enough why Fultz did not need to send any more OSS agents in, Albanian-born or otherwise), Fultz advised Stefan to "find out what is on the mind of this lad you are dealing with and perhaps get some ideas across to him."

Fultz, who knew the history of Albania and of the Balkans well, told Stefan that Hoxha's "performances and actions are being watched carefully not only by our people but by others. People are wanting to know whether he has the qualities of a serious, responsible leader or whether he and the men associated with him are merely another group of Balkan politicians."

Fultz said that Hoxha's decision to ban further OSS agents of Albanian stock from his country could be viewed "either as an expression of hostility to Americans, or as an indication of weakness on his part in that it is an attempt to cover up things that are happening over there." This was apparently in reference to the killing of prisoners. In the next paragraph of his message Fultz said, "Summary executions of prisoners, military and political, are looked upon with disfavor by almost everyone. Labeling a person 'a traitor' and shooting him out of hand may be an easy solution of an immediate problem which doesn't solve anything."

"It is such brutalizing spectacles that the world objects to most in the Fascists and Nazis' codes," Fultz said, pointing out that "the French have enough sense of fitness of things to give a reasonable fair trial to so-called traitors and collaborators" before shooting them.

Fultz said it was time for Hoxha to begin to think about conciliation, tolerance, balance and binding the wounds of war once the fighting was over. It was one thing to wage a successful guerrilla war, Fultz said, it was quite another to govern in peace, to make sure that that there is someone around "to set their foot down and make it quite clear that hell-raising in the Balkans no longer pays."

"People outside even now are wondering what the peacetime performance of the FNC may be. Under the stress and excitement of war time conditions they have organized successful guerrilla warfare, or reasonably successful guerrilla warfare. Working under conditions of peace is quite another matter and some ask 'Have they the guts to settle down to the drudgery of peacetime living and really do something for their people?' Minus the slogans, the flag waving and the fanfare can they overcome the vast inertia which has always existed and move their people inch by inch along the road to something better?

"Will their fourteen and fifteen year old youngsters get the same thrill out of hoeing row after row of corn that they have got out of spraying submachine gun fire? They will not and then what are they going to do about that? What are they going to do about hoeing the corn, breaking the rock, building the roads, erecting houses, making brick and doing all of those prosaic things when they find that it requires more courage for these than for the other things?

"If your Cinc wishes to be recognized as a serious responsible leader he would do well to contemplate seriously on such questions as these now."[21]

Orders came for Lts. O'Keefe and Kukich to head north. Partisan forces were headed toward Tirana and the OSS wanted to be on hand for the final push toward the Albanian capital. O'Keefe finally was able join Col. Myslim Peza, who was southwest of Tirana, while Kukich would hook up with Gen. Mehmet Shehu who with his 1st Partisan Division was coming in from the east.

Stefan, newly promoted to captain, remained with Hoxha at his headquarters. He was the highest ranking American military officer in Albania. He was Hoxha's confidante. He had his ear, or so he thought. Albania was a small country, to be sure. Yet he was an important man in the small country. He could deal with that.

6

North

The two lieutenants marched at the head of the OSS column as it left Partisan headquarters at Odriçan and headed north toward Tirana. It was September 11, 1944, and the weather was still hot.

The men were divided into two units. One was called the Perry Unit and was headed by O'Keefe. The other was the Peat Unit with Kukich in charge. O'Keefe had with him Cpl. Milton Tassi, an Albanian-American radio operator. Sgt. George Chekani, another Albanian-American radio operator, would join O'Keefe by parachute when they got close to Tirana. With Kukich was Sgt. Vangel Kyrias. Although Hoxha had insisted that Kyrias could not go with O'Keefe to Peza, he allowed him to travel with Kukich to join Shehu's forces. Kyrias, a linguist who could speak English, Greek, Serbian, and Italian, as well as his native Albanian, was a trained radio operator.[1]

The Americans had with them two Albanian mule tenders to care for five mules, as well as a political commissar called Agim. Agim was assigned to them by Hoxha. His job was to watch the Americans and to report back to Hoxha anything the Americans or the others might say or do that sounded suspicious. The men walked in single file except for O'Keefe. He rode a horse he had purchased from some Gypsies who had passed through Odriçan.

Their goal was the small village of Pajanja just south of Tirana. It was there that Col. Myslim Peza, with the help of the British, forming the 22nd Partisan Brigade, which would join his division for the assault on Tirana. Once there O'Keefe and his Perry Unit would remain with Col. Peza while Kukich and his Peat Unit would join up with Gen. Memhet Shehu and his 1st Partisan Division that was just east of Tirana.

Peza, 53, was probably the oldest of the Partisan fighters. It was said of him: "Although he knows very little about reading and writing he knows a great deal about how to fight."[2] Peza had fought against King Zog and was forced to flee to Yugoslavia after he killed a colonel in Zog's army. He returned to Albania following the Italian invasion, took to the mountains and began a movement against the Italians. Later he joined in with Hoxha and the Partisans. Hoxha welcomed him with open arms.

The Americans carried M-1 rifles as well as .45 caliber handguns. The Partisans liked the M-1 rifle because it was good for the long-distance shooting that the Partisans favored. It was accurate, semiautomatic, and easy to handle and keep clean. Compared to the old Italian rifles they had captured, or were given by the Allies, the M-1 was a combat luxury. In their baggage they had several Thompson submachine guns.

Hardly had the men started on their journey when Stefan was notified that Hudson would be parachuted in to confer with him and Hoxha. Although Stefan had been in Albania longer than anyone else, Hudson had made something of a name for himself by making numerous trips to the Albanian coast where he picked up pouches of valuable intelligence left there by his agents.

Stefan and a group of Partisans met Hudson when he parachuted in at Kosine, a four-hour march from Odriçan, on September 23. He carried a pouch for Stefan. They gathered the supplies, loaded them onto the mules and headed for headquarters. Although Hudson did meet Hoxha, he remained in Odriçan only a few days before he headed for the coast. Hoxha throughout the war remained very suspicious of any American OSS officer who worked with the hated Balli Kombëtar before joining him, and Hudson was no different. In addition, Hoxha's suspicious nature was further aroused because the British launched a series of actions along the southern coast of Albania without his consent or knowledge at the time of Hudson's visit. Hoxha, who lived in fear that his drive toward power would be cut short by the British, often viewed such military actions as hostile toward him, even though they were carried out with local Partisan support and were against the Germans. There were some Partisans that Hoxha did not trust.

Hudson and a mule train left Odriçan for the coast two days after arriving. He carried an intelligence pouch from Stefan. Salim Doda traveled with him, as did Kember Elmas, an Albanian-American OSS radio operator, and an American airman who had been found roaming the mountains after he had parachuted from his bomber. It rained steadily. Streams and rivers flooded and trails turned into mush. Hudson and his group crossed paths with Gus Routsis and his party, who were escorting five Rhodesian airmen to Borsh along the coast. The Rhodesian Allies had bailed out of their bomber after engine trouble.

Both groups bedded down in a burned-out house in Borsh. The village was "completely destroyed by the Jerries," Gus Routsis recorded in his diary. "Terrible rain, terrible nights. Wet all day, wet all night. Still raining like it never rained before."

After getting all the men evacuated for Italy by boat on September 28, Hudson went further down the coast to Saranda, where the British commandos had launched their attack. A week later he was back in Bari. Gus Routsis, with the sound of mortars and gunfire in his ears, headed to Odriçan.

Kukich, O'Keefe and the men heading north traveled high in the mountains in order to avoid the Germans, who stuck mainly to the roads below and the larger villages. The Germans at this point in the war had become very wary of ambushes the Partisans liked to set up whenever German patrols ventured into the mountains.

The country the men traveled through had already been visited by the Italians and the Germans and there was little left to damage. Destruction was everywhere. Yet it was beautiful country. The high mountains, covered with snow at the top, plunged down into fertile valleys. Streams bounced down among the rocks carrying fresh water. Canny Albanian travelers always seemed to know where the best drinking water was. They often had long debates over the virtues of one stream over another. The days in September were hot. The trails were rocky and difficult. One man rode in front on the lead mule, setting the pace, while the rest followed on foot, except for O'Keefe. He had his horse and this gave him the freedom to ride away from the group when the landscape permitted. This was not often because of the many steep hills. Still, O'Keefe, a native of Arkansas, fancied himself a cowboy, and who was to argue?

Despite the intense heat that enveloped the walkers when they climbed a hill, they were suddenly plunged into coolness when they descended into a valley where the sun did not shine. It grew cold at night. There were no lights and the nights were very dark. They dared not light a fire. The Americans, unused to such darkness, were surprised at the immensity of the night sky filled with countless stars they had not seen before. The Albanians barely looked up. The Americans found it easy to focus on the natural beauty of the land despite the presence of so much man-made destruction all around.[3]

A special OSS agent Fultz sent earlier spent six weeks in the region in August and September studying the destruction that O'Keefe and Kukich had just left or were passing through. The unnamed agent was an

Albanian American intellectual and activist who had lived most of his life in the United States but who knew the region and the people well.

After listing the destruction of hundreds of homes in a score of towns and villages, the agent's report not only blamed the Germans and Italians for the destruction of property, but the Ballists as well. When the groups attacked a village suspected of harboring Partisans, they simply burned the houses down while the inhabitants fled to the mountains. "Bands of Ballists occasionally were not content, say, to force a Partisan who they had heard was being sheltered in one of the homes to flee. They went on to smoke out his stench from the home, with the obvious result.

"The condition of the people is pitiful. Ignored and even exploited by a government established to cooperate with the Germans, living in fear of their lives while the Germans launched another drive, confused by the fratricide between the father in a family and the eldest son, wandering helpless in the fields and mountains, the people have learned a lesson in steadfastness never before equaled in their country," the OSS agent reported.

"How some of the people live is a mystery," he reported. He found people living in crude shelters made of leaves and straw. Others lived openly in the fields they once cultivated. "Although houses have been systematically destroyed, some part of the structure might remain, and here people have moved themselves and all their belongings. Many times the roof is open sky, and if they are lucky they have managed to construct something that will pass for a roof. Perhaps it leaks, but they know that many others cannot live even that secure from the elements."

Ironically, the same Germans that many Albanian peasants looked upon with hatred and contempt were once viewed as friendly invaders because the Germans treated them at first better than any other Balkan invaders had ever done. "Gradually, the troublesome Partisans, growing stronger and more audacious day by day, provoked the Germans to acts of destruction in the southern areas and this snapped any chances the Germans might have had for successfully enjoying a quiet occupation of the country.

"Each time the Partisans grew too strong for comfort, the Germans rolled in with cannon, tanks, artillery, mortars, and ruthlessly applied their now-famous terrorist measures, destroying homes deliberately to teach the people a lesson, conducting spot checks, taking prisoners for no understandable reason, ruining the crops, taking the livestock. Thus the Albanian villager and peasant began a silent hatred of this invader, and waited hopefully for the tide to change. Thus, too, the Partisan movement gathered momentum, for it was the only movement in Albania that acted, no matter how roundabout, against the Germans," the report stated.[4]

Kukich could sense the warmth of the people as they made their way north. After hours of walking and riding through the silent countryside, with only the sound of the hooves of the animals ringing out from the rocks, the group occasionally came across a shepherd on a grassy plateau grazing his flock. It was not at all uncommon to have the shepherd invite the Americans to share a meal of roasted goat. They often gave the Albanians their C-rations in exchange.

"Many times they would not even accept any money from us, even though they were in need," Kukich said. "They knew we were Americans helping them fight the Germans. And that was enough for them. But we usually left them money anyway."

Other times they bought food from villagers who were still able to grow vegetables in small plots of land around their gutted homes. Frequently they came across fig trees bearing fruit and they stuffed themselves and pocketed what they could not eat. Things in the countryside seemed to slowly improve as the group made their way north.

The first order of business was to get around the city of Berat. Hardly two days into their journey, they came across heavy fighting between the Partisans and the Germans on the outskirts of the city, one of the most ancient and historic cities in the country. They decided to circle the fighting and make camp at a secluded high spot in the Tomori Mountains above the Osum River, which ran through the city. From there O'Keefe and Kukich radioed Bari.

"Germans have disarmed all gendarmes in Berat in fight of Sept. 12. They are using two Italian fighter planes to locate Partisans in Berat area," they radioed. "Partisans of the 7th and 8th Brigades in Berat area are not properly clothed or shod for fighting. Many are barefooted. Food is difficult to get."

Bari radioed back: "Supplies to Partisans limited by transportation facilities. Under these conditions FNC often asks for arms in preference to clothing. Please find out if possible if these Partisans have asked for shoes and clothing and failed to get."

Bari then radioed Stefan at Odriçan: "O'Keefe and Cooky [Kukich] report Partisans of 7th and 8th Brigades in Berat area fighting without proper clothing and with some barefooted. Does C-in-C know this? Has he asked for and failed to receive such stores?"

Stefan relied: "Moisiu [Gen. Spiro] says Shtab knows about situation reported in your last. He claims they have asked for such repeatedly and have not received."[5]

With supplies or without, the Partisans later took the city of Berat as the Germans retreated toward Elbasan and Tirana.

6. North 125

The group left the Berat area and continued north. They passed through such villages as Çorovoda, Kapinove, Karkagos, Roshnick, Mollas, Zherijë and Belsh. Some of the villages were on the map, but most were not.[6] It would have been a fine tour were it not for the death and destruction.

In one village they came across an Italian soldier the villagers had hired to dig a well. His name was Carlo. He had been at the job for two weeks, working for food and a small sum the villagers had just paid him. Carlo was proud of his work. He gave them water from the well. The men drank from the new well and invited Carlo to eat with them. They spent the night in one of the empty homes in the village. The next morning as they were about to leave, Carlo complained to O'Keefe and Kukich that the commissar Agim had taken his money.

Kukich confronted Agim. He demanded the money back. "Most of the Partisans were totally honest," Kukich said, "but there were exceptions, and this was one of them. He told me that he was going to give the money to Hoxha. And I said, 'Is that right?' I then got the radio and told him I was going to radio Hoxha. That did it. He gave the money back. I don't know why Hoxha sent this one with us. Maybe it was because he wanted to get rid of him."

Carlo joined their group. He could cook and he knew how to handle the mules. The following day the men came across two Partisans struggling on the road heading toward them. One was wounded in the foot and was being helped by the other. The wounded man was barefoot while the Partisan helping him had on sandals made from pieces of tires tied with rope. The two had been in a skirmish with Germans north of Berat and had been separated from their group.

Kukich sat the wounded man down by a stream and washed the wound. The man, a young boy really, had been shot in the foot. Kukich treated the wound with an antiseptic before bandaging it up. They took the two men to the next village where they spent the night in a barn. Both Kukich and O'Keefe carried a pair of extra boots. They gave them to the two Partisans.

When Kukich checked on the two men the next day, he found that the wounded Partisan was not wearing the new boots, but had on a beat-up old pair of cardboard shoes. "*Këpucë, këpucë,* [shoes, shoes]," Kukich said in Albanian, pointing at the man's shoes. Agim had taken the wounded man's new American boots for himself and had given him his old ones. Kukich was furious. He confronted the commissar with his .45 and demanded the return of the boots. "I told him I was going to shoot him, and that if I didn't shoot him I was going to report him to Mehmet

Shehu in Tirana. I think he was more afraid of Shehu than of me shooting him," Kukich said. Agim returned the boots. "The closer we got to Tirana the more frightened he became thinking I was going to report him to Shehu. I would have, too, but by then he had disappeared."

The men marched for a week. Even though they came across destroyed villages, dead animals and burned crops along the way, all was not grief and sadness for the Albanians. In one of the last villages in their path they came across a wedding. "It must have been a Sunday. We had been walking for hours and we were hot and tired. And there was this wedding in the village square. The people invited us to join in," Kukich said. "They had this fellow playing a box accordion and they were playing and singing all kinds of songs. Tassi pulled out a handkerchief and joined in the Albanian wedding dance. We ate lamb and drank raki with all the rest of them and ended up sleeping in a hayloft."[7]

The men arrived at Pajanja late in the day on Sept. 17 and witnessed the formation of the 22nd Partisan Brigade, which the British were charged with supplying. Kukich radioed Bari about the formation ceremony. "Peza [Col. Myslim] requests more Yank missions. Attended inauguration of the XXIInd Brigade. Speeches interrupted by men yelling 'We want arms.' We saw approximately one thousand men and at least ten per cent of these were not armed. Peza stated that he has fifteen hundred men in reserve without arms."[8]

The next day, Kukich radioed: "Peza stated that British neglected to send a mission to supply him for a period of seven months. Kupi was being supplied. Now Allied battle dress is being worn by quislings and gendarmes of Tirana. Jemal Heri, one of Kupi's men, was selling Allied supplies to Partisans. This man is now dead."[9]

What the Albanian Partisans could not understand—nor could some of the Americans—was why the Partisans were dependent on the British for arms, arms that frequently did not arrive. Why couldn't the Americans supply them with arms? The arms were American, weren't they?

O'Keefe, in a pouch-delivered letter to Fultz, wrote: "The Partisans in this area are suffering from lack of clothing, shoes, food and arms. The men I saw in the south were much better equipped in every way and seemed to be doing less fighting. All Americans here seem to be very popular and everyone is most courteous to us, but we are continually asked why we can't supply them with arms etc. Why can't we have an American supply officer in Albania to do the same type of work that Greaser is doing in Yugo? It is amazing to me the determination and plain guts that some of these Partisans have. I have seen them suffering from wounds that would kill an ordinary person, but they never complain. If they had the equipment they need and deserve, I am sure the Germans would be out of Albania much sooner.

"I don't want you to think I am promoting an American supply system among the natives. I tell them that our job is only intelligence and that I am not a supply officer. It seems to be impossible to make them understand this as they keep asking us for help."

Hoxha continued to badger the British over the supply situation. He accused the British of bad faith, of breaking the promises made at the conference at Bari. In an October 5 message from Odriçan to Bari, Stefan radioed: "After talking with SHTAB I find they feel that the British are using every means to get out of fulfilling agreement." He said that Hoxha felt that the British were not delivering on the supplies promised. "Anti-British feeling becoming more intense every day because of these actions."

When the British accused the Partisans of allowing supplies to rust and rot on the beaches because of lack of transportation to haul the supplies inland, Hoxha became furious. "It was the first time I had ever seen Hoxha lose temper," Stefan radioed on Oct. 7. Stefan quoted Hoxha: "Commandos on coast eating good food while Ptzs in same sector rely on starvation rations. If British not satisfied with our end of agreement, why don't they break it. If this business continues, I will take drastic action." Stefan, in his own voice, added: "We don't feel that we should press these issues at least temporarily until he cools off."[10]

Another serious problem for Hoxha was the British habit of conducting raids against the Germans in Albania without Hoxha's knowledge or permission. To him it was simply another example of British arrogance. He knew the British did not like or respect him, and the feeling was mutual. But even as Hoxha protested, the British continued to launch raids along the coast and inland, sometimes with Partisan support. They also dropped in troops by air. The British did not inform Hoxha about these raids in advance, and he usually found out after the fact.

Stefan had radioed Bari on Sept. 17: "Shtab objecting to British sending in special troops. Claims that they have the manpower to carry out task. They say send us arms. If we want specialists we will ask for them. Palmer [Lt. Col. Alan] Palmer and I talked to [Partisan Gen. Spiro] Moisiu and political commissar [Bedri] Spahiu this morning regarding this question. Apparently they feel that they might be shown up. Furthermore I am under the impression that they do not want the Huns to be destroyed too soon. At least not until they get the maximum amount of arms."[11]

The British ignored Hoxha and the Shtab. No sooner had O'Keefe and Kukich arrived at the Partisan base at Pajanja than thirty-five men of the British Long Range Desert Group (LRDG), headed by Col. David

Lloyd Owen, arrived by parachute. Contrary to orders by Hoxha that no British officer could arrive in Partisan territory without his permission, these soldiers landed anyway. There were there to fight Germans no matter what Hoxha said or ordered.

Hoxha in early October requested through Stefan that he be allowed to send a military representative to Washington. Fultz, in a letter to the State Department accompanying the request, said that although he sympathized with the Albanians he urged that the request be denied. Instead he recommended that the United States make "some friendly gesture" toward Hoxha.

Albanians seem to feel, Fultz wrote, that the British were following "a frankly cold-blooded and selfish policy" toward them and that the Americans were indifferent. "This I think explains in part at least why they turn to the Russians as their one best hope for achieving a fair measure of freedom and an opportunity to develop their country and their people under the conditions of peace."

Fultz added: "I see nothing to be gained by sitting supinely by and allowing friendly people to slip into an attitude of doubt and of possible mistrust of our ultimate motives merely because we are loath to make a few simple gestures of reassurance. Should we sit by and allow the Russians to make all such gestures?"[12]

Kukich and O'Keefe split up on September 21. Kukich and Sgt. Kyrias left Pajanja to join Shehu and his 1st Partisan Division east of Tirana. O'Keefe remained at Pajanja with the British and the newly formed 22nd Brigade. No sooner did Kukich and Kyrias leave, however, than the Germans began to shell the area, in an attempt to catch the new brigade in the open. But the brigade had moved to another location the day before.

O'Keefe, working with the British, was on hand when the British paratroopers arrived. Col. Owen, the commander of the LRDG group, was severely injured in the jump. A week later a British doctor by the name of Michael Parsons was parachuted in to treat Owen. O'Keefe said that Dr. Parsons not only treated Owen, but provided medical treatment for numerous wounded Partisans. "He undoubtedly saved a number of lives," O'Keefe reported. At the same time an English-speaking Albanian arrived from Tirana. He was Leandro Millo. He had been a prisoner of the Albanian gendarmes for several weeks and had been tortured before escaping. "During this time he was badly beaten and came here suffering from shock and bad treatment. He was beaten with a chair, rifle, cow's tail and had needles stuck in his hands and feet. He managed to escape through the help of a friend and is with us now. He has a contact in Tirana which should furnish us with some good intelligence." Part of the intelligence

Millo provided was a list of names of the Balli leaders who were still in Tirana.[13]

It took Kukich and his party a day to circle Tirana and make contact with Shehu and his 1st Partisan Division. Shehu had just arrived in the Biza area east of Tirana following a successful battle with the Germans for the town of Dibra, just over the border in Kosovo. Now Shehu was closing in on Tirana. Shehu sent patrols into Tirana from the east and from the north, testing German strength. Kukich sent out radio reports to Bari from Shehu's headquarters, including information about market days in Tirana and other cities and towns so that the Allies could avoid killing civilians during bombing and strafing raids.

"Sizeable Hun transient camp located inside Tirana stadium," Kukich radioed on Sept. 23. "Camp consists of one five large tents and one zero zero Huns. Four zero Hun trucks parked underneath stadium seats. One small tank placed inside water fountain near Bashkia."

Sept. 24: "Six zero Huns with six mortars have been shelling us from Petrela Castle. Please bomb the castle."

Regarding the inaccurate and inconsistent Allied supply system—where supplies were wrongly dropped or stolen—Kukich radioed on Sept. 29: "Mehmet Shehu stated that on the 4th of February he bought Allied battle dress and ammunition for his men from a high merchant of Gurri Bardh. Receipt is now at Shtab HQ."

In a different message on the same day, Kukich warned about the lack of supplies. "Mehmet Shehu stated to us on the 28th of September that if Major Oliver [British liaison officer J.F.P. Oliver] does not receive arms and ammunition soon he will be compelled to have Oliver leave the First Division area.... It is over two weeks now that First Division has not received any supplies. October will be the most decisive month to fight the Huns and we are in great need of arms and ammunition."[14]

Kukich, upon meeting Shehu, was impressed with the man. Most Allied soldiers were impressed with Shehu. Kukich said, "Shehu was very strict and the men obeyed him. They were afraid of Shehu." The men and boys who made up the Partisan army respected Hoxha, but they feared Shehu. "They were more afraid of Shehu than they were of Hoxha. Everybody was afraid of him. He was a warrior. He had fought in Spain and he knew how to fight. He had the training. He was well qualified, and he could speak English. He was a graduate of Fultz's school. We didn't need an interpreter," Kukich said. "He was a soldier's soldier."

Kukich presented Shehu with his M-1 rifle as a gift. Shehu admired the weapon but said it was too awkward for him to carry and he gave it to a subordinate to carry for him. He told Kukich that he much preferred a

Thompson submachine gun, and Kukich said he got him one. The Thompson, although a pound heavier than the M-1, was easier to handle. The Albanians considered it a weapon of prestige.[15]

Reginald Hibbert, who met Shehu during the first battle for Dibra in June 1944, wrote, "He was obviously a man of decision and resolution and we were immediately swept up in his retreat into Macedonia. The speed with which he acted took us by surprise after so many months of inaction by every Albanian we had met."[16]

Kukich said that Shehu, bold in battle, was essentially a cautious man when it came to politics. Although a confirmed Communist, Shehu displayed little interest in anything that did not pertain to military matters. He avoided talking about political matters. "But he was a true believer in Communism," Kukich said. "He wanted to be a general, and that was that. I don't think he wanted to be in Hoxha's place."

"When I got to know him better I used to talk to him about taking over from Hoxha. Personally I wanted Shehu in there. I said to him, 'You could take over if you wanted to.' And he said to me, 'Niko, don't even mention anything like that to me. I'm going to stay the hell away from you.' Hell, Shehu knew Hoxha was not a military man, even though he dressed the part. Shehu knew he could have taken over the country. He could have had Hoxha shot. But he didn't want anything to do with politics," Kukich said.

After a conversation like that, Shehu would insist that when Kukich met Shehu they would meet in an open field where no one could hear them rather than in Shehu's command tent. "He would give me reports on how many Germans were killed that day and so on and I would send the stuff to Bari," Kukich said.

Nearing Tirana one night, Kukich, separated from his party, came across a group of British soldiers in a deserted village. There was a German patrol in the area so Kukich stuck with the British. It was raining hard and one British soldier insisted on sleeping inside the village church. He left his duffle bag with Kukich and another British soldier for safekeeping. "I told him not to go near the church because that would be the first place the Germans would look," Kukich said. The Germans returned during the night and captured the soldier. Left with the soldier's bag, Kukich and the other soldier went through it, coming across a Leica camera and eighteen gold sovereigns. The British soldier took the Leica and Kukich kept the gold. Later on, it bothered him that he had taken the gold, so as soon as Tirana was taken, he spent half the money on people who needed assistance. The other nine pieces he gave to Tom Stefan as a wedding gift when Stefan got married in Tirana.

6. North

The situation was fluid. The Germans wanted to leave Albania but they still held Tirana. The Germans sent patrols out from Tirana in order to test the strength of the Partisans while the Partisans sent their patrols into the edges of the city. Since Sgt. Kyrias was from Tirana, where his mother still lived, Kukich depended upon him even though Shehu, like Hoxha before him, did not trust him. Both felt that Kyrias had too many connections with the Balli Kombëtar. Like Shehu, Kyrias was a graduate of the Fultz School and they may have been school rivals.

As Kukich's party approached Tirana one night, Kyrias suggested that they camp on the grounds of the ancient castle of Petrela, just east of Tirana, which the Germans had abandoned. The castle was built during the 1400s to serve as part of the defense system that Skanderbeg, the national hero, constructed to ward off the attacks of the Ottoman Empire. Two men from Tirana approached the group and asked for Kyrias. The men told the sergeant that his mother wanted to see him. Kukich did not like the situation. "How did these two men know we were here? Who were they? Ballists? I had the feeling this was a set up. I told Kyrias not to go. He said he was going to go because he wanted to see his mother. We argued about it. I could have pulled out my .45 but I didn't, and he left with the two men," Kukich recalled.

It was dark. The mules were restless. Carlo kept repeating "No bono, no bono." Kukich did not like the situation at all. He signaled to the Albanian mule men to move out to another location. They circled around a grove of trees where they had been resting and came into a bridge that led to a wide castle entrance below the castle itself. No sooner did they reach the safety of the entrance than heavy gunfire broke out aimed at their previous position. "All hell just broke loose," Kukich said. "There was machine gun fire, tracers and grenades exploding. They were either Germans or Balli or both. We all would have been killed had we not moved. It was an ambush."

Kukich suspected Kyrias had something to do with the incident and he threatened him when he came back the next day. "I grabbed him by the shirt and shook him. He denied everything. Shehu found out about it and told me to get rid of Kyrias because he was too friendly with the Balli. "The Balli were grasping at straws. They were losing the war. Some thought that by killing an American officer and blaming the Communists for it the United States would get more involved in their cause. Shehu came to me and said, 'I want Kyrias out of the country. You have nothing to say about it. That's an order.' I sent a message to Fultz. 'Mehmet Shehu wants Kyrias out' and Fultz ordered him out. Kyrias jumped all over me, blaming me. I told him 'No, you made the mistake. You tried to play both sides by siding with the Balli.'"[17] Kyrias left Tirana for Bari on November 27, the day before the celebration of the fall of Tirana.

O'Keefe and Kukich frequently worked together, moving from one group of Partisans to another as the Partisans gathered strength in late September and October for a final assault on Tirana. Shehu in late September told the pair of OSS officers that the most important German in Albania was Major Franz von Scheiger, an Albanian-speaking German "who has inspired Hun politics in Albania." He also gave them a list of Albanians who worked with the Gestapo and were considered war criminals.[18]

Back in Odriçan, Enver Hoxha and the Shtab prepared to go to Berat for a conference regarding the future of Albania. Berat fell to the Partisans on October 12. Hoxha invited Stefan to attend. This time Stefan was not going to be the only member of the Allies to attend the meeting, as he had been at Përmët. This time the British and the Russians, especially the Russians, would be on hand. Stefan, accompanied by Cpl. George Routsis and Albanian mule men, left Odriçan the next morning.

He could not have been unhappy to leave Odriçan, a small, dusty village with no electricity and no running water. Stefan and the OSS had lived at Odriçan and Helmës for months, moving from one village to the other, depending on German activity. Berat was a real city, a city with real homes that had running water and, perhaps, even electricity, despite the destruction from all of the fighting.

The conference represented an important turning point in Albanian history and politics because for the first time the Communists would establish a government that would take over and run the country once Tirana was taken. Stefan would be an eyewitness to the story.

Cpl. Kostas "Gus" Routsis, George's brother, and Cpl. Spiro Thanas, another Albanian-American OSS radio operator from Boston, plus an Albanian cook, were the only ones left at Odriçan when Hoxha, his staff and Stefan left for Berat. They found there was little to do but "eat, read and sleep," as Routsis recorded in his diary.

"Monday, Oct. 16, 1944. The weather is perfect today. Four Spitfires flew in direction of Korcë—only three returned. Germans withdrew from Fieri.

"Tuesday, Oct. 17, 1944. Went and picked grapes with Lilo, who is the owner of the house we're staying in, in the morning. There is plenty of German movement between Jannina and Korcë.

"Wednesday, Oct. 18, 1944. The mule men have returned with the mules. We plan to leave tomorrow for Berat. Everything is ready.

"Thursday, Oct. 19, 1944. Started out from Odriçan at 7.45 A.M. About dinnertime it started raining. The River Osum from Çepan to Çorovodë is lined by precipices ranging up to two hundred feet straight up from the bed of the river. I spent the night in Izet [mule man] father's house. All that night it rained cats and dogs and there was plenty of thunder and lightening. Spiro got drunk on raki and threw up. We passed some wonderful sights down this River Osum.

"Friday, Oct. 20, 1944. Started at 7.30 from village next to Çorovodë. About an hour later it started raining. On the way one of the mules got scared and jumped into the swift and dangerous river to an island in the center of it. The mule man went with the horse to rescue the mule. He was almost drowned himself in doing so. Further on it took us three hours to get the mules across a swift, swelling, ice cold little stream. Three of us crossed to the other side on a log and with a long rope pulled the mules across one by one. This stream is very cold because most of the water comes from the snowy peak of Tomori. Every one of us was soaked through to the skin. Still further one of the mules turned while another fell with the load. That night I slept on top of a pile of corn in a little village about five hours from Berat.

"Sat. Oct. 21, 1944. Started out at 7.00 A.M. Just outside the village I left Spiro and the mule man behind. Walked to Berat alone. Arrive in Berat at 11.30 A.M., exactly four and a half hours later while the boys with the mules got there two hours later than I did."

Gus Routsis found that about one third of the town had been burned by the Germans before they left. They also had blown up the important Hasan Bey Bridge that spanned the Osum River. Partisans were forced to use makeshift rafts to ferry animals and supplies across the river. The Germans, Routsis noted, had done "a wonderful" job in blowing up the bridge. He met Stefan and his own brother George, as well as Albanian cousins from his village who were fighting with the 8th Partisan Brigade.[19]

Stefan, meanwhile, not only had a ringside seat at the conference, but he addressed the meeting as well, as did the mission chiefs from Britain and the Soviet Union. The difference was that Stefan talked to the group in their own language, which surprised some Albanians but pleased them all. He mingled with the delegates, drank with them and made friends. He was looked upon with respect. He was not only an American officer, he was and an American officer of Albanian heritage who spoke Albanian with them. He was open. He spoke directly. He spoke about the United States, democracy and the land of opportunity. He represented the dreams of many of them, or the dreams they had for their children. Go to America, work, raise a family, become American, and be free. It is what Stefan's parents had done. It is what many of them wanted to do.

Stefan radioed Bari that Hoxha still complained about "the Allied failure to furnish enough arms." Yet, even as Hoxha demanded more arms and ammunition, the Allies already began to cut back on its commitment to help. Earlier in October the OSS called a halt to its intelligence-gathering activity along the coast near Dukat and further north at Vlora, evacuating all agents.

At Berat the Communists formed the Anti-Fascist Committee of National Liberation which in turn became the provisional government of Albania with Hoxha as it head. Hoxha, resplendent in a new uniform, accepted the post of prime minister of the new government while the delegates to the conference applauded and cheered wildly. Nishani was appointed foreign minister. His first order of business was to seek official Allied recognition.

Stefan radioed on Oct 23: "On the afternoon of the 22nd all hell broke loose when Hoxha accepted the post of Prime Minister of the new democratic government. Shouting and exultation continued well into the night."[20]

A week later Stefan flew from Berat to Bari for a meeting with Fultz about Hoxha, the Berat conference and the future. When he returned he brought with him supplies for his men as well as winter clothing.

While both Kukich and O'Keefe remained in the vicinity of Tirana with Shehu and his 1st Partisan Division reporting to Bari on the Partisan offensive, Stefan remained in Berat with Hoxha, well away from the main battle. The Routsis brothers, working in shifts around the clock, relayed his messages to Bari.

"Tirana fell today," Gus Routsis wrote in his diary on Friday, November 17. "The people and Partisans were shooting all kinds of weapons to show their happy feelings. Others are gathering at Enver Hoxha's door shouting Enver Hoxha, Enver Hoxha."

Not everyone was celebrating, however. Gus Routsis told of meeting one man, an American, who wanted to go home. "A World War [One] veteran, an American naturalized citizen,* came today asking for to get back to the states as soon as possible. I wish I could help them."[21]

Stefan found time to write a letter to Earl Brennan, head of the OSS Albanian Desk in Washington, thanking him for his promotion to captain

---

*This American was one of several thousand American citizens who were caught in Albania during World War II and could not get out. Following his break with the United States, Enver Hoxha shut his country down. No one could leave. These Americans, fearing for their lives and the lives of their families, hid or destroyed their American citizenship documents and suppressed their knowledge and use of English. Anyone speaking English was suspect. The vast majority of these Americans died in Albania without ever returning to the United States. However, since their children were American citizens, they were eligible to come to the United States upon the fall of Communism in 1990. Thousands of them did.

and two letters of commendation. Stefan also implied that his knowledge of Albania and its political leaders might be useful in the future when Hoxha took over the country.

From Berat on November 14—three days before Tirana fell—Stefan wrote, "At this writing the military picture is gradually drawing to a close, with an interesting political future in the making, and we are all set up to report it.

"It has been our good fortune to be with the leaders who will run the country. I know every one of them from Hoxha right down through, their weaknesses, their strong points, and their ideologies. There is no other group who is so close to the situation as our section. No one realizes this better than the British.

"After we settle in Tirana, and upon Mr. Fultz's coming to Albania, I hope that it will be possible for me to make a short trip to Washington, to give you an eye picture of the situation, as well as to be briefed by you on future policy."[22] Stefan thought he might have a friend in Brennan, who was also from New Hampshire. Brennan, who served a term in the New Hampshire House of Representatives before the war, had also served as U.S. Consul in Rome and Florence.

Stefan, like Hoxha before him, would not get invited to Washington.

Two days later Stefan informed Fultz that Hoxha, who was not intimate with combat, planned to remain in Berat and watch the Battle of Tirana from afar. He would stay in Berat and come to the capital when Shehu and the Partisans cleared Tirana of all "dangerous elements."

On November 17, the day that the capital was captured from the fleeing Germans, Stefan cabled: "Shtab now plan to move to Tirana soonest. Berat literally going mad as name of Hoxha resounds throughout the city. Hoxha requested I remain here and enter the capital along with his staff."[23]

It would not be much of a parade as parades go when Hoxha, with Stefan marching in the third row, led his entourage into Tirana. But it was the only parade they had, and it was all theirs.

7

Tirana

Gen. Mehmet Shehu welcomed the order to liberate Tirana. The order to attack the capital came from Enver Hoxha in Berat to Shehu at his 1st Partisan Division headquarters outside of Tirana on September 15, 1944.[1]

It was only fitting that Shehu would lead the effort to rid the capital of German occupiers and their Albanian collaborators. Shehu, although only 31 years old, was the most experienced officer in the Partisan Army. He was both respected and feared by his men, as well as by the Italians and the Germans. The battle for Tirana would be the biggest battle in the war. He was ready for it.

If Shehu showed any concern over whether his army was up to the task of pushing the Germans out of Tirana he did not show it. The Albanian Partisans at this point in the war had an army of some 40,000 spread across the country. Most had only superficial military training. But what they lacked in experience they made up in spirit. The vast majority of the men and boys who made up the army were poorly educated peasants who knew little about politics or military matters, let alone what Communism was. What united them was a shared hatred of the Germans.

Shehu had trained his 1st Partisan Division as well as he knew how, considering the circumstances. Often the men had little in the way of food. Frequently they slept outdoors in all kinds of weather. They did not look much like an army, considering their lack of clothing, and their mixed collection of weapons of all kinds from various armies.

"The men who call themselves soldiers have little experience in army discipline and training methods," a September 1944 OSS report stated. "True, there are some former [Albanian Army] officers serving the Partisan cause, but these are relatively very few and scattered in the various units. 'Army,' in the meaning of that term known by the modern world, has no significance to these rough, bearded raki-drinking men. Consequently as new arms come in, be they captured German mortars or Allied rifles, there are some accidents. The men do not even know how to hold their guns.

"All arms possessed by the Partisans are small-arms. There is a mixture of guns: Greek and Italian rifles, a few American guns, German and Italian mortars (of which the German mortars are superior). Arms are what they can get, most of them captured from the enemy, the rest furnished by the Allies.... All 40,000 front-line troops have weapons of one sort or another, in the same manner as their clothing goes. If one man has a tommy-gun, another has a pistol, and so on," the report said.

"Some brigades are dressed adequately, others very poorly. The Partisan dress in what they can get, and they have an odds-and-ends mixture of clothing. Many have Allied clothing which has been dropped in to them, but there is no rule of uniformity. If one Partisan has an Allied field jacket, the other wears Allied pants, and so on. No member of the FNC army knows what a complete single uniform is. A Partisan would be glad to own just one complete uniform. The clothing that is dropped to them is distributed from the top down to the rank-and-file, the higher ranks naturally getting the better clothing."

The same went for the food that the Allies dropped, which, like the arms and clothing, was in Partisan eyes never enough. "The Partisans manage to eat but their rations are slim. They exist and that is all. All food supplies dropped by the Allies, source stated, go to the Partisans, not to the people.

"The morale of the troops, however, is very good. As military men, the self-made leaders provide alert leadership and experience is improving their effectiveness. Although the men do not understand high-faluting talk about principles, they are united in one common cause: hatred of the German invaders.

"The Albanian Partisan is by nature a fierce, unafraid fellow," the OSS observer wrote. "The feeling of each man is this: 'Let the Allies supply us and we will clear the Germans out of our land. Give us heavy weapons to combat their heavy weapons and we ask no more. This is our battle. We want no Allied troops. We know how to fight enemy.' The Albanian, at the same time, is by nature a lazy fellow, not used to taking precautions. Fierce and war-like, much of the courage displayed is unwarranted though gallant, and many mistakes are made."

The Germans, the report said, always lost heaviest when they fought the Partisans in the rough, mountainous terrain that the Partisans knew so well. The Germans, with heavy weapons, tanks and planes, defeated the

Partisans whenever the Partisans engaged them in pitched battles. This slowly changed in the favor of the Partisans as they learned from experience, and from the fact that the Germans, on their way out of Albania, fought more rearguard actions. "Today the odds have been considerably reduced and more pitched battles are being fought."[2]

In front of Shehu and the Partisans now was the biggest pitched battle of the war. It was in contrast to all the hit-and-run skirmishes of the past. The Germans were on the defensive now and under attack as they fought to leave the Balkans. The roles had been reversed. It was the Germans who were now holed up in houses and buildings, and it was the Partisans who would root them out.

Shehu was confident. He knew *his* men were trained and ready. He had trained them. "The fighting formation which remained well ahead of all the others in training, equipment, battle experience and morale was Mehmet Shehu's 1st Division, and within that division, his old 1st Brigade," Reginald Hibbert wrote. "It was these troops under Mehmet Shehu's command ... who were given the task of fighting the last serious battle of the war in Albania, the battle of Tirana, which began in earnest

Downtown Tirana, with dead Germans, horses and donkeys. Dajti Hotel is on the right where the animals graze (courtesy Kostas "Gus" Routsis).

at the end of October and ended up in the occupation of the capital on 17 November."[3]

Shehu was different from Hoxha. Even though, like Hoxha, he was a true believer in Communist doctrine, Shehu did not dabble in party affairs. He spent most of his time during the war fighting the Italians and the Germans rather than attending party meetings that were usually dominated by Enver Hoxha. Shehu was a man of action who was more comfortable in the field than behind a desk.

Hoxha was not a military man, even though he dressed the part and liked to play the role of a general. "Shehu wore the same uniform all the time, day in and day out," Kukich said. "It was an old Italian Army uniform, all worn out. Unlike Hoxha, who always put on a good front, who always tried to impress people, Shehu did not care what you thought."[4]

Although Hoxha was commander in chief of the Albanian National Liberation Army (ANLA), he actually had little experience in fighting. He had been in close guerrilla-like encounters with the enemy, as he had been when the Ballists and Germans captured General Davies, but he had never led men in battle. There is no record of his leading troops against the Italians, Germans or Ballists. He conquered no villages or towns. He personally killed no enemies in battle, although he did order the execution of enemies, prisoners of war, alleged traitors and spies.

German prisoners of war being marched to the airport (courtesy Kostas "Gus" Routsis).

Hoxha understood the importance of images. He loved the uniforms the Allies provided him. As the amount of supplies from the Allies increased, so did the quality of the uniforms Hoxha wore at his headquarters. Photos of Hoxha taken during the early period of the war at his hideouts in the mountains of Albania contrast sharply to those taken later. In the early pictures Hoxha looks as unkempt as the rest of the Partisans around him. He looks as though he made a habit of sleeping in his clothes, which he probably did. His uniforms are a mixture of pieces of clothing from various armies, like the clothing wore by the rest of his men. He is unshaven and his hair is uncombed. In later photos, when the war begins to go his way, Hoxha is a different person. He is sleek, well-groomed and well-dressed. His uniforms are cleaned and pressed. Naturally handsome, the six-foot-tall Hoxha *looks* like a general. Save for the Allied officers around him, Hoxha towers over everybody else. Whether riding his black horse around the countryside at his headquarters at Helmës or Odriçan, or pictured standing over a war map of Albania, the Communist Party leader cut an attractive, romantic figure that appealed to the oppressed, poverty-stricken young people of Albania.

Hoxha was a politician who successfully used his combative instincts and skills to win the internal battles for leadership of the Communist Party in Albania. He could be ruthless and he could be charming, depending on whether a competitor needed to be destroyed or won over. He was an intellectual who seemed to relish outmaneuvering his opponents or getting his hands dirty when power was at stake. He understood from the beginning that whoever won control of the Communist Party in Albania would control the army. The man who controlled the army would control the country. He wanted Albania to be free from the Italians and Germans, just as the leaders of the other resistance movements did. Hoxha wanted the Communists to take over the country. The Balli Kombëtar and Kupi's northern tribes also wanted to take over the country. But they wanted to keep things in Albania as they were, with them in charge, and perhaps bring back King Zog as well. This meant fighting the Communists. The BK was willing to collaborate with the Germans to beat the Communists and maintain the status quo. Hoxha was a radical. He not only wanted to take over the country, he want to revolutionize it, and he had behind him men and women who were willing to fight and die for the cause.

Stephen Peters, a Harvard-trained Albanian-American OSS agent, covered the treason trials of Balli Kombëtare leaders in Tirana in 1945. Some of the BK leaders, he reported, testified that they thought it was in the interest of the Americans and the British that the Communists be beaten. "These were not, of course, the real reasons BK fought the FNC [Communists]. BK fought because it wanted to be in power after the country was liberated. It was a matter of the old conservatives or the young radicals; there was no possibility of compromise. The young radicals won because they didn't hesitate to make sacrifices; because they were daring and brave; because they had good organizing ability; because they were determined to put their radical ideas into practice. BK lacked comparable leadership, lacked fundamental principles, lacked the courage to sacrifice."[5]

Communism in Albania was imported. Hoxha became a Communist in France. He was born to a well-to-do family in Gjirokaster, a fine old city in the south, on October 16, 1908. His father was a landowner. Hoxha studied at the French Lycee of Korcë. He was a good student, so good that he was awarded a state scholarship by the government of King Zog to study at the University of Montpellier in France. He was fluent in French, studied Marxism and joined the French Communist Party. As a result of his pro–Communist and anti–Zogist activities, he was stripped of his scholarship in 1933.

Hoxha went to Paris in search of work and a law degree. There is no record that he found either. However, through "his own efforts and the assistance of some Albanian friends," Hoxha was appointed as a clerk in the Albanian consulate in Brussels. That government job did not last long. "For his revolutionary activity, which came to the notice of the agents of Zog, in 1936 he was dismissed from his position on the grounds that he had turned the consulate into an arsenal of Marxist literature."[6]

It is noteworthy that Hoxha, an active critic of the Zog government, was able to win a government job, even after losing his state scholarship, from the regime he made a habit of attacking. It is true that he lost both, but the fact that he was able to get them in the first place indicates that his family had friends in high places in the Albanian government.

Despite his dim prospects at the time, Hoxha never appeared to be short of funds. Pictures of him taken in Paris, Antwerp, Brussels, Montpellier and Bari in the early 1930s show him dressed like any other well-off and carefree Parisian *boulevardier*. There is little in these photographs of Hoxha that point to the hard-core Communist revolutionary he was destined to become.

Hoxha returned to Albania in 1936. He went to Korcë, where he taught at the Lycee. He mingled with workers, sought out recruits for the party and helped create the first Communist Party cell in the city. He came under the suspicion of the police. He moved to Tirana in 1940 and opened a wine and tobacco shop called Flora. Under the guise of a shopkeeper, Hoxha used the store as a front for his party activities. He participated in demonstrations against the Italian occupation and traveled the country and held organizational meetings. He became head of the Communist Party of Albania in 1941.

Mehmet Shehu, younger than Hoxha by five years, had trained as a soldier. Shehu went to Fultz's American Vocational School in Tirana, graduating in 1932. He learned English there. He had a romantic streak in him and wrote poetry. One of those poems was published in the school's magazine Laboremus in December 1931. Fultz, who ran the school at the time, said later that Shehu's failure to win a job in the state's Department of Agriculture upon graduation played a key role in his turn towards Communism. He went to Italy where he attended the Naples Military Academy. He was expelled from the school for his Communist Party activity and he returned to Tirana in 1936. He was 23 years old.

Unlike Hoxha, who remained in Albania, Shehu volunteered to join the Republican forces in the civil war in Spain. He became a member of the Spanish Communist Party and rose to become the commander of the 4th Battalion of the Garibaldi or 12th International Brigade. After the Fascist forces of General Francisco Franco defeated the Republicans, Shehu was sent to internment camps in France and Italy before he returned to Albania in 1942. He joined forces with Hoxha, who now was in command of the Communist movement in Albania.

Although he was a loyal party member, Shehu was not an organizational Communist. He was not on hand when Hoxha initially formed the party at secret meetings in Korcë and Tirana. He was not in on the ground floor of the movement in Albania, as it were, and he was not personally close to Hoxha. Having missed those early meetings, Shehu had not bonded with Hoxha as others had. He did not attend the important meeting Hoxha later held with the British at Labinot or the conference at Permët. He deferred to Hoxha in the matter of party and politics. He was a soldier who preferred to be with his soldiers in the field. That is what he knew.

Now here Shehu was outside the gates of Tirana planning to attack while Hoxha, his leader, was one hundred miles away in Berat discussing the victory parade. Yet if Shehu harbored any animosity toward Hoxha at that time he did not show it. Perhaps he wanted it that way. Kukich, who believed Shehu should have been the man to take over the country, recalled mentioning the possibility to Shehu on several occasions.

"He could have taken over," Kukich said. "He was doing all the fighting. The Partisan soldiers favored Shehu. There was closeness between him and the men. The people liked Shehu as well because he was a fighter fighting for his country. He had a good reputation from fighting in Spain. He came back to Albania as a hero. He was a solid disciplinarian and very strong. He was respected. Hoxha let Shehu take care of the fighting, and

Shehu left the politics to Hoxha. I don't think Hoxha had a plan for the battle of Tirana. He left that up to Shehu. I told Shehu, 'Mehmet, the men love you. The people love you. You should take over. You should run the country.' He said to me, 'Niko, don't ever talk to me about things like that. Politics is Hoxha's business, not mine. Stay away from me, Niko.'"

Shehu held briefings for Kukich and fellow Allied officers attached to his 1st Division at his headquarters in an abandoned house just northeast of Tirana. Shehu conducted the meetings in Albanian, although he sometimes spoke English or Italian. When Kukich wanted to speak with him alone Shehu would meet him in an open field where they could talk without being overheard. "That's when I would tell him that he should take over. He *knew* he could have taken over the country. He could have had Hoxha shot. But he didn't want to hear it."[7]

While Kukich thought highly of Shehu, some other Allied officers, namely the British of the SOE, had a different opinion. Major Peter Kemp, who met Shehu in the spring of 1943, wrote fifteen years later: "The Brigade Commander was Mehmet Shehu, a grim, energetic and efficient soldier who has since become Prime Minister of the Albanian People's Republic. Unlike most of the Partisan leaders he already had some practical experience of serious warfare, for he had commanded a company of the International Brigade in Spain; unlike most of them, also, he spoke good English. A sour, taciturn man of ruthless ambition, outstanding courage, and sickening ferocity—he had personally cut the throats of seventy Italians after a recent engagement—he admired the soldier qualities of [Major Billy] McLean and [Major David] Smiley and valued the help they gave him."[8]

Smiley, in his memoir of the war published in 1984, repeated some of what Kemp wrote. "Mehmet Shehu was a short, wiry, dark, sallow-faced man of about thirty who seldom smiled except at other people's misfortunes. He spoke good English, was very capable, and had far more military knowledge than most other Albanians.... He had a reputation for bravery, ruthlessness, and cruelty—he boasted that he had personally cut the throats of seventy Italian *carabinieri* who had been taken prisoner. I got along with him at first, for as soldiers we had something in common; but he did little to conceal his dislike of all things British, and my relations with him deteriorated."[9]

That Shehu was a capable commander, had a reputation of being ruthless, hated the British and could speak English is pretty much accurate. That he cut the throats of seventy Italian prisoners of war is not only open to question, but extremely doubtful. There are no documents to support the allegation. Outside of Kemp, and Smiley's rewrite of Kemp, there is no confirmation that any such incident took place. The Shehu story reads more like Sterling Hayden's tale about his Serbian shipmate shooting thirty Italians holed up in a cave.

Kukich scoffed at Kemp's story about Shehu. "I think it's ridiculous. I never heard of it," he said. "It could not have happened. Word would have gotten around. Albania is a small country. We would have heard about it. We would have known. I was with the Italians. They would have said something. Gen. [Adolfo] Infante would have said something. The Italian government would have said something. Tom Stefan, who spent a lot of time with the British, would have said something. They never did."[10]

One of the main reasons Kemp disliked Shehu stemmed from the Spanish Civil War. Only a few years before arriving in Albania, Kemp had fought as a volunteer on the side of the Nationalists (Fascists) in Spain while Shehu had fought on the other side with the Republicans Loyalists (Communists). Now Kemp was fighting *with* the Albanian Communists *against* his former comrades—the Italian Fascists and the Nazis. No small wonder then that Shehu not only returned Kemp's dislike, but also never trusted him.

Shehu estimated that there were some 1,500 to 3,000 German soldiers in Tirana, mostly of the 297th Infantry Division, along with 300 to 400 Ballists and pro–Zogist German collaborators. The Germans occupied most of the buildings in downtown Tirana around Skanderbeg Square, where the Mosque of Ethem Bey and the Venetian Campanile stood. The population of Tirana was only about 35,000 at the start of the war. That number had increased to about 100,000 as thousands of refugees fled the fighting in the countryside and sought safety in the city. Those with money jammed the already overcrowded hotels while others moved in with friends and relatives, if they could. The more unfortunate slept in city parks, in cemeteries or under bridges that crossed the Lana River.

Most of the buildings in the city were private homes built on winding, narrow streets and alleyways. The whitewashed residences had gates that enclosed gardens and ensured privacy. The gates were all closed.

The Italians had knocked down many of these homes when they built grand government buildings in the downtown area. Several of these Italianate buildings were adorned with projected heads, like gargoyles, of helmeted Italian soldiers who looked like Mussolini. The Italians built the elegant Dajti Hotel, where visiting high-ranking Italian Army officers and government officials stayed when in Tirana. Italian officers held weddings and parties there and Count Galeazzo Ciano, Mussolini's son-in-law, often made the hotel his headquarters when he visited the country.

The Italians built wide boulevards, the widest of which was named Mussolini Boulevard. Stemming out from the boulevard were roomy apartment

7. Tirana

View of Skanderbeg Square after the Battle of Tirana. The top of the tower of the Mosque of Ethem Bey has been sheared off by a shell while the Venetian Campanile is intact (courtesy Kostas "Gus" Routsis).

houses built to accommodate Italian officers, bureaucrats, colonists and their families, turning the area into a small Italian city within a city. The Italians built as though they intended to remain in Albania for a long time.

The Germans and their collaborators, lying in wait for the Partisan offensive, set up defensive positions in the government buildings and on the rooftops. They took over hotels, homes, shops and the parks. According to Shehu the Germans also had combat positions in the city's hospitals, schools, mosques, churches, banks, movie theaters, and the empty American legation building. The Germans mined the roads leading to the center of the city as well as the streets around the buildings. They set up obstacles and strong points at intersections and aimed artillery pieces at already calibrated crossing points. Artillery observers and snipers were lodged atop the campanile. Italian tanks with German crews patrolled the perimeter.

The British wanted Shehu to attack right away, but the general had other plans. Shehu, in his book, described a testy October 18 meeting he had at his headquarters with three British officers of the SOE. The officers, Majors Victor Smith, M.J. Thornton, and Captain J.F.P. Oliver, insisted that Shehu launch the attack immediately. Shehu refused. He told the British officers that he would attack when he was ready, and not before then. Shehu said that the British raised their voices and accused the Partisans of being afraid of the Germans. Not one to mince words, Shehu shouted back: "The Germans know if the Partisans are afraid or not, and not you. You are in Albania now and here it is the Albanian Partisans and the people who command, and not British officers. When and where we attack is our business, not yours."[11]

Shehu began his attack on Tirana on October 29 at 6 P.M., eleven days after the meeting with the British. He estimated that it would take his forces nineteen days to liberate the city, given that they had no artillery, but only captured mortars. Shehu would have Allied air support, but he did not give that much importance. He was certain of victory. The Germans soldiers were worn out and practically surrounded. German armies were in retreat everywhere. Increasingly the army in the Balkans relied on foreign conscripts like Armenians, Bulgarians and others to fill its depleted ranks.

Forces of Shehu's 1st Partisan Brigade spearheaded the attack from the north. The Partisans came over and around Dajti Mountain and swept through a broad pass that opened up like an invitation to the city. The plan was for the 1st Brigade to fight its way toward the center of the city and join forces with Colonel Myslim Peza's 4th Brigade that came from the southwest.

Shehu was proud of the 1st Brigade, which was the hammer of his 1st Partisan Division. He had commanded the 1st Brigade when it was formed. It was the first organized military unit the Partisans had put together. "It must be remembered," Shehu wrote, "the First Brigade had accomplished all of the duty entrusted to her right from the start."

Coming into the pass, the 1st Brigade rolled over an old cemetery before it ran into heavy fighting on a hill called "Bastard Hill" or "Son of a Bitch Hill" (*kodra e Kopilit*)—so named after an unmarried woman gave birth to her child there. Several times the Germans launched counteroffensives around the hill, but each time they were beaten back. British officers of the LRDG, who were with the Partisans, called in air support from the Allied air base in Foggia. Allied planes swooped in and bombed and strafed the German positions and the Partisans broke through. Although Shehu acknowledged the Allied air support in the battle for the hill, he wrote that the bombing actually did little damage to the Germans, but did raise the morale of the Partisans.[12]

The 8th and 9th Partisan Brigades, meanwhile, came up from Peza in the southwest to join in on the surrounding of the city. The move came as the Germans withdrew troops from Greece and headed north toward Tirana. The Germans intended to leave Albania and head north toward Montenegro. In order to do so the Germans had to travel along the coastal road from Greece to Durrës. From Durrës the Germans could either head east and reinforce the garrison in Tirana or follow the road north toward Montenegro. They traveled north, bypassing Tirana. However, the Germans who retreated from Kosovo traveled southwest toward Elbasan. It was from Elbasan that the German 22nd Corps attempted to march northwest and relieve the troops in Tirana.

Meanwhile, parts of downtown Tirana were in flames, with smoke billowing above the city. Kukich reported that large fires broke out along the main boulevards. He radioed Bari that the Partisans held the eastern part of Tirana while the Germans held onto the rest. The Germans, he said, looted homes, hospitals, shops and hotels. "Huns in Tirana have been drinking very heavy and been drunk [sic] while fighting," Kukich cabled. "Barracks near air field have been blown up by Huns on Nov. 1. Hotel Berlin was burned by Huns on night of Nov. 2."[13]

Not all of the Germans were drunk, however, because the Germans inflicted serious damage on the Partisans before fleeing, surrendering or dying. "The fighting was house to house," Kukich said. "I was going house to house. I went into five or six houses and came across a dozen dead Partisan soldiers. They would spread the curtains, raise the windows and shoot. And by the time they did this, they were dead, killed by German snipers. Hell, they could have shot *through* the windows. But they didn't know. They weren't trained. For many of them it was their first fight. I told Shehu and he straightened it out.

"There were a lot of dead and wounded Germans lying in the streets. Partisans would be stealing their boots even if they were still alive. Hell, it was war. Many of the Partisans had no shoes."[14]

Allied bombing of German positions in Tirana played an important role in the battle. The Germans had no aircraft in the skies. The few planes they did have at the Tirana airport were destroyed by Allied bombing and strafing runs. In one day the British RAF (Royal Air Force) sent in twenty eight rocket-firing planes to attack German gun positions and troop concentrations in the city.[15]

Following one bombing run, Kukich and British Captain Oliver came across a group of German soldiers who sought to surrender. Fearing reprisals from the Partisans, the Germans—there were more than a hundred of them—wanted to surrender only to the Americans or British. "One of the Germans came out with a white flag that had a note attached to it," Kukich said. "I sent one of the Partisans to get it. It said they wanted to surrender only to us. I looked at Oliver. What were we going to do? We couldn't take prisoners. There were one hundred and twenty-five of them. So we called Shehu at his headquarters. He told us to get out. They would take care of the prisoners. He said, 'You are to go out, both of you.' And we did." The Partisans marched the prisoners to the airport, which was now in Partisan hands. Kukich did not see them again.[16]

Shehu began the final phase of his attack on Tirana on November 11. He wrote that the morale of the German soldiers and the Albanian collaborators among them was low as a result of the Partisan offensive, disjointed as it was. Some German units had already left the city for Shkodra in the north while others prepared to do so. Kukich reported that the Albanian quislings were also leaving. Still, German units held important strongholds in Tirana, including a retaken Bastard Hill and the entire main square. They would not leave without a fight.

Although the fighting in the city was fierce, an unexpected but bigger battle took place just outside the city when the German force from Elbasan sought to hook up with the besieged German units in Tirana. This was the battle of Mushqeta, the name of a small village on the outskirts of Tirana.

The German 22nd Corps, made up of some three thousand men with tanks and artillery, had come from Struga in Macedonia to Elbasan. En route they had fought several skirmishes with Partisan guerrillas. After the men regrouped in Elbasan, the 22nd Corps headed for Tirana. Before it got there, the long column was caught in the open by Allied aircraft just after it traversed the winding mountain road at Qafe e Kerrabë (Kerraba Pass) and was destroyed at Mushqeta.

Shehu took full credit for the destruction of the German column, which saved Tirana for him, even though his Partisans did not attack the stunned Germans until after the planes had done their damage. Kukich said it was the bombing and strafing of the column by the planes that paved the way for the Partisan attack on what was left of the Germans. "We called in and Americans and British planes came in and bombed and strafed and knocked out all of the tanks and artillery. Once that was done, the Partisans came in and picked off the Germans," Kukich said.[17]

Hibbert wrote that the planes were called in by British officers of the LRDG and the planes attacked the column "with somewhat mixed help from the Partisans [who] had their minds set on moving to Tirana for the final kill."[18]

Lt. O'Keefe, who was in contact with Captain Stan Eastwood and his

LRDG as well as with Shehu on that day, witnessed the fighting. "At that time about 80% of Tirana was in Partisan hands. The fighting between the Germans and Partisans in Tirana and along the Tirana-Elbasan road was quite heavy during this time. The Partisans were greatly assisted by the RRDG patrols and Allied air strikes. In the last few days of fighting in that area, a large German force attempted to break through from Elbasan to relieve Tirana. The LRDG succeeded in destroying an important bridge across the Erzen River in the vicinity of Musgete [sic]. The Germans were not able to bring any equipment across the destroyed bridge and very few men got through to Tirana. Most of the Germans were either captured or killed by Partisans and Allied air bombardment."[19]

After the bombing, Partisans of the 1st and 8th Brigades came down from the hills that bracketed the road and killed many of the Germans who had been caught in the open by the Allied planes. This action took place between Mushqeta and Petrela. The Germans on the road were weak and vulnerable following the air attack. Their tanks were destroyed or disabled, their artillery pieces were smashed. The soldiers were dead, wounded or dazed. The Partisans first opened up with mortars and machine guns, and then came upon the Germans with rifles and pistols.

Shehu estimated that the Partisans killed some fifteen hundred Germans, wounded one hundred and fifty and captured another one hundred and fifty. The rest went to the hills seeking to escape. Very few headed for Tirana. He said the Partisans captured two working tanks along with eighteen trucks loaded with supplies. "The convoy from Elbasan was completely liquidated," Shehu wrote. "The battle of Tirana was decided at Mushqeta."[20] OSS reports estimated that some one thousand Germans had been killed while five hundred had made their way to Tirana.

Shehu toured the battlefield in person, overwhelmed at the destruction he had helped bring about. The bodies of men and dead horses were intermingled with destroyed or burned vehicles. The dead soldiers and their horses had so many holes in them, he said, that they gave the impression of having been stabbed repeatedly with knives and not killed by bullets. Weapons, the types of which he had not seen before, were strewn about, thrown by the side of the road, along with explosives of various kinds. There were twisted artillery pieces, wrecked trucks, mortars, machine guns, rifles, medical equipment and clothing all along the road. In the midst of the rubble was a child's pillow that must have been taken from some family along the way. Nearby was the body of a dead colonel sitting in a burned car between two destroyed motorcycles with sidecars. "You could count the bodies up to Berzhitë [a nearby village] but you couldn't count any further even if you walk slowly because there are so many. Look to the left and look to the right and you see a torrent of blood.

"There are German bodies in the nearby forests, soldiers who had attempted to flee the carnage, and there are dead Germans in a stream that flows red with blood, like a slaughter canal," he wrote. There were two tanks that were hit and turned completely around as though headed toward Elbasan, the direction that they came from, and not Tirana. "The destruction of these forces saved Tirana from a massacre," Shehu wrote. He marveled at how his forces, numbering some twelve hundred men, could inflict such a lopsided defeat on the German column, while he suffered only minimal losses. He estimated that he suffered only twelve Partisans killed and thirty wounded.[21]

The fact of the matter is that acting alone Shehu could not have inflicted such casualties on the German column. He had no air power of his own and no artillery. He had only a few machine guns. The only mortars he had were captured Italian or German mortars and they would not have been capable of causing such damage, even if the Partisans knew how to use them. The Partisans could not have destroyed or damaged tanks. As brave as the Partisans were, they did not have the firepower to inflict such damage on the Germans. It was Allied air power that destroyed the German column while the Partisans carried out a successful mopping-up operation. Still, it was a victory, and Shehu was quick to claim it for himself and the Partisans. The Allies appear not to have objected.

With the German relief column out of the way, Shehu turned his full attention back to Tirana. On November 15 he moved in on downtown Tirana, where a fanatic rearguard force awaited the Partisans. Many of the Germans had already evacuated the city, along with a number of Albanian collaborators who sought to escape to Austria. Some Germans left the road north and fanned out into the mountains. "Twenty Germans disguised in shepherd clothing have been captured here," Kukich cabled Fultz.[22]

As the Partisans closed in they found that much of the damage done to the city had been caused by Germans as they left Tirana. They left behind them a string of blown-up and burning buildings. There were many Germans dead in the streets.

A minor controversy broke out when the political commissar of the 1st Division told Kukich that civilians in Tirana had thrown hand grenades at the Partisans. This incident told the Allies that perhaps Hoxha and the Communists were less than welcome in Tirana. Hoxha denied that the incident even happened. He told Stefan that the Partisans were welcomed in Tirana and had control of the city.[23]

The battle for Tirana came to an end on November 17. Shehu estimated that the Partisans killed two thousand Germans, including three colonels, in the city and captured three hundred. He estimated Partisan losses at one hundred and twenty killed and two hundred and ninety wounded. "So fierce was the fighting," Shehu wrote, that a captured German officer said that half of his battalion enroute from Corfu to Tirana was liquidated at Ibë while the other half was killed at headquarters in the city."[24]

If the estimates of the numbers of Germans killed by the Partisans seemed high, they probably were. Shehu again failed to factor in the significant impact of Allied air power in the battle.

In a pair of after-action reports, the OSS said that the Germans had had substantial forces in the city but had no real plan to commit the entire force to defend the city. "In the battle of Tirana, the Germans never made a full commitment of forces. At the very beginning, there were about 4000 Germans in the city, but the tactical plan, according to source, appeared to be an emphasis upon retreat northward while maintaining holding forces in the capital whose number varied slightly around the 1000 figure," the report said.

The Germans used an outer ring of defense systems that commanded the approaches to the city and all the roads that led to the city center. These positions were manned mostly by Albanian gendarmes. After these strong points crumbled under Partisan attacks, the Partisans then faced positions manned by German troops, which gave them considerably more trouble. These rearguard actions conducted by the Germans took place at the same time that other Germans left Tirana and headed north. Some fifteen hundred men housed in barracks in the west side of the city toward the Durrës road broke out and went north. One company of the unit was trapped in the barracks and killed by the Partisans, according to the OSS.

The OSS agreed with Shehu's assessment of two thousand Germans killed in the fight for Tirana. However, the OSS report said that some of those dead Germans were wounded prisoners who were killed by the Partisans. "The ANLA policy toward German wounded, according to source, was not to have German wounded. Thus, most Germans who were found wounded were killed outright, with no mercy shown. Source did not see any living German wounded. Very few prisoners were taken by the ANLA."

The Germans who fought in its rearguard action fought tenaciously, often to the last man. "Although Germans battled grimly to the very end and at times refused to surrender, even when cornered by twos and threes in houses, they fought always in terror for their lives, having heard that they would be killed outright upon capture." Other German soldiers left

German soldiers killed in the battle (courtesy Kostas "Gus" Routsis).

in panic, however, killing civilians, burning down houses and looting shops. "Toward the end the low morale, coupled with heavy drinking and the realization that their cause was hopeless, brought about ruthless behavior of German troops. As the Germans retreated, they began to enter homes and take out reprisals on innocent civilians."[25]

Kukich, O'Keefe and their radio operators headed for the American legation building just off the center of the city on Elbasan Road, but they were held up by the Partisans. Their commander, Gen. Dali Ndreu, was concerned about meetings Kyrias had had with his relatives in Tirana. Kyrias' relatives were suspected by the Partisans of being sympathetic to the Balli. Kukich lost his temper and complained to Bari. The Partisans relented and Ndreu apologized for the delay. The Allies apologized as well. Kukich cabled Bari on November 15. "The goddam war seems to have entered a period of chivalry. The generals appear to be so busy apologizing that one wonders when they have time to fight. Now that the boys can speak to the civilians, what the hell are they going to talk about? Of what use is freedom if one has nothing to talk about?"[26]

The Americans passed wrecked and burned German vehicles with dead Germans in them as they headed toward the city center. There were dead Germans and Albanian gendarmes lying side by side in the streets. There were dead horses and donkeys still attached to smashed wagons along the roads. Stray dogs sniffed the dead. Smoke hung over the city as buildings still burned. There were no people in the streets and the city was eerily quiet.

The American legation building was empty when they got there. Although the building was intact, it was damaged. The Germans had used the building during the battle, had trashed it, and had taken the caretaker prisoner when they left. Kukich quickly had repairs done and cabled Fultz. "Roof damage for the entire legation from bullets and bombs amounts to two rocks [gold pieces]. Work is done but the bill has not been paid. Work to be done includes plastering inside and out of various buildings which will cost two [additional] rocks. Also repairing of doors and windows throughout the legation which will cost four rocks. 80 windows are broken. We will need sufficient glass and putty for this."[27]

The men ran the American flag they had brought with them up the flagpole in front of the building. It was the first time the flag had flown at the legation in five years. The Germans had taken everything with them that they could. The men were in need of food and clothing. All of the shops and markets in the city were closed. A recent supply drop had gone astray and landed in Biza. The British had gotten to it first and ransacked it. A disgusted O'Keefe cabled: "The British are smoking American cigarettes."

O'Keefe also told Fultz that many Albanians, who noted that the American legation was once again in American hands, descended on the building seeking to get out of the country. "Many have indicated they would like to leave Albania. Some have offered bribes to us in order to get out." Fultz warned his men to be "scrupulously careful" about being drawn into "disagreements" with the Partisans over these civilians and to avoid "open criticism" of either the Partisans or the British. "There are many civilians in Tirana who have grievances, so be careful that contacts with them do not put you in a false position," Fultz cabled back. "Select your contacts very carefully, choosing only the most reliable persons from whom you might be able to obtain important intelligence."[28]

Tirana was tense. People were fearful. They remained locked in their homes. The city was firmly in the hands of the Partisans, but no one knew what to expect. People who had sided with the Balli Kombëtar were especially afraid. If the Partisans treated them the way they treated the German wounded, then the future was truly grim. Many hoped that the Americans would exert a softening influence on the Partisans. Albania had, after all, many ties with the United States. Surely the Americans would not let Albania slip away and fall into the hands of the Communists. Things did not look good.

The Partisans cleaned up the city for Hoxha's expected arrival. They used prisoners to pick up bodies from the streets and quickly buried them in makeshift cemeteries. Dead animals were collected and burned. Partisan wounded were taken to hospitals for treatment, even though there was nothing to treat them with. The Germans had looted the hospitals and stolen all of the medicine and equipment. Wrecked vehicles were cannibalized for parts and towed away. Rubble was cleared from the main boulevards and thoroughfares. Mines were deactivated from around the airport and the airport was declared open, although no planes landed. Hotels reopened and shopkeepers were urged to open their shops.

Kukich and O'Keefe, after surveying the scene in Tirana, cabled Fultz on November 24. "Apparently attitude of majority of civilians towards Partisans is not good. On November 28 change for the better is expected by many. In parade on that day, flags of three Allies will be carried in a parade. Indications from many [Albanians] that they would like to withdraw from Albania. Bribes from some to us in order to leave."[29]

Stefan cabled Fultz from Berat the day Tirana fell. "Shtab now plan move to Tirana soonest. Berat literally going mad as name Hoxha resounds throughout the city. Hoxha requested I remain here and enter the capital along with his staff."[30]

It was an honor for Stefan to march into Tirana with Hoxha, an honor he no doubt felt he deserved. He had been with the Partisan leader longer than anyone else. He had been closer to him than any other of the Allies assigned to the Shtab. He spoke the same language as Hoxha. They had come under fire together. "They were like brothers," Kukich said. Like brothers they sometimes irked one another. At times they argued and fought. But in the mountains of Albania they seemed to have bonded. Now Stefan would march into Tirana at Hoxha's side. It was a long way from clearing tables at the Arch Street Tavern.

8

Victory

The celebration of the liberation of Tirana began early in the morning of November 28, 1944, when six British Halifax bombers swept in low over the city and dropped leaflets of greetings and congratulations. The planes, which had contributed so much to the Partisan victory, then swooped over the airfield and dropped packets of food that were quickly snatched up by hungry Albanians.[1]

Although the British bombers did not land, the airport had actually opened the day before when Captain James Hudson came in on a C-47 with supplies and three reporters. That was the same day that Sgt. Vangel Kyrias was sent back to Bari and an early trip home to the United States.

Although food was available in Tirana—at inflated prices—there was a shortage of bread. Bakeries and shops that had shut down during the fighting did not reopen as nervous merchants and citizens awaited the arrival of Enver Hoxha and the future he brought with him.

Following the departure of the British planes a 21-gun salute, mainly from captured German and Italian guns, was fired off and Hoxha entered Tirana at the head of a group of his commanders for the victory parade. The day had been chosen because it was the anniversary of the day in 1912 when Albania first declared its independence from the Ottoman Empire in the city of Vlora.

Hoxha, commander in chief of the army and head of the new provisional Albanian government, wore a new uniform with a Sam Browne belt and a cap adorned with a red star. He had gloves. His boots shined. He radiated confidence, as well he should have. He was now back in the city that he had been forced to leave following the Italian occupation. Back then he had run a small shop. Now he ran the country.

Hoxha had earlier arrived in Tirana from Berat. Leaving Berat he was

8. Victory

given a warm sendoff by cheering Partisans and residents who lined the streets and handed him flowers, or threw flowers in his path. From there he and his entourage slowly made their way over rough roads and around bombed-out bridges to get to the capital. Ordinarily the trip from Berat to Tirana took three hours. However, because the roads and bridges were so damaged it took Hoxha two days, with an overnight in Elbasan. Hoxha and his party set out from Berat on November 26. They rode in captured German and Italian cars and motorcycles with sidecars. These vehicles had to be left behind because the bridges crossing the Osum River had been blown. After crossing the river by mule and raft, they boarded a bus that waited on the other side. The bus was also left behind when they came to another destroyed bridge. The ordeal was repeated several times as they came across more damaged and destroyed bridges. After spending the night in Elbasan, Hoxha and his group set out again for Tirana. They drove through the Kerraba Pass and up to Mushqeta, where the remains of the recent battle there still lined the sides of the winding road.

Mushqeta Battle Memorial erected after the war. It reads: "On this road from Mushqeta to Petrela the fate of the war for the liberation of Tirana was decided. On November 14–15, fighters form the 1st, 4th, 8th and 17th Brigades ambushed a convoy of 3,000 Germans and destroyed them" (author's photograph).

Hoxha described what he saw this way: "Along the road we saw overturned tanks and armored cars, burnt-out trucks shifted a little in order to open the road, piles of spent machine-gun cartridges, enemy soldiers' helmets, and so on. The closer we approached Tirana, the more destroyed enemy weapons were to be seen on both sides of the road. There was something beautiful and symbolic in this scene. The victors passed proudly among the smashed weapons and remnants of the defeated invaders."[2]

Hoxha was met by Shehu and Myslim Peza on the outskirts of the city. The two combat leaders described the battle for Hoxha. Shehu pointed to two captured Italian tanks that the Partisans had captured. They were now manned by Partisans.

Peza stayed at Hoxha's side as the march of the leaders into the city to the parade reviewing stand began. Shehu dropped behind. Baba Faja, the jovial wine-guzzling Bektashi leader, was in the front row along with Dr. Omer Nishani, who had been named Minister of Foreign Affairs. Koçi Xoxe, a tinsmith from Korcë who was now a general, jostled for a place at Hoxha's side, as did Gen. Spiro Moisui, Hoxha's chief of staff. These men had been among the first to join in with Hoxha when he took to the mountains to begin the war against the Italians and the Germans, and they all had remained close to him. Stefan marched in the second or third row, depending on the changing of positions. Beside him most of the way was Shehu, British Captain Marcus Lyon, a Russian officer and a Yugoslav.

Crowds came out to watch Hoxha and his commanders make their way to Skanderbeg Square. The people were generally unenthusiastic, and the welcome was not near the warm reception he had received in Berat. The people of Tirana, generally sympathetic to the Balli Kombëtar, or even to King Zog, were in a state of shock. They found it hard to believe that these men, this ragtag army, these *Communists* had been able to defeat the Balli, and force the Germans to abandon Tirana. "The people of Tirana were utterly amazed that these men had come down from the mountains and taken the city," Kukich said. "And there was Tom marching alongside Hoxha as though he was Hoxha's number three or four man. That's how close to Hoxha Tom was."[3]

Hoxha, who towered over his Albanian comrades, strutted in front. He and his group made their way down the broad street still called Mussolini Boulevard to Skanderbeg Square. The mosque there had been damaged, the top of its tower sheared off. The clock tower beside the mosque had also been hit by mortar shells. More people now lined the street. Hoxha headed toward the Dajti Hotel where a reviewing stand had been set up. Only days before, prisoners had removed the bodies of several Germans and their dead horses and smashed wagons from the side and front of the hotel.

8. Victory 159

The hastily built reviewing stand stood on the site of a former German strongpoint in front of the hotel. It was where Hoxha, his staff and special guests watched the victory parade. The stand was decorated with red and black bunting, Albania's colors, and displayed the flags of Albania, the United States, Great Britain, the Soviet Union and Yugoslavia.[4]

Hoxha climbed the stairs to the reviewing stand. A band played and the Albanian flag, a black double-headed eagle on a red background, was raised. Hoxha and the others saluted. Hoxha, the center of attention, surrounded by his commanders and his staff, approached the microphone. It was his moment. To Hoxha's left stood Dr. Nishani. To his right was Koçi Xoxe. On Xoxe's right stood Stefan. He wore an American pilot's cap set at a jaunty angle along with a pilot's leather jacket that had American flag on the shoulder. With clothes no doubt borrowed from an American airman, or airmen, he had helped rescue, Stefan looked about as prominent on the stand as any of Hoxha's generals, if not more so.

Kukich stood among the people in the crowd who awaited Hoxha's speech and the parade that was to follow. So did Cpl. Gus Routsis. Routsis had arrived in Tirana from Berat by bicycle the night before. It had taken him a full day, but he had made the trip faster than Hoxha had. He and a Partisan soldier had bought bicycles in Berat and traveled together, hitching rides with their bikes on trucks and crossing rivers by raft. He counted five bridges blown from Berat to Tirana. In Tirana Routsis met with his cousin Vangel of the 8th Brigade, who had fought the Germans days earlier at Mushqeta. Routsis wrote in his journal: "He says out of three thousand Germans in the convoy, one thousand were killed, about three hundred prisoners, and the rest are still hunted down up in the mountains where they dispersed to save their necks. A lot of them will probably starve to death."[5]

Some 30,000 to 40,000 people waited for Hoxha to speak. To most people of the city Hoxha was nothing more than a stranger. The people did not know who he was, although they had heard about him. And what they had heard came from German and Balli propaganda machines, and it had not been good. The way he was dressed, the way he looked, the way he carried himself, he could have been from one of a number of armies that had passed through Albania.

The crowd spilled over the boulevard and filled the park across from the grandstand. Loudspeakers had been set up on light poles at the corners of the streets around the hotel. People who could not get close to the grandstand huddled around the various loudspeakers.

Hoxha took the microphone and got right to the point. Sid Feder of the Associated Press, who covered the event, wrote in cables to Rome that

Hoxha "entered liberated capital today with defiant promise from new premier that Albania is ready to fight to preserve southern boundaries fronting Greece." Feder described Hoxha as an "ex-school teacher who heads both Partisan Army [and the] government which took over capital on 32nd anniversary [of the] declaration [of] Albanian independence.

"Speaking from stand [in] front palatial Hotel Sejti [sic], which [is] like something out [of] Miami Beach, Hoxha addressed 30,000 to 40,000 of populace massed on Boulevard Mussolini in first capital of Europe freed entirely by own Partisans," he reported. "Hoxha also pledged Democratic government [for] Albania," Feder reported. Feder also noted the presence of Stefan, even though he got his name confused with Stefan's home town. He wrote that Hoxha "entered city by walking entire length of Mussolini Boulevard with staff, Allied officers, including Captain Thomas Stefan Laconian or Laconjan, as crowds threw flowers [and] cheered."

Radio reporter Morris Rosenberg of the OSS's Psychological Warfare Board (PWB) estimated the crowd outside the Dajti Hotel at 30,000. Rosenberg, in his same-day report to Bari radio, wrote: "Hoxha said government would work for promptest restoration of the country with economic, social, cultural reforms and people would control the country in democratic manner. Lauded the deeds [of] ANLA which [is] now driving [the] last Germans from the NW of country. Told crowd ANLA with the help of Allies rid Albania of Germans and praised the Red Army and Yugoslav Partisans especially and said that Albania must ally with Tito."

Allied observers noted that Hoxha heaped praise on the Soviet Union and Yugoslavia, neither of which had contributed anything to the Partisans' victory, but barely mentioned—let alone thanked—either Great Britain or the United States, which had. It was a clear sign that Hoxha had every intention of driving his country away from the west and into the orbit of Tito and Stalin. The reference to Greece was a message to Great Britain that Hoxha would fight if Greece sought to annex part of Albania. Hoxha lived in fear that the British would agree to Greek claims to a portion of southern Albania, which the Greeks called Northern Epirus. Hoxha suspected that British commando raids along the coast in the summer had been a prelude to a British-led Greek takeover of the south of Albania.

After Hoxha's speech the army passed in review. The parade included the 1st, 4th, 8th, 10th, 12th and 15th Brigades of the Partisan Army. All of the brigades, except for one, carried the Albanian flag—a black two-headed eagle on a red background. One unit carried the hammer and sickle, the flag of the Soviet Union. They were followed by the Antonio Gramsci Battalion, a unit of Italian soldiers who had joined the Partisans in a brigade

8. Victory

named after Gramsci, an Italian poet and Communist with Albanian roots. Behind the Gramsci Battalion came the two sputtering captured Italian tanks, and a unit of Armenian deserters from the German Army.

Stefan radioed Fultz that while the parade had been "quite impressive," the people who watched the parade were less than enthusiastic, however. "It looked as if the people were stunned. The cheers I heard sounded almost as if forced by the occasion. There was not the wild display of enthusiasm demonstrated in the south."[6]

No sooner had all of the leading figures gone into the hotel for a victory party than a controversy erupted over the display of flags in the capital. The British, in a show of "unity," displayed the American flag along with the Union Jack at the British residence during the parade. Its failure to raise the flag of the Soviet Union, the third member of the Allied Alliance, brought a howl from the Russians. Both the Soviets and the Albanians complained to Stefan, who was now the ranking American officer in Albania. Stefan cabled Fultz and recommended that either the British fly the flag of the Soviet Union or that the Stars and Stripes be taken down. Somehow the issue was resolved and the party at the ornate Hotel Dajti continued. Hoxha and all of his generals and colonels, dressed in their best uniforms, were there. Some, like Shehu, brought their wives, although most did not. There is a rare photograph of Fiqret Shehu sitting between a pair of British officers and Shehu at a well-provisioned dinner table. Stefan changed into a dress uniform, as did Lts. Kukich, and O'Keefe and British Colonels Marcus Lyon and Alan Palmer. The Allied officers mingled with the Albanian generals and several Soviet and Yugoslav officers who were also on hand. Stefan invited his Albanian-American radio operators George and Gus Routsis and Albert Tolie. The three radio operators were the only enlisted men at the party. White-coated Hotel Dajti waiters, who had worked for the Italians, served dinner on tables set with the hotel's fine china. The raki, whiskey, vodka, cognac and wine flowed as toast after toast was proposed to the liberation of Tirana.[7]

The cocktail/dinner party was the first, and last, of its kind in Tirana. Hoxha and his staff would not again meet and mingle with the Allies at such a social event.

Captain Stefan took charge of the OSS unit at the U.S. legation. This consisted of himself, Lts. Kukich and O'Keefe, as well as a dozen enlisted men, practically all of whom were Albanian-Americans and could speak Albanian. The OSS unit was scheduled to stay in place until a civilian unit of diplomats could relieve it.

November 28, 1944, in many ways was the highest point in Stefan's life. The pinnacle he reached was reflected in an Associated Press story by

Celebration in downtown Tirana, November 28, 1944. Captain Tom Stefan is at center, smiling and with emblem on cap. Directly over his left shoulder is Lt. Nick Kukich (courtesy Nick Kukich).

Feder about Hoxha that mentioned Stefan prominently. The *Boston American*, where Stefan had newspaper friends from his restaurant days in Boston, picked up the Associated Press story and added its own touches. *Dielli*, the Albanian-American weekly newspaper in Boston, reprinted the *Boston American* story beneath a picture of Stefan with a cut line that read: "Local Law Student Becomes Key Man in Albania."

"It's still the land of opportunity," The *Boston American* story read. "Thomas Stefan was a bus boy in the Arch St. Café two and a half years ago. Today, at 27, he is an Army captain, representing the United States as liaison officer with Prime Minister Enver Hoxha, Partisan general and prime minister of Albania. When Hoxha, 36-year-old college professor, marched with his hosts into Tirana, Albanian capital, recently after the Nazis and their puppet government had been ousted, Capt. Stefan was at his side. Stefan was in Albania long before the Nazis lost control. How he got there and what he did are still a military secret, but the Albanians and the Americans of Albanian descent rejoiced December 2 when they read that Stefan was Mr. Uncle Sam, officially in Albania.

"He was born in Laconia of Albanian parents, studied at Ohio State

8. Victory

College [sic] after graduating from Laconia High School, then had to give up college due to the death of his father. Judge Harry E. Trap of Laconia encouraged him to study law.

"He came here, got a job as a busboy at the Arch Grill and studied at Suffolk Law School nights. That career, too, was interrupted, this time by war. Stefan enlisted in the Army and was eventually sent to Washington to study the language of his ancestors.

"No one was more delighted than his former employers, Christo Thanas, James Keko, George Gelany and Paul Johan. They sent him an Albanian dictionary and regularly the weekly Albanian newspaper published here, the *Dielli*. 'And don't forget our compatriots when you go to Albania,' they urged him.

"He did. And now the ex-busboy is advisor on American affairs to the head of the government of Albania."[8]

In the days following their victory, the ANLA moved quickly to establish order in the city, putting the city and country under virtual martial law. Although Hoxha declared an amnesty for people who had sided or sympathized with the Balli Kombëtar and the Germans, the "amnesty" was ignored or quickly forgotten. The ruthless Koci Xoxe, who was essentially an uneducated laborer, was named Minister of the Interior with full police powers. Hundreds of people were jailed, their homes ransacked and their property taken. Suspects were arrested on the street. There were reprisal killings and secret executions. People disappeared. While Partisan supporters celebrated the liberation of Tirana, thousands of other Albanians who had supported the opposition, or who had sat out the war, lived in fear. And well they should have. Among other things, the Partisans were anxious to find and punish the members of the Balli Kombëtar who had killed some eighty Partisan supporters in the streets of Tirana on February 4, 1944. They wanted reprisals, and they got them.

Late in December the deteriorated bodies of twelve Albanians were discovered in the basement of the Hotel Bristol in downtown Tirana. One of the dead was a woman who had worked with the Germans and the Balli. Her husband, a captain in the Gendarme, had earlier been executed by the ANLA in Korcë. Another of the dead was a newspaper editor. Still another victim was known to have helped the ANLA while working for the Germans. He was killed by mistake.[9]

Many Albanians, whether they were German and Balli collaborators or sympathizers—or just plain bystanders—lived in fear, not only in Tirana but throughout the country. "In general the people of Korca dislike and fear the FNC," Stefan reported in December. "A part of this attitude grows out of the fact that key positions in the organization are occupied by

Moslems. [Korcë was an Orthodox region.] It also grows out of the fact that the people have accepted the propaganda which presents the movement as communistic. There are also many persons who have put on the red star and have pillaged and plundered. These are now group leaders and a great deal of resentment has been stirred up thereby. Because of the heavy percentage of Moslems in the FNC organization some of the people are referring to it as the rebirth of the Turkish era."[10]

Many suspected collaborators in Tirana turned to the Americans and the British for help, claiming to have been duped by German propaganda into backing the Germans. They worked with the Germans, they said, in order to save their country from the destruction that would have followed had they opposed them. They had only the interests of Albania at heart, they said. Some of those who sought out the Allies were prominent Albanian businessmen who made money out of the war by selling goods to the Germans. But was that not to be expected? Others were landowners who had gravitated toward the Balli and the Germans because of the stability that they represented. Established old-line Albanian families, the elite of the country, with names like Toptani, Vrioni and Konitsa sought to work their way into the good graces of the Americans and the British as a means of protection. They were well-educated, well-to-do and they spoke English. They believed in democracy. They were also Balli Kombëtar sympathizers who hated and feared the Communists. They threw fine parties for the Allied officers. They did not believe that the Allies would allow the Communists to take over the country, and they said so.

Captain Stefan attended many of those parties, as did Lts. Kukich and O'Keefe. The three American officers were dashing and very popular. The three were young, unmarried and they had money. Stefan was especially well-liked. He was not only the ranking American officer in Albania, he was an Albanian-American who spoke the language. And he was charming. He was also close to Hoxha and the other Partisan leaders. He could get things done. He could pick up information. He also could pick up women, which he did. In no time at all he accumulated several attractive girlfriends. Some of these young women later paid dearly for their American friendships, including a woman friend of O'Keefe's.[11]

The Americans of the OSS in Tirana developed a routine as they sought to continue to gather information. They not only went to parties, but they hit the bars as well. OSS Sgt. Edward E. Nichols of Wisconsin, a radio operator who arrived in Tirana in January 1945, said, "There was little doubt in the minds of the Albanian authorities as to our mission—political intelligence. The OSS teams were welcome when the Partisans were in the hills fighting the Germans. Our teams could call for air strikes, supplies, even gold. But now they just wanted us to leave." Nichols said, "Most evenings we would make the rounds of what passed for night clubs, picking up such information as we could. We would always sign the bar checks. One of our group had the task each morning of going about town settling the bar checks that we had signed the night before."[12]

There came a time though when Kukich and O'Keefe, who were also not exactly known as wallflowers, decided they should cut back on attending the parties and hitting the nightclubs because the Communists frowned on Allied fraternization with Balli sympathizers. Fultz did too. Being straitlaced Communist ascetics, they also looked down on the open social contact between the Allies and Albanian women. Increasingly Albanians who fraternized with the Americans and the British were subjected to questioning by Albanian authorities.

"The parties were thrown by Balli sympathizers, and I knew Hoxha disliked them," Kukich said. "So O'Keefe and I decided not to go to any more of them. But Tom couldn't be talked out of going. He was starting to drink a lot."[13]

The economic situation in Albania was a shambles. Not only had the fragile infrastructure of the country been destroyed, but thousands of villages had been burned and crops ruined. In addition, the Germans upon leaving Albania had systematically looted the country. Government workers who had not been paid in months, now found themselves without jobs. There was no industry, no commerce and no jobs. Many were forced to sell their clothes and other belongings on the streets of Tirana. There was so little money around that the provisional government could only pay its new high ranking ministers fifty dollars a month, the pay of an American private.

Hoxha needed help. He soon found that his two new friends, Stalin in the Soviet Union and Tito in Yugoslavia, had deep economic problems of their own and could hardly afford to provide any meaningful aid for Albania. Hoxha, despite his animosity toward the Allies, was forced to turn to the Allies for economic assistance, even though the United States and the United Kingdom had not granted recognition to his government.

Hoxha in many ways was a man caught in the middle. Which way to go, east or west? He had people around him like Nishani who generally admired the United States and urged Hoxha to make an accommodation with the Americans. On the other hand were a group of Communist hardliners like Koci Xoxe who pushed Hoxha toward the Soviet Union and Yugoslavia. Hoxha worshiped Stalin, and would do so for the rest of his life, even though the Soviets had been only spectators at the fighting in Albania. Hoxha distrusted the Americans. He believed that the British led the United States around by the nose. He had a burning hatred for the British. He was convinced the British planned to overthrow him and cut Albania in half, giving the south to the Greeks. Had not the British supported his enemies before? And were not the British and the Americans now providing sanctuary in Italy for Albanian traitors who had escaped?

Despite Hoxha's success in taking over a country, neither he nor any of the people around him had any experience in governing anything—not a village, not a town, not a city—let alone a country. They were young and inexperienced and the country was on its knees.

In early 1945 the State Department sent OSS M/Sgt. Stephen Peters, 39, to Albania to assess the political, economic and social situation. Peters was an Albanian-born, Albanian-speaking American who was a graduate of Harvard. He had taught school in Boston as well as in Albania. He was considered to be an intellectual with a firm understanding of Albania who could be relied upon to come up with an objective report on what was taking place in the country. He knew many people in the country.

His visit came at a crucial time. In the first week in February 1945 the Big Three—Roosevelt, Churchill and Stalin—met at the peace conference in Yalta in the Crimea to work out the future of a partitioned Europe and set the agenda for a United Nations conference in San Francisco in April.

In a penetrating, unvarnished series of reports, Peters painted a dark picture of Tirana. Although only about one-fifth of the city had been destroyed during the fighting, nothing seemed to be working. "The streets are dirty, unkempt, full of gaping holes. No one appears to be working to clear the rubbish in the ruined sections or fill the holes in the main streets," Peters wrote in his first report, dated February 8, 1945. The government controlled newspapers "are full of big talk about the great reconstruction work being done by the FNC and give abundant publicity to the ephemeral 'Labor Brigades,' but there is very little evidence to show that any actual work is being done. Even the Skanderbeg Square, the pride of Tirana in peace time, in front of the government palaces looks like a dilapidated place. No damage at all was done to the square or the surrounding buildings, but no one is taking care of them. Very few street cleaners are seen about the city."

Peters was surprised to find that well-stocked stores were open for business despite the fact that many stores and businesses had been burned to the ground. The stores seemed to have everything for sale—shoes, tobacco, chinaware, Swiss watches, jewelry, and cameras, as well as meat and vegetables. However, very few people had the money to buy anything since "money is the scarcest thing of all."

The people of Tirana, in Peters' view, seemed as grim as the streets.

8. Victory

"Even with its small population, Tirana before the war was very crowded and its streets were full of well-dressed people, new vehicles, and clean carriages. In those days there was fast moving traffic and everybody seemed busy. Today, in spite of its tripled population, the city seems to be at a standstill: during the day the streets appeared deserted, the crowds are small, ragged, dejected, and forlorn; the vehicles are few and worn out; the carriages are old, dirty, and about to fall apart. The pre-war cafes and restaurants are almost always empty. There is very little business activity. Most of the storeowners and their apprentices sun themselves outside and appear as if a sudden blow stunned them. Practically everybody seems to be sunning himself in calm resignation. In most residential sections people, the majority of whom are dirty, sick looking, emaciated, ragged, barefooted, just loiter idly at the street corners or sit under the eaves when it rains. Almost all of them convey the impression of a hopeless lot; there does not appear to be any life in them, any ambition, any desire to stir about."

Peters took note of the plight of the country's civil servants, whom he described as "the most desperate and dissatisfied people in Tirana." At one time, under the rule of King Zog, these people were "the most numerous and prosperous" people in the city. Now, after being stripped of their jobs by the Communists, they "are in dire circumstances. Almost all of them appear to be against the present setup and say so in private, though they do not have the courage to protest in public. They do not know where to turn for assistance. Somehow the FNC has filled them with terror."

Their plight was in sharp contrast to the way they lived under King Zog, Peters noted. "Before April 1939 [when King Zog fled] Tirana was the city of Zog's expansive court, of the diplomatic corps, of a large number of well-fed, well-dressed officers (Zog's army consisted roughly of 10,000 men, about 2,000 of whom were comparatively highly paid officers), of deputies, ministers, and a large number of lesser state functionaries. At that time the majority of the people of Tirana were civil employees, for Zog's government seldom employed one man where two or three could be conveniently used."

Now these unemployed civil servants were having a hard time finding anyone who would or could help them. Although most of the Albanian people, including the Partisans, were friendly toward the Americans at the beginning of the war, that began to change. These now jobless civil workers dared not ask the Americans for help, nor could they expect anything but grief from the Partisans.

Peters, who roamed the streets of Tirana at all hours, was not impressed with the "motley-dressed" Partisan soldiers who patrolled the city. "They are the queerest bunch of soldiers one can imagine. It is hard to see two of them dressed alike and still harder to see two of them carry the same arms. Their dress represents the uniforms of almost all European armies. A Partisan soldier may have an Italian cap, a British battle blouse, a pair of American trousers, and a pair of German shoes. And their arms, which are carried in all shapes and manner, in accordance with the wishes of each individual soldier, may be an Italian rifle, a German pistol, or a British Tommy gun. Most of the soldiers, both men and women, are on the whole in their late teens. There is nothing soldiery about them in their bearing and their walk. They slouch along as if they carried an enormous load. They appear serious, but there is no vivacity in them, no apparent enthusiasm. They look underfed and unhealthy (the current typhus epidemic broke out among the FNC Army because of its uncleanliness and lice). These soldiers are a sorry looking bunch in the city and appear like prisoners freshly captured from some international brigade. They are boys and girls from the mountains who have descended down and taken control of the capital."[14]

There is little to doubt the accuracy of Peters' observations regarding the Albanian military on duty in Tirana in February 1945. However, by the time Peters arrived in Tirana, the best-trained and most motivated troops of Gen. Mehmet Shehu's 1st Partisan Division that took Tirana had moved on to new assignments. Following the liberation of Tirana, Hoxha had two veteran divisions fighting alongside Tito's Partisans in Yugoslavia, taking heavy losses. While one division fought with the Yugoslavs in Kossovo, a second division moved north to the Albanian city of Shkodra and into Montenegro following the Germans in retreat northward from Tirana.

The soldiers who occupied Tirana during Peters' visit were replacements, most of them new to the military. They were simple village people. They were very young, poorly dressed, ill-trained and ill-educated. None had seen any fighting and their discipline was a work in progress.

Ismail Kadare, Albania's most famous writer, later took a more romantic view of the events that took place in Tirana during the winter of 1945. Kadare wrote that the day the Partisans took over Tirana "was really a sort of holiday." And though there were arrests, imprisonments, secret executions and the confiscation of private property, these acts were all hidden behind a façade of merrymaking. After all, there was a lot to celebrate. Fascism had been defeated.

"At the time, nobody dreamed of criticizing the victors. They were the fortunate ones," Kadare wrote. "And their good luck was redoubled because of the immediate sympathy they aroused: most Partisans were young and dapper, and many of them were high school boys. There were also professors and university students who, interrupting their studies in Rome, Vienna or Paris, had come to fight; sons of the idealistic bourgeoisie who, fascinated by communist theories, had renounced their parents and their wealth; later, priests and other religious people from various confessions joined with them. Young women were another important element in the wave of popular sympathy.

"Throughout the memorable autumn of 1944 and the winter of 1945, young women partisans, together with thousands of others, crowded the streets, having a good time, becoming engaged to boys they had known in the marquis, or to others whom they had just met, happy as you please. At the Hotel Dajti, where the upper middle class amused themselves, the day would dawn while the knights-errant were still dancing ... and no one knew what was hatching beneath the scenes: intrigues, ongoing power struggles, the poison and knife the leaders were preparing for one person or another."[15]

Although there may be some accuracy in what Kadare wrote, Kadare, who was nine years old at the time, did not publish his observations until 1995.

In any event, Stefan, Kukich and O'Keefe took Peters under their wing. They gave him access to their files and provided him with backup information. Although Peters technically was a radio operator, his real assignment was to provide the OSS and the State Department with information that he, with his Albanian language skills and contacts, could provide. He quickly found out, however, that academics he had previously known in Tirana were too frightened to talk with him. "They all wanted to talk to me at length but did not dare lest they found themselves in prison the next day," Peters reported.

He noted that Allied personnel were "diligently watched" and their movements curbed by the government. "There is evidence that the commissars have orders to note and report whenever possible any person seen visiting or talking to Allied personnel," he noted. He reported that "a few people who associated with Allied personnel soon after Tirana was liberated were either locked up for a day or so or directly or indirectly warned or threatened by the commissars."[16]

Peters found that Hoxha and his leadership team seriously favored the Yugoslavs and Soviets over the Americans and the British, even though Hoxha paid lip service to friendship toward the United States. "Both the Russians and Jugoslavs [sic] have the confidence of the Partisans, while the Americans and the British, especially the latter, are looked upon with suspicion and even distrust," Peters wrote. He also quickly found out that the Hoxha government, which was made up of "many Russian-minded members," preferred secrecy to openness. "Following the early Russian example of almost complete blackout on internal information for the outside world, the present authorities in Tirana, suspicious as they are of the Anglo-American intentions for the current regime, are attempting to carry on with their program with as much secrecy as possible," Peters reported. "Perhaps they are just following blindly the Russian policy of suppressing news without having clearly understood the Russian aims. There is a vogue currently in Albania to imitate the Russian ways of doing things."

Peters noted that many "large landowners, conservatives and pro–Fascists are counting on the British for their salvation. As for American influence, it is as high today among the rank and file of the people as it has ever been." Yet, he added, there was "no question that key men like Enver Hoxha and Sejfulla Maleshova [Minister of Popular Culture who studied in Moscow] are trying to sell Russia to the Albanian people. To succeed in this they must somehow minimize the American influence. Also, so long as the present government is not recognized by the Allies, it is expected to act unfriendly and look with suspicion and concern on the Anglo-American intentions. As an unrecognized government, it does not seem to feel secure, even though it is convinced that it has the backing of the great majority of the people. All members of the government are very much afraid of England and believe that the British may encourage the reactionaries and pro–Fascists and make common cause with them to bring about confusion and discontent among the people."[17]

Enver Hoxha, despite all of his outward obsequiousness toward the Soviets and the Yugoslavs, was deeply concerned about what the Allies would do about Albania. On the night of February 11, 1945, the day that the Big Three released the text of the agreements reached at Yalta, a worried Hoxha made a most unusual visit to the American legation. Although other members of the Albanian government like Nishani, Shehu, Çitaku, Baba Faja, Ndreau and others had dined at the legation, the unexpected visit by Hoxha, the prime minister and commander in chief, was his first. It broke precedent. He had always paid his respects to the British first. Yet he was so concerned about the fate of Albania that he went to see Stefan and the other Americans in an attempt to obtain information. He brought with him Omer Nishani, the foreign minister, who was friendly with the Americans and admired the country greatly.

Stefan, in his report to Bari on the meeting, said "The General [Hoxha] appeared nervous and lacking his usual self-composure. Over a period of ten months [I] have not seen him as he appeared this evening." Stefan said that during the meeting, which lasted for an hour and a half, "Nishani carried the conversation, with Enver saying very little." He said

8. Victory

On the reviewing stand in front of the Hotel Dajti. Captain Tom Stefan, with emblem on his cap, is fifth from the left. Koçi Xoxe, with stripes on his sleeve, is to Stefan's left. Hoxha, the taller man with the cap left of Xoxe, approaches the microphone (courtesy Nick Kukich).

the main topic of conversation was the meeting of the Big Three and "if we had received any information regarding it." Stefan reported that Hoxha was "obviously disturbed" why relief from the United States had not arrived, and why "all publicity being given [to] Tito for actions that his formations are carrying out" against the Germans in Yugoslavia. Hoxha was also disturbed over the fact that the United States had not recognized his government. "The visit was an unusual one, broke all precedents," Stefan reported. "Cannot recall the General in any activity paying his respects to us before he had done the same to the British. The call certainly was not made because of Hoxha's professed friendship for the U.S. On the basis of his general attitude toward the British it appears that this gesture can be interpreted as the first open step to play off the Americans against the British. Believe that there are enough other reasons to substantiate this contention."[18]

Whether Hoxha or Stefan knew it or not, Albania at Yalta was hardly thought about. While the Big Three carved Europe among them into spheres of influence, Albania was not even mentioned. Albania remained under the British sphere of interest even though the Partisans had set up their own government. To add insult to injury, Albania was not invited to attend the April organizational meeting of the United Nations in San Francisco. "What could be more insulting for the Albanian people," one Albanian official told Peters, "than to invite to the San Francisco Conference states like Liberia, Egypt and Turkey, all of which have not lost a man in this war, and to ignore completely Albania, which has lost thousands of men. The Allies know it [Albania] has done more than its share."

Other countries invited to the conference whose contributions to the defeat of Hitler were negligible included Haiti, Honduras, Costa Rica, El Salvador, Bolivia, Paraguay and Mexico. It became clear to many Albanians that the United States, following the lead of the United Kingdom, was determined to give Albania and its new government the cold shoulder. But the signs had been there all along. Washington and the State Department ignored numerous requests from Hoxha that he be allowed to send a representative to Washington to discuss military aid and relief.

When Peters met Hoxha on February 19, the Albanian leader complained bitterly about the lack of information from the Yalta Conference on the future of Albania. It had "upset" him and his government, Hoxha said. "Lack of recognition, or any information at all on the intentions of the Big Three for Albania and the present regime, is equally disconcerting to all members of the government, who feel they are unjustly treated and their country blockaded from the rest of the world," Peters reported.

Peters said that he served as the interpreter for reporter Peter Furst of the Rome Bureau of the *Stars and Stripes*, who interviewed Hoxha for an hour. Although Hoxha was friendly, he complained about the Allies,

Enver Hoxha. Autographed to Nick "Cooky" (courtesy Nick Kukich).

8. Victory 173

Captain Tom Stefan at the Hotel Dajti during a reception hosted by Enver Hoxha following the victory parade (courtesy Nick Kukich).

who had stopped supplying his two divisions that were still fighting in Yugoslavia. Peters reported that Hoxha said his men in Yugoslavia were fighting under "appalling conditions." "He read a cable he had just received which stated that the Sixth Albanian Division in cooperation with the Fifth Yugoslav Brigade, had captured Vishegrad, near Sarajevo, with large losses to the enemy as well as [to] the Albanian formations." The two Albanian divisions, Hoxha claimed, "are fighting with the weapons and other supplies captured from the enemy. They fight for a day or two, he explained, then they reorganize and take stock of the material they have captured and have on hand, lick their wounds, and plan their next engagement. He stated that because of lack of sufficient supplies, the Albanian formations in Yugoslavia have lost heavily in every engagement, but, he added, they are going to continue fighting the common enemy to the end." Hoxha insisted that his two main requests from the United States were "recognition and relief." Peters said that Hoxha repeated "again and again that we must have aid from America."[19]

Despite his requests for "recognition and relief" from the United

States, Hoxha repeatedly placed obstacles in the realization of either. Hoxha grew increasingly strident at the fact that his new government had not been officially recognized by the United States, and that Albania had not been invited to the organizational meeting of the United Nations in San Francisco. It was something of a *Catch-22* situation. Recognition of his new government by the United States depended on the recommendation of a group of civilian State Department officials whom Hoxha refused to allow into the country.

Hoxha also balked at signing an agreement with representatives of either the U.S. Military Liaison (ML) or the United Nations Relief and Rehabilitation Administration (UNRRA) to discuss the handling and distribution of humanitarian aid shipments to Albania. Ever suspicious, Hoxha insisted that all relief supplies be turned over to his government on the docks at the harbors of Durrës and Vlora. Hoxha would then see to the distribution of the supplies to needy Albanians by his government. Representatives of UNRRA insisted that they be in charge of the distribution of supplies to ensure that the aid did indeed go to people who needed help most and not to Hoxha's henchmen.

There was also the question whether the new Albanian government was capable of handling the shiploads of supplies of humanitarian aid waiting to be delivered, unloaded, stored and dispersed. "Taken as a group Albanian officialdom is full of words and empty of constructive acts," a February 1945 OSS report on relief said. "It is characteristic of officials and many others that they will assume cheerfully and with all self-assurance almost any responsibility whether or not they understand the complexities involved. They will assume readily such responsibility on paper or in nicely worded speeches without knowing in the least how they are going to carry through. They think in terms of magnificent sweeps of the imagination and refuse to be bothered with details. They have proven themselves many times over as lacking in talent for effective organization and in capacity for sustained hard work.

The report stated that Albanian officials were sure to tell the Allies that they could move ten thousand tons of monthly supplies from ship to shore and had sufficient warehouse space to store the supplies as well as enough trucks for distribution.

"They will say all of this with appearance of perfect self-confidence knowing that there is one lighter at Valona [Vlora] and none at Durazzo [Durrës], knowing that the season is in the middle of its rainiest, that probably there is insufficient warehousing, that they cannot place into operation as many as fifty serviceable trucks throughout the country, that bridges are down and rivers are swollen to a point where north and south road traffic has been out for three weeks. They will give such assurances and three, four or six weeks later will have perishable goods scattered in the mud and the rain from Durazzo to Elbasan to Berat to Delvina. Having brought things to such a pass they will bow politely and say, 'What can we do? It is the will of God that it rains.' From their point of view perhaps they are right for, after all, American supplies and the rains are supposed to fall with even-handed liberality alike on the just and the unjust."

In the same sarcastic vein, Kukich reported on the activity of some twenty blacksmiths who were "the only ones that can be seen doing any work here in Tirana." While many young people were organized into work groups they did not seem to be doing much work. "The Albanian youth can be seen playing and singing in the streets, carrying small pieces of lumber and others dragging shovels, brooms, etc. Some can be seen carrying placards saying PUNË, meaning work, but the locals look upon this as a big joke." The blacksmiths, who were mostly Italian, were different, Kukich reported. They took the metal from old Italian tanks and hammered the metal into farm tools—spades and hoes. Then they sold them.[20]

Increasingly hungry Albanians came to the American legation seeking humanitarian assistance, despite the risks involved. Stefan, in a message to Fultz, urged him to send supplies to Albania regardless of the political situation. "Not much is solved by sitting on stockpiles of food in Italy," he told Fultz. Stefan brought up the matter of UNRRA relief to Hoxha and asked the Albanian leader when he would help expedite the arrival of the much-needed aid. "The reply [from Hoxha] was in the next few days," he cabled Fultz. "Pointing out the need for immediate relief, I cited the number of people who consistently came to the legation looking for work and asking only food for pay. In an arrogant manner he denied the existence of the present state of affairs, holding out the progress made by his government in creating social relief agencies, emphasizing in particular community messes and soup kitchens. Comment: In regard to the latter, only the lower class of men and in some cases, gypsy children, take advantage of this service. Many families in dire need consider it beneath their dignity and pride to stand in a chow line."[21]

While Hoxha haggled over control of UNRRA aid with American and British officials, he also launched a vast investigation into alleged war criminals, headed by the much-feared Xoxe. Xoxe at this point was Hoxha's equal in party affairs and was known to be a man to watch. While Hoxha in party circles was viewed as an "intellectual," Xoxe was a seen as a crude representative of the "workers" of Albania, a man willing to get his hands dirty. Stefan radioed Fultz: "Have known this man for a long period and my impressions of him are not good ones."[22]

A Central Investigating Committee was set up in Tirana to deal with cases of alleged war criminal and political prisoners. Similar committees were also established in cities and towns throughout the country.

In a reign of terror, thousands of suspected Balli Kombëtar sympathizers and their families were arrested and jailed, including Hoxha's brother-in-law Bahri Omari, who had been a member of the Balli Kombëtar Central Committee. Omari was married to Hoxha's oldest sister Fahrije. Also arrested were Tefik Mboria, Qemal Vrioni and Kol Tromara, all from prominent Albanian families. Mboria, a friend of Italian Foreign Minister Galeazzo Ciano, Mussolini's son-in-law, had at one time sheltered Hoxha and Nishani in his home when they were on the run in 1943. Peters, who attended the Omari trial, said that several prominent Albanians attempted to intercede with the OSS in order to save Omari and Tromara, who was tried with him.

Both men were leaders in the Albanian-American organization "Vatra" in Boston both before and during World War One. Tromara, according to Hoxha, committed the additional "crime" of ridiculing Hoxha by referring to him as "Mr. Red" during pre-war political discussions. Both Omari and Tromara were found guilty of war crimes and were executed, along with scores of others. Mboria and Vrioni were also found guilty and sentenced to death. However, their sentences were reduced to thirty years and life in prison respectively.[23]

The ongoing trials, some of which were held in movie theaters, began each morning at 9 A.M. They were broadcast over loudspeakers, like sporting events. Signs were posted throughout Tirana that announced that "The hour for war criminals has come." People were also urged to report any war crimes their neighbors may have committed. The death penalty by the Communist-controlled investigation was handed out liberally. *Bashkimi*, the party newspaper, regularly printed like football scores the numbers and names of people who had been executed in Tirana, Korcë, Vlora, Erseke and elsewhere.

Members of the BK and German sympathizers hopelessly argued that they had the interest of Albania at heart when they worked with the Germans. They wanted to save their country from irreparable damage as a result of war. They said that they were victims of circumstances and that the real war criminals had escaped to Italy where they lived under Allied protection. Peters apparently agreed. He reported, "The great majority of those who committed crimes intentionally are now either in Allied camps in Italy or in Germany. Documents produced so far in court seem to point out that there are quite a few war criminals currently being harbored by the Allies in Italy."[24]

8. Victory

Hoxha repeatedly sought the return of these men so that they could stand trial in Tirana, but the Allies turned down all requests. Hoxha rightly suspected that these men were opponents of his regime who were in Italy under Allied protection conspiring to seek its ouster. They had either accompanied the Germans in their retreat from Albania, or had been whisked out of the country by the Allies as the Partisans sought to arrest them. In either case they ended up in camps in Italy. As far as Hoxha was concerned, the Allies were as bad as the Germans when it came to harboring his enemies.

In an April 1945 report to General Donovan, the OSS, under the heading "Albanian Anti-Hoxha Refugees in Italy," reported: "130 Albanian refugees were in a camp near Bari. They are opponents of the FNC government and were brought to Bari in Allied ships from Albania where they were hiding in the countryside. Midhat Bey Frashëri is the head of the group. He reported that the more important figures of this group have been released from the camp, and the Bari camp transferred to Lucca.

"Zogist Group in Italy: Zogist and Nationalist forces in Italy are said to be crystallizing around three non–Communist Albanian leaders: Mehmet Koniça in Rome; Midhat Bey Frashëri in Bari; and Ekrem Bey Delvina in Florence. They aim to form a party on democratic lines to participate in the Albanian Government along with the Communists, who at present control the government.

"Although many members are Zogists, the group is in substance agnostic in regard to the constitutional question. Many republicans and monarchists are in their ranks. As part of the work of the organization, conferences and contacts are taking place among the various Albanian groups scattered through Italy. This work of the organization is carried out in absolute secrecy. The promoters of the movement feared that if they let their plans be known, Communists would find a way to hinder their preparations and would persecute their relations in Albania.

"The leaders of the new Albanian party hope keenly for Allied support, so as to insure for Albania a democratic government with participation of Nationalists and Zogists. However, they do not know whether Anglo-Americans consider it opportune at this time for the party to come out in the open or whether it should continue behind the scenes for the time being."[25]

Stefan frequently traveled from Tirana to Bari and Rome and met with the Albanian dissident leaders. Not only did Stefan socialize with Balli Kombëtar sympathizers in Tirana—much to Hoxha's disgust—he also did so in Italy, which made Hoxha furious. These Albanians in Italy who had fled their country were Hoxha's enemies. He considered them to be collaborators, traitors and war criminals and he wanted them all sent back to Albania where they could stand trial and be shot. He bitterly railed against the Allies for providing them sanctuary.

Stefan moved with ease among the dissident Balli Kombëtar members in Italy just as he had done in Albania. He attended their parties in Rome just as he had attended their parties in Tirana. In Tirana Stefan was seen frequently at BK parties with Lulu Vrioni, an attractive and well-educated woman from a prominent family of Balli supporters. The Partisans had arrested several of Lulu Vrioni's relatives. Among them was Qemal Vrioni, her uncle, who had been given a prison sentence of life at hard labor. Stefan's relationship with the young woman did not go unnoticed in Tirana.

Hoxha, through intermediaries, complained to Fultz that Stefan had become overly aggressive toward Hoxha's government as he socialized with his friends in the Balli. Stefan was becoming too friendly with the Balli, just like Sgt. Vangel Kyrias had. Fultz, who once counseled Stefan to get as close to Hoxha as he could without compromising himself, now told Stefan to back off a bit.

Fultz, in a March 12, 1945 memo to Stefan, said "Kadri Hoxha [no relation] the other day dropped the comment that seemed to indicate that they regard you as too inquisitive about affairs which to their way of thinking is none of your business." Fultz said that Kadri Hoxha, who was head of the ANLA delegation in Bari, implied to him that "you were not being too subtle about such things and were perhaps creating some suspicions as to your good intentions."[26]

Stefan reported to his

Lillian (left) and Lulu Vrioni, Tirana 1945 (courtesy Nick Kukich).

superiors that the Albanian dissidents in Italy were ardent anti–Communists and were willing, with Allied help, to return to Albania and overthrow Hoxha and the Communists. In a June 27, 1945 report, Stefan wrote: "In conversations I had with some of these [leaders] in Rome on the evening of 25 June, it was disclosed that all of these former leaders, who once constituted the backbone of Albanian leadership, believe that it is Allied policy to fight the spread of Communism in the Balkans, since it would be very detrimental to the welfare of the British Empire, and for other reasons.

"They are under the impression that their group was the only one which acted in concert with Allied interests and in carrying out the fight against Communism in Albania. Although in some instances we were forced into collaboration with the Germans, they pointed out, the Western Allies clearly understood our difficulties and, we are certain, they added, that Great Britain, in particular, will not let us down, and that a means will be found for our return to the fatherland."[27]

Stefan's reports, en route to Washington, now went through OSS Cpl. Robert Mantho, who was acting head of the Albanian Desk in Bari. Mantho, 23, was an Albanian-American who was born in Alliance, Ohio. His parents had migrated from Korcë, as had the parents of Stefan. Mantho was a graduate of the University of Michigan and had worked as a newspaperman before the war. He was fluent in Albanian and was considered by his superiors to be very intelligent.

Mantho forwarded Stefan's reports about the Albanians in Italy to Earl Brennan, head of the Albanian Desk in Washington. When he did so he also added his own somewhat critical comments on Stefan's observations. It is not known what relationship, if any, the two men had with one another. But there are hints that it could have been an adversarial one. Stefan was a captain and a star. He was still the ranking American officer in Albania and chief of the OSS Mission in Tirana. He had been in the country longer than anyone, and he knew all of the principal players. Mantho was only a corporal and he was new. Even though he knew the Albanian language and was a college graduate, he was not an officer. He had not been to Albania, either. It would have been unnatural then had there not been some sort of envy on Mantho's part toward Stefan.

In his report to Brennan on Stefan's activities dated June 29, Mantho complimented Stefan for his "considerable value" to the State Department before he cast doubt on some of Stefan's observations.

Stefan basically reported that there were two groups seeking a *coup d'etat* in Albania, one made up of dissatisfied army officers, merchants and intellectuals, and the other composed of dissidents in Italy. Mantho said these were unsubstantiated "wild claims." He added: "I still feel that this information is highly tendentious in spite of the good captain's assurances to the contrary; however, I pass it on to you for you disposal in the back of your mind. If it turns out that this is a serious threat to the existing regime, we will be greatly surprised from where we sit, but we will also be sure to pass any results onto you soonest."[28]

The Albanians in Italy were right to operate in secret. Enver Hoxha had a long reach. He had spies everywhere and Italy was not that far away.

When Nick Kukich went to Rome in September 1945 he met his old friend Xhelil Çela. Çela told Kukich that he was afraid to return to Albania because the Partisans were looking for him. Although Çela had faithfully worked for the Americans and the British, as was well known, he had once been a member of the Balli Kombëtar when the BK fought the Italians. After the BK began to collaborate with the Germans, Çela broke with the organization and went to work for SOE Major Gerry Field at Seaview. Concerned about the Partisans back then, Çela got Field to write a letter to the Shtab explaining his new role. Fultz hired Çela to work for the OSS, and wrote a glowing letter of recommendation. After the Partisans took Tirana, Çela wrote a letter to Fultz pleading with Fultz to vouch for him with Hoxha and the new Albanian government so that he could return without fear to his farm in Dukat.

Çela told Fultz all he had done for the OSS and the SOE—he opened his home to them, provided agents with food, housed the American nurses upon their rescue, and gathered intelligence. He told Fultz that he had refused payment in the past because he worked not for money, or for political parties, but for what was good for his country. "Please if possible make this clear over to the Albanian Government. I judge you [sic] for this because you are the only one that knows what was my position ... only you and your officers know this," Çela wrote.

Fultz did not buy it. He believed that Çela found the life in Rome to his liking and simply did not want to return to Albania. Fultz, in a message to his counterpart Major Eliot Watrous, said, "I have the feeling that Çela's reluctance to return home at this time probably grows as much out of his disinclination to get back and settle down to the rigorous conditions of Albanian living as it does out of fear. While his thinking may have a small admixture of fear I think it has more of a desire to prolong his stay in the more comfortable surroundings of Italy as long as possible." He said the OSS would not provide Çela with any more funds and he advised Watrous to follow suit. Watrous agreed.[29]

Kukich found Çela living in the streets of Rome. "He had no home. I took him to my hotel, the Grand Hotel, and invited him to stay with me, but he said it would only get me killed. He said he could not go home. The Communists were looking to kill him because he had not only been with the Balli, but he had helped us. 'America let me down, nobody wants to talk with me,' he said. 'I have no home because of what I did for the Americans. Now nobody wants to do anything for me.' I felt sorry for him. I gave him three gold pieces. He left. Three days later they found him floating in the Tiber River. He had been killed. That was Hoxha's doing. He got rid of everybody he could who had fought against him or who worked for us."[30]

Despite Hoxha's mistrust, obstructionism and paranoia, some humanitarian assistance did reach the country. The UNRRA program, before it was shut down, provided some $27 million in aid, one fourth of which went for food, while the rest was spent on agriculture, and the drainage of the swamps around Lake Maliq.[31]

Sergeant Peters saw first-hand the success and popularity of UNRRA relief during two tours of the country, one in the north and the other in the south, which he took in May and June 1945. "A good deal of favorable comment was heard all along the north on Allied relief," Peters reported. "Practically all civilians encountered had been informed of the supplies coming in from the Western allies and were profusely grateful to the Anglo-Americans." In the south, where the destruction and destitution were greatest, Peters found that the needs of the people were overwhelming. The supplies of food from UNRRA "have enhanced tremendously American influence in the whole area. Whenever trucks of flour passed by, cheers for American were spontaneously uttered. It is evident that, small though the amount of supplies has been so far, people feel themselves closer to American than ever.[32]

Meanwhile, in Tirana Hoxha and his Communist government confiscated the land of some one hundred of Albania's biggest landowners, mainly in the south and in central Albania, the only areas where there was fertile land. Private property was abolished and church buildings and land taken. A retroactive war profits tax was established and businessmen who could not pay it were jailed. Arrests, trials and executions continued. Hard labor internment camps were set up and whole families were sent to them for punishment. The government initiated a draft for everyone from the ages of seventeen to thirty-five. The allies in Tirana increasingly found their movements restricted. They were followed everywhere.

Stefan, Kukich and O'Keefe continued to file intelligence reports with Fultz. Their duties, whether military or social, still brought them into contact with the military leaders of the country, as well as the ever-diminishing number of people who had made up the social elite of Tirana. Kukich, who remained in contact with Shehu as well as with Hoxha, reported on a gunfight between Shehu's bodyguard and chauffeur. At first it was thought to have been an attempt on Shehu's life, but it turned out to be an argument over a rifle, which the bodyguard won.[33]

Kukich several times went hunting boar in and around Dajti Mountain with several Albanian friends. At one meeting with Shehu, also a hunter, the general showed Kukich an English-made Holland and Holland 12-bore Royal 30 shotgun with an elaborately engraved stock. Shehu told him that Stalin had given him the gun when he was in Moscow in 1945 visiting the Voroshilov Military Academy. Shehu told Kukich that the shotgun had originally been given by Hitler to Romanian Gen. Ion Antonescu when Romania joined the Axis and sent troops to help in the German invasion of the Soviet Union. The Soviets took the shotgun when they invaded Romania and captured Antonescu. Romania surrendered on August 24, 1944, and Antonescu was executed. The Soviets sent the shotgun to Stalin. Now it was in Shehu's hands. Shehu said he got along very well with Stalin. There were some who believed that the Soviet leader would not have been upset if Shehu had taken over the Albanian government, according to Kukich.

"I think the Russians trusted Shehu more than they trusted Hoxha," Kukich said. "Stalin liked him. I think they wanted Mehmet to take over the country. That's why they invited him to Moscow."

While some members of Hoxha's staff distrusted the Soviets—and wanted Albania to throw their lot in with the West—Hoxha continually played up to the Russians. According to Kukich, Hoxha referred to Stalin as his "big brother," as in "Big brother will take care of this" or "Big brother will take care of that." When the Soviets sent Albania a shipload of corn that had rotted en route, Kukich said he went to see Hoxha. "I told Hoxha about it. I said, 'See what your big brother did for you. He sent you corn that even the swine won't eat.' He got mad. He told me to shut up. He didn't want to hear any more about it. Even though he was mad, I could still talk to him."[34]

In July, Stefan reported that some 16,000 Italian soldiers had been evacuated back to Italy during the previous five weeks and that the remains of nine American flyers in their wrecked plane had been located on a mountaintop in Dibra, just over the Albanian border in Kosovo. The bomber had crashed returning to Italy from a bombing run over Yugoslavia.[35]

The days of the OSS operations in the Balkans were coming to an end. The soldiers would be replaced by diplomats. The OSS closed its Albanian Unit in Bari in March 1945. Fultz transferred from the OSS to

8. Victory

the State Department. He joined veteran diplomat Joseph E. Jacobs, who headed a civilian mission to Albania. Their job was to recommend whether the United States should grant recognition to the new Albanian government. The contingent from the State Department arrived in Tirana on May 8, 1945—VE Day.

For Fultz the return to Albania after an absence of twelve years should have been something of a homecoming. But it turned out to be anything but that.

Stefan, Kukich, O'Keefe and the rest of the OSS Tirana Unit stayed on until September, when they packed up to leave the country.

Despite his desire for official recognition by the United States, and for inclusion in the United Nations, Hoxha continued to obstruct Allied aid projects and reject Western assistance. He increasingly allied his country with Stalin and the Soviet Union. In the Cold War that had already begun, Hoxha joined the side of the Soviets.

Jacobs and Fultz remained in Albania until October 10, 1946, when a junior official replaced them. Any chance of official recognition of Albania by the United States and Great Britain came to an end following the Corfu Channel incident, on October 22, 1946, when two British warships hit Albanian mines, killing forty-three British sailors and severely damaging the ships. Albania refused to accept responsibility, and all relations came to an end. All the Americans and the British left Albania for good.

Albania plunged into a brutal police state nightmare that would last for forty-five years.

9

Home

Nick Kukich sat in the sun at the outdoor café near the Hotel Dajti and watched the people walk by. It was a warm September day. He had begun to pack his things for the long-awaited trip home. They were leaving in a few days. The war for him was over. The OSS Tirana Unit was about to disband, replaced by civilians who had already moved into the crowded legation building.

He sipped Italian wine and waited for his friend Tom Stefan, who was to meet him at the café that they had gotten to know so well since they had arrived in Tirana almost a year earlier.

Earlier in the day Kukich had visited Hoxha at his office in order to pay his respects. Kukich brought with him a half-pound bag of beans he had bought in the market. Hoxha had recently ordered the installation of hundreds of sharpened wooden stakes around the Tirana Airport. He had his soldiers plant the stakes in the ground like beanpoles. The idea was to thwart any landings by British paratroops that Hoxha thought might invade his country. The Cold War had begun and Hoxha had chosen the other side.

"I poured the beans out on Hoxha's desk and told him that we should plant the beans out at the airfield and split the profits when they grew up the poles. We could be partners, fifty-one per cent for me and forty-nine per cent for him. He laughed. He liked a good joke. 'Niko, Niko, what am I going to do without you?' he said. He told me I should take the beans with me and plant them in America because I was the capitalist, not him."[1]

Stefan arrived with two women, one on each arm. They were the Vrioni sisters, Lulu and Lillian. Both were attractive and prettily dressed. Stefan had been seeing a lot of Lulu, the prettier of the two. Kukich had met Lulu with Stefan at parties. She spoke English well and she was quite intelligent. Their family was part of the Tirana elite that Hoxha hated. These were the landowners, intellectuals and merchants whose property he confiscated. They were Balli members or supporters who were earmarked for investigation, arrest, interrogation, trial, imprisonment and execution. Some were whisked off the streets, never to be heard from again. Others were tortured, killed and buried in unmarked graves. The lucky ones escaped to Italy. The rest were stuck in Tirana. Very few people picked up were ever let go. Lillian's husband, a member of the Balli, had just been arrested and was in prison awaiting trial. She did not know what prison he was in. Their uncle Qemal Vrioni had barely escaped execution. Tried by Hoxha's special court as a war criminal, Qemal was found guilty and sentenced to death. However, his sentence reduced to life in prison at hard labor. All seventeen of his co-defendants were found guilty and executed that same day, April 15, including Kol Tromara and Bahri Omari, Hoxha's brother-in-law. The Vrioni family, like many others in Tirana, had been prosperous and well-respected. Hoxha had confiscated their holdings, but he could not confiscate their name. Lulu would get out. She was one of the lucky ones. Lillian was not so lucky. She remained behind.

Stefan told Kukich that he had just quietly married Lulu. It had been a civil ceremony, just the two of them with Lillian as a witness. Kukich was surprised, not only because of the marriage, but also because it had been a secret civil ceremony. Albanians were famous for their elaborate weddings which lasted for days. Weddings were extremely important family events, even under the Communists. The new Hoxha government might have attacked the churches and mosques, but it left weddings alone.

Kukich kissed Lulu and ordered a bottle of champagne. He had doubts about the wedding. Lulu was happy but nervous. Lillian was just nervous. He took nine pieces of the British gold he had with him in his money belt and gave it to them as a wedding present. Stefan gave the gold to Lulu. Stefan talked about plans to get Lulu out of Albania. There was no question of Lillian leaving; she was determined to stay behind and help her husband, if she could find out where he was being held. There was little time for Stefan to work out the legal arrangements to get Lulu out since the Americans had to leave for Rome in several days. Perhaps Hoxha, if he found out about the marriage, would not let Lulu leave at all. They first thought to smuggle Lulu out with a group of Jewish refugees that they were helping get to Rome, but Stefan vetoed the idea. "I'll get her out myself," Stefan said.

He had to get her out. Crossing the borders was out of the question. Hoxha had sealed off the country. People caught crossing the borders were shot out of hand and their families sent to concentration camps. But Lulu was married to an American officer, although Stefan at this point was somewhat estranged from Hoxha. Lulu and her family were considered to be Balli Kombëtar, the enemy, and Stefan had married into it. That could only hurt her chances of getting out. Stefan knew that the Balli smuggled people in and out of Albania by sea through its still functioning network. He of course had friends in the Balli. But that was too dangerous, and perhaps unnecessary.

"I don't know if Tom married her for love or to get her out of the country, or both," Kukich said. "Tom did not even say goodbye to Hoxha. They were not getting along. Tom started drinking heavily in Tirana and he was going to all kinds of parties with the Balli. The Balli were he only ones who could afford to throw the parties. The Partisans didn't have any money. Hoxha disliked those parties. I told Tom and O'Keefe that we'd better stay away from these parties. O'Keefe and I did, but Tom continued to go to them and then he met Lulu. And Lulu, of course, was on the other side. I don't know that when Hoxha found out about him marrying Lulu, he got very angry. Hoxha did not like it at all."

Kukich added: "Tom was on the outs when he left Tirana. He talked about becoming ambassador to Albania, or a diplomat, or getting a job with the State Department or something like that. One thing he did mention was that if he didn't get a job with the State Department he was going to travel the world and visit each member of the OSS. I think he did a pretty good job of that."[2]

The plan Stefan put together to get Lulu out of Albania was the simplest. He would take her with him. On the last day of duty in Tirana, Stefan packed his gear in a jeep and drove to Lulu's home and picked her up. Then, along with Kukich, O'Keefe and several other members of the OSS Tirana Unit in another jeep, they drove to the airport. Although Hoxha had tightened security in and around Tirana, the daily military flight of the Dakota C-47 from Rome to Tirana had become so routine that airport guards simply waved the Americans on and off the plane. Often the Americans handed them a bottle of Scotch, or cigarettes. Stefan was so familiar to them that they paid little notice when he boarded the plane with the others, including Lulu. Three hours later Tom and Lulu Stefan were cracking open a bottle of champagne in the Hotel Excelsior in Rome.

Jacobs and Fultz arrived in Tirana on May 8, 1945, to meet with Hoxha, now head of the People's Republic of Albania. Whether the U.S. government would extend diplomatic relations to Albania replied upon the Albanians meeting there two conditions. The first was that Albania hold free and open elections. The second condition was that Albania recognize the validity of treaties concluded between the U.S. and Albania prior to April 1939. The condition of free elections was one of the principles articulated by the Big Three at Yalta. The treaty condition was a principle of the United States that dated back to the end of the eighteenth century. Albania held one party elections on December 2, 1945, which Hoxha and the Communists, naturally, won. The recognition of treaties prior to 1939 was rejected by the Partisans when they met at the Conference of Përmët in June 1944. Those treaties had been signed under King Zog. The Partisans abrogated both the king and his treaties.

There is a telling photograph of Fultz taken outside of the Fultz School sometime in 1945. He stands surrounded by some forty of his former students, some dressed in Partisan uniform, outside the school building in something of a class reunion pose. It is obvious from the picture that the students, all of whom came from peasant backgrounds and mountain villages, looked up to Fultz. He was, after all, the man who had given them an education and trained them to better themselves and their country. The extraordinary thing about the school was that many of its graduates had fought for the Partisans, the Balli Kombëtar and the OSS.

It was not long after the picture was taken that Fultz was to observe first-hand his former students killing one another in Tirana. In a letter to a colleague in July 1946, Fultz noted that Major Frederick Nosi, head of a military court in Tirana, and a Fultz school graduate, presided over the trial of thirty-seven men charged with being "enemies of the people." Nine of the men were sentenced to be executed and the rest sent to prison. "Among the nine men who were taken out on the hill the other morning and shot were Shaban Balli and Ali Jonuzi, both of whom you will recall as students at the school."[3]

Jacobs and Fultz nevertheless persisted in their attempt to coordinate and distribute aid from UNRRA, which was financed mostly by the United States. Thousands of Albanians depended on UNRRA food for survival. However, the two Americans found that they increasingly had to deal with obstructionist bureaucrats who were influenced by the increasing number of specialists Hoxha brought in from the Soviet Union. Hoxha continued to create difficulties. He adamantly insisted that all UNRRA food and supplies be dropped off at docks and that no foreigners be allowed to distribute aid to the Albanian people.

The British withdrew their military mission from Albania in April 1946 and did not replace it with a civilian one, as the Americans had. The British blamed the Albanians for the deaths of their sailors in the Corfu Channel incident of October 22, 1946. Hoxha refused to take responsibility for the incident. The British broke off all relations with Albania and promised to keep Albania's pre-war gold it had captured from the Germans.

The United States a week later announced it would follow the British lead and not recognize Albania. The Americans shut down their Tirana diplomatic operation and recalled Jacobs and Fultz. Five days before the departure of Jacobs and Fultz, another two graduates of the American Vocation School went on public trial. Abdyl Sharra and Beqir Kujtimi were accused of conspiring with Fultz and another American to sabotage a draining project at Lake Maliq, a project that had been undertaken by UNRRA. The two men along with several others were found guilty and executed.

Fultz believed that Hoxha had the two men killed for several reasons. Both came from prominent families in Vlora and therefore were "class enemies"; both had brothers who had escaped to Italy, one of whom had taught at the school; the government needed a scapegoat after it botched the Lake Maliq project; and that the trial could be used to discredit Julty, the school and the United States.

Writing from Rome to a colleague, Fultz said, "If you recall the atmosphere back in 1933, fourteen years ago, you will have a fair idea of what prevails now, except you must remember that men can pick up a lot of devilishness in 14 years. Methods and tactics have been intensified, improved and stepped up any degrees. Those in power exhibit a stubborn ignorance devoid of any sense of decency, of human kindness or of tolerance. They neither want Americans nor anything that Americans stand for. Of this one fact, there can be no doubt whatever."[4]

Hoxha suspected all those who had attended the Fultz school of being American spies, except for rare exceptions like Mehmet Shehu. (Hoxha would accuse Shehu of being a career American spy thirty-five years later). Hoxha rounded up all Albanians who had attended the school and had them jailed or executed. This included graduates like Kadri Hoxha, the ANLA officer in Bari who had complained about Stefan. He arrested all Albanians who had associated with the Americans, like one of O'Keefe's woman friends. Even Albanians who spoke English were suspected of spying for the Americans.

Fultz and Jacobs left Tirana in October 1946. It was the second time that Fultz had been forced to leave Albania, the country he loved and wanted to help.

Stefan and Lulu sailed from Rome to New York in May 1946. Stefan had with him a copy of a letter of commendation that Fultz had sent to Gen. Donovan. He also had been awarded the Legion of Merit and the Bronze Star. Stefan brought his bride Lulu home to Laconia, New Hampshire, where his mother still lived. He gave his address as the Ambassador Hotel in Laconia. He and Lulu then drove to Washington where he was discharged the following week.[5]

9. Home

If Stefan thought he could parlay his Albanian expertise and network of contacts in the country into a job with the State Department, he was disappointed. There is no record that he met with Brennan, head of the OSS Albanian Desk, in Washington, or with anybody else at the State Department. Brennan had never answered him when Stefan wrote from Albania and asked for a meeting during the war, nor did he reply to similar requests from Hoxha. So there was no reason for Brennan to meet with Stefan now that the war was over. Brennan was probably out of a job as well.

Like hundreds of thousands of other returning American war veterans, Stefan found that there no longer was any need for him or his experience. The war was over. The size of the military was drastically reduced. Men were discharged at a dizzying rate. One day you were a decorated and respected military officer who had helped Gen. Enver Hoxha take over a country, and the next day you were being shown the door by your government.

Nobody was interested in Albania anymore. Hoxha turned his back on the west and the United States. He railed against the west at the Paris Peace Conference. He shut his country down, isolated it, and turned it into a Soviet-styled police state.

Stefan communicated with Suffolk Law School to obtain the law degree he had worked toward before the war. Although he did not attend classes in Boston, he apparently did enough law school work by mail to get a degree. He did not take the Massachusetts bar examination, however. Nor did he practice law.

Stefan landed a job with the Veterans Administration in Washington where he handled disability claims. Kukich and his new wife Rose visited Stefan and Lulu in 1949. "They were living out of a suitcase in a rooming house near Dupont Circle, eating out all the time," Kukich said. "He was working for the VA. He wanted to fix me up with a disability pension because of the injury I had to my hand. I told him to forget it. We could see that Lulu was very unhappy. We went to a restaurant. Rose said Lulu was crying when they went to the ladies' room. 'This is no life for me,' she told Rose. She was very unhappy. Tom was drinking. He kept talking about going back to Albania. He couldn't let go. I knew there was no way he could go back to Albania. He was dreaming.

"He wasn't happy to be where he was," Kukich said. "He had been on top of the world in Albania. Hell, we *all* had been on top of the world. But it was over. Now we were at the bottom and we had to start over. It was rough. I felt the same way. It was hard to adjust. I went back to the coal mines after the war and worked there for four months until I could land a decent job."

Kukich believed that Stefan could have played an important role dealing with postwar Albanian issues. But Albania was yesterday's news. Nobody cared. In addition, Stefan had burned his bridges with Hoxha when he became friendly in Italy with the leaders of Balli Kombëtar, who wanted the United States to help them overthrow Hoxha. The final break with Hoxha probably came when Stefan married Lulu Vrioni.

They talked about their old friend Sterling Hayden, who was in the news as a result of his divorce from Madeleine Carroll and the new Hollywood movie *El Paso* Hayden had just made. They would talk about Hayden again in 1951 when Stefan visited Kukich in Indiana, where Kukich had gotten a job. Hayden was again in the news as a result of his brief 1946 membership in the Communist Party. Hayden testified before the House Un-American Activities Committee in 1951 that he was first recruited for membership in Boston in 1940. He said he joined the party in Hollywood after the war but quit after six months in revulsion against the party's totalitarian ways. Joining the party, he said, had been a mistake.

Hayden, described in newspaper stories as "a Marine hero," earned the committee's friendship and respect when he named members of his Hollywood cell and talked about his wartime OSS exploits. Hayden told the committee how he had run guns, agents and supplies from Bari across the Adriatic Sea to the coast of Yugoslavia. He said it was there that he developed respect for the Communist Partisans and their resistance to the Nazis.[6]

Kukich was disturbed by the 1951 meeting with Stefan. Stefan came off the train wearing his frayed army uniform even though he had been discharged years ago. "He was unshaven and his uniform was dirty. He was drinking. He was living in his uniform. I believe the feds were looking for him for impersonating an officer. Lulu threw him out. It was sad. He was lost. He had been such a good dresser. We had dinner. He wanted to borrow a hundred dollars. I didn't have a hundred dollars. The banks were closed. I gave him twenty-five dollars and took him to the train. It was all I had. I also gave him bottle of liquor. I shouldn't have, but I did. It was the last time I saw him."[7]

Ironically, the day after Stefan left, Kukich received a letter from Gus Routsis warning him that Stefan had passed bad checks.

Gus Routsis along with his brother George returned home after the war and worked in their father's restaurant in Middleton, Connecticut. The brothers, both of whom had been Stefan's radio operators in Helmës, Odriçan, Berat and Tirana, were surprised to find Stefan still in his army uniform.

"It was sad," Gus Routsis said. "Here he was separated from the army and he was impersonating an officer. He pretended that he was working as a purchasing agent for the government. We took him in. We were happy to see him. Then he ran short of cash. We cashed a check for him and it bounced. I tried to call others who knew him just to warn them. In most cases it was too late. He never got over being in the OSS. He was the highest ranking officer we had over there at the time. He mingled with the higher ups in the regime, and then it came to an end."[8]

Lulu Vrioni, who quickly became disappointed with Stefan, separated from him and then filed for divorce. They had no children. Stefan disappeared. He wandered from one OSS friend to another. He visited John O'Keefe in Lonoke, Arkansas, where O'Keefe worked for the U.S. Post Office. His OSS friends said that he drifted down to Texas and then to Mexico where they heard he had been killed in a Mexican prison. They shook their heads. Soon they forgot about Stefan.

British SOE participants in the Albanian war who wrote books about their experiences—men like Smiley, Amery and Kemp—made no mention of Stefan. British writer Jon Halliday, in his book on Hoxha and the war, demeaned Stefan. In a footnote in his book, Halliday, apparently influenced by Hoxha's vituperative comments, wrote: "The first OSS mission did not arrive [at Hoxha's headquarters] until May 1944. It was headed by a very ineffectual figure, Tom Stefan, whom Hoxha treats with some disdain."[9]

Hoxha, in his memoirs written decades later, was dismissive of Stefan. Hoxha said Stefan was a spy sent to harm the Albanian people. He also treated Stefan with disdain, but Hoxha treated practically all of his one-time friends and associates with disdain. Sometimes he had them executed as well.

Hoxha described his dealings with the "degenerate" Stefan this way: "About the end of April or the beginning of May 1944, I don't remember clearly, Thomas Stefani [sic], with two others, presented himself to our staff at Helmës. He was about 30 years of age, a short, thick-set man. Sometimes he spoke English, sometimes Albanian. But he spoke neither of them well and with an accent as though he had a mouthful of porridge. He had plenty to say but not with much sense.

"'I've been sent to the Albanian partisans by Air Force Headquarters as liaison officer,' this American lieutenant told us at the first meeting we had with him.

"'When were you sent?' we asked him.

"'It's wartime, gentlemen,' he said. 'We set out some time ago, but we were obliged to spend several months, first at Karaburun of Dukat and later as guests of Mr. [Skënder] Muço. But he....'"

"'We knew he [Muço] was bound to come to a bad end,' we told him.

Several times we appealed to him to join the National Liberation Movement but he didn't want to and he was shot like a stray dog."*

"'We three are of Albanian origin,' Thomas Stefani hastened to say, to get off the subject of Skënder Muço, 'we are from Korça.'"

"'That is good to hear. As Albanians we shall get on well,' I said."

"'First, I am an American, then an Albanian, gentlemen. Such is my duty.'"

"'But what is your duty?'" I asked.

"'As Liaison officer, I shall ensure communications between you and my headquarters and will report from time to time as the need arises. I have special instructions from General Stawell to gather intelligence information on the enemy, especially number-plates and other information which will help support the actions of your military forces against the occupier.'"

"This was the 'duty' of this degenerate Albanian, who so foolishly boasted to us that he was 'first an American.' However, we knew that he had been sent to throw dust in the eyes of the Albanian families of economic emigrants in America in order to say to them: 'You see, we too have come to help the Albanian people.' He had come to prepare the ground and the premises for the notorious Mr. [Harry] Fultz, who was to organize plots and blackmail against our people's state power from the first months of the liberation of Albania."[10]

Reginald Hibbert, who also served with the SOE and wrote about it, was the only British writer to say anything positive about Stefan. Hibbert, who met Stefan in southern Albania in the spring of 1944, commented on Stefan's understanding of Albania. "We also met Captain Tom Stefan, the U.S. liaison officer with the Partisans. He was of Albanian origin and appeared to have a thorough grasp of the situation in Albania. Unlike the British officers in Albania who were conditioned to disavow an interest in politics and professed to be focused exclusively on fighting Germans, Stefan spoke freely of being briefed by the State Department through the Office of Strategic Services. This openness did not seem to cause him any difficulties."[11]

Unlike their British counterparts, the Americans of the OSS in Albania were not literary men. They did not write books or articles about their

---

*Skënder Muço, a young, aggressive and well respected lawyer from Vlora, was a prominent organizer of resistance groups opposing the Italian Fascists. He became an anti–Communist leader in the Balli Kombëtar but attempted to get them to fight the Germans rather than collaborate. He and ten others were arrested by the Germans. Muço and two others were separated from the group, placed in a car headed for Tirana. The three men were later found along the highway shot to death with their hands tied behind their backs. Enver Hoxha was suspected to be behind the killings.

war experiences in Albania. The Americans had no Julian Amery, David Smiley, Reginald Hibbert or Anthony Quayle. They did have Sterling Hayden, who touched on his war exploits in *Wanderer*, his autobiography. But Hayden spent most of his time in Yugoslavia, not Albania, and he did not meet any leaders of the Albanian resistance. The American OSS story in Albania was never told. Albania remained a British story told by British writers. In 1995 James Hudson self-published his memories of Albania in *Beyond the OSS*.

I came across the Albanian OSS story quite by accident. As happens in life, I went looking for one thing and found another. I sought to do a book about Enver Hoxha from the point of view of the Partisan soldiers who fought for him in 1943 and 1944. I wanted to find out what kind of a man he was back then. What did his men think of him? Toward that end, with my Albanian companion Agim Prodani at my side, we interviewed a half dozen of so of these old Partisans in Tirana in 2002. I met them in their smoky veterans' club in Tirana, or in restaurants and cafes, or in their homes.

As I interviewed these ancient warriors I discovered that although they had indeed fought that good fight against Fascists and the Nazis with Enver Hoxha—and liberated their country—and although they were proud of their achievements, they had difficulty in remembering Hoxha the man. There were very young at the time, boys, really, around fourteen, or fifteen, or sixteen years old. Hoxha, the commander, was thirty-five years old back then. He was a distant, almost mythological figure to these young boys. They knew about him but they did not know him. They never talked to him and he never talked to them. They rarely even saw him. He was the hero-general of Albania, the savior of his time, a man far above their lowly station in life. They worshiped him but they did not know him.

I came across a picture of Hoxha and his men marching in their victory parade in Tirana on November 28, 1944. It was in Hibbert's book. There in the third row was a man identified as Captain Tom Stefan, a U.S. Liaison Officer.

Outside of Captain Lloyd Smith, who had helped in the rescue of the American nurses, I had not known that the OSS had been in Albania. Who was this Captain Thomas Stefan? And what was the OSS doing in Albania? The Albanians did not know. Most Americans did not know. The British did not care. Hoxha had written the history of the period but not in a truthful way. He had written the story the way he wanted the story to come out. The British were part of the story, but the way Hoxha told it the British were always treacherous. Americans were not even worth mentioning. When Hoxha did refer to Fultz or Stefan, he ridiculed them and called them spies and lackeys of the British.

Tom Stefan's gravesite (author photograph).

I decided the book on Hoxha could wait. I began to research Stefan's life and the OSS effort in Albania. This book is the result of that effort.

Then toward the end of my search for Tom Stefan he disappeared. After losing his wife and his job, and after scamming money from his OSS friends, he drifted away. Nobody around Boston remembered him. There were no signs of him in New Hampshire. Nick Kukich, Gus Routsis, Jim Hudson and Semeon Simollari all thought that he had died in Mexico, killed in a Mexican prison some time in the fifties. That did not turn out to be true.

Stefan ended up in California, perhaps in search of movie star Sterling Hayden, his old OSS drinking companion. Perhaps he found him. Perhaps Hayden, who commanded a lot of money when he chose to make a movie, had given Stefan some financial help. Perhaps they hit the bars of Sausalito and relived the old drinking days of Bari. If so there is no record of it. There is no record that Stefan ever tracked down Hayden as he had tracked down other old OSS friends.

Tom Stefan died on the streets of Los Angeles on September 6, 1959. He was alone. He had no known address. He was homeless. He was 42 years old. Six months earlier Hayden had left Hollywood for Tahiti aboard his schooner *Wanderer*, a fugitive from justice. He had taken his four

9. Home

children with him, despite a court order prohibiting it. Stefan, also a fugitive, and Hayden had other things in common, like Boston, for instance. They both were alcoholics. Both former OSS officers were drinkers, dreamers and drifters. Unfortunately, only one of them could afford to do all three.

The *Laconia (N.H.) Evening Citizen* ran Stefan's obituary a week after he died. The obituary, complete with a picture of a smiling Stefan in his Army uniform, referred to him as Major Thomas Stefan. If Stefan was a major, he had promoted himself.

"He collapsed on the street and was pronounced dead on arrival at a Los Angeles hospital," the obituary said. He was alone and he had no home address. When I checked with Los Angeles police officials about the cause of his death, the police said that records of such deaths where no foul play was involved were destroyed after ten years.

The *Laconia Evening Citizen* listed his three sisters as Stefan's survivors, but made no mention of Lulu Vrioni.

Tom Stefan was buried September 14, 1959, in Union Cemetery in Laconia. The cemetery is located just off the center of town behind the courthouse, not far from where Stefan once lived. Taps were sounded by a bugler from the local Salvation Army Corps. His sisters attended the burial, as did a few friends from New Hampshire and Massachusetts. Lulu Vrioni did not attend. Nor did any of Stefan's comrades from the OSS. They did not know he had died.

Epilogue

Nick Kukich, after the war, returned to the coal mines before he landed a job with DuPont. He retired from DuPont in 1978. He lives with his wife Rose and extended family in Delaware. He turned 91 in January 2007.

Kostas "Gus" Routsis, 83, lives in retirement in Naples, Florida, and keeps in touch with Nick.

James Hudson worked as a consultant for Value Engineering of Maryland. He also keeps busy writing. He is active on the OSS website. He recently published *Beyond the OSS*, a memoir of his war years. He lives in Maryland.

John O'Keefe returned to Lonoke, Arkansas, where he worked in the U.S. Post Office, becoming deputy postmaster before retiring. He never married. Nor did he ever talk about his OSS service in Albania. He died in 1989 at the age of 72.

Anthony Quayle died in London on October 20, 1989, following a distinguished acting career. He largely played himself—a British Army officer behind enemy lines in World War II Greece—in the movie *The Guns of Navarone* in 1961. He was knighted by Queen Elizabeth.

Sterling Hayden, who appeared in a string of memorable movies, died in May 1986 in Sausalito, California. He was 70. One of his last movie appearances was in *The Godfather*. Hayden and Quayle never worked together in the movies, nor is there any record that they met after the war.

Angelo Metro went to the Massachusetts Institute of Technology after the war and graduated with a degree in electrical engineering. He operated Metro Marine Company in Chelsea, Massachusetts. He died in 1975.

Stephen Peters worked for the State Department following the war. He died in 1989.

Epilogue 197

Enver Hoxha died of natural causes in April 1985 at age 77. He ruled the Albanian Communist police state he created for 41 years. Communism officially fell seven years after his death.

Nexhmije Hoxha, Hoxha's wife, was briefly jailed after Communism fell. She lives in Tirana and can be counted on to come to the defense of her husband.

Lulu Vrioni worked for the Voice of America in Washington, D.C., for many years before her retirement. She died in a Washington nursing home in 1995.

Mehmet Shehu "committed suicide" on December 18, 1981, following a break with Hoxha. Hoxha accused Shehu of being both an American and British agent. Many believe Hoxha had Shehu killed. Shehu was 68 years old.

Koçi Xoxe, Minister of the Interior, and a Hoxha rival, who was responsible for the execution of thousands of Albanians, was himself executed by Hoxha in 1948.

Myslim Peza, the veteran Partisan leader, was one the few associates of Enver Hoxha to live a long life and die in his bed. Peza died in 1984 at the age of 87.

King Amhed Zog died in France in 1961. He was 65 years old.

Harry T. Fultz died December 30, 1980. He was 92. He served as secretary to the Pan American Board of Education in Chicago from 1948 to 1962, when he retired. He returned to Indiana to farm. He is buried in Salem, Indiana, the town where he was born.

In 1992 the first post–Communist government of Albania secretly exhumed the body of Enver Hoxha from its honored marble gravesite at the Martyrs of the Nation Cemetery just outside Tirana. This action came after rioting Albanians tore down three statues of Enver Hoxha the Communists had erected in Tirana, Korcë and Gjirokaster. Hoxha's remains were turned over to his family and he was reburied in a common plot of land. Communism in Albania was buried along with him.

The American Vocational School—the Fultz School—was reestablished in 1993 and continues to educate and train Albanians, just as Harry Fultz would have wanted.

Chapter Notes

Chapter 1

1. National Archives: Record Group 226, Entry 154, Box 16, Folder 232. (Hereafter NA: RG.)
2. Nick Kukich interview.
3. Kukich interview.
4. Max Corvo, *The OSS in Italy 1942–1945: A Personal Memoir* (New York: Praeger, 1990), p. 17.
5. *Ibid.*, p. 18.
6. Kukich interview.
7. Reginald Hibbert, *Albania's National Liberation Struggle: The Bitter Victory* (London and New York: Pinter Publishers, 1991), p. 70.
8. Hibbert, p. 70.
9. SOE Maj. Anthony Quayle Report, February 23, 1944. Nick Kukich files.
10. *The OSS: America's First Intelligence Agency* (Washington, DC: Central Intelligence Agency), pp. 8–9.
11. Kermit Roosevelt, *The Overseas Targets: War Report of the OSS*, vol. 2 (New York, Walker Publishing Co., 1976), p. 125.
12. Roosevelt, p. 125.
13. NA: RG 226, Entry 154, Box 7, Folder 235.
14. Julian Amery, *Sons of the Eagle: A Study in Guerilla War* (London: Macmillan & Co., Ltd, 1948), p. 50.
15. NA: RG 226, Entry 154, Box 6, Folder 100.
16. Enver Hoxha, *The Anglo-American Threat to Albania* (Tirana, Albania: The "8 Nentori" Publishing House, 1982), p. 34.
17. Hoxha, *Anglo-American Threat*, p. 39.
18. Amery, p. 59.
19. David Smiley, *Albanian Assignment* (London: Chatto & Windus, The Hogarth Press, 1984), p. 67.
20. Peter Kemp, *No Colours or Crest* (London: Cassell & Co., Ltd., 1958), pp. 121–122.
21. Hoxha, *Anglo-American Threat*, p. 57.
22. NA: RG 226, Entry 210, Box 476, Folder 10.
23. Kemp, p. 97.
24. H.R. Tilman, *When Men & Mountains Meet* (Cambridge, UK: University of Cambridge Press, 1946), pp. 114–115.
25. Smiley, p. 36.
26. NA: RG 226, Entry 108B, Box 32, Folder 304.
27. Hibbert, p. 61.
28. Kukich interview.
29. Kukich interview.
30. NA: RG 226, Entry 108, Box 78, Folder GB 2900.
31. Anthony Quayle, *A Time to Speak* (London: Barrie & Jenkins, Ltd., 1990), p. 273.
32. NA: RG 226, Entry 108, Box 71, Folder GB 180.
33. Brigadier Edmund Frank "Trotsky" Davies, *Illyrian Venture* (London: The Garden City Press, Ltd., 1952), pp. 171–172.

Chapter 2

1. Quayle, *Speak*, p. 265.
2. *Ibid.*, p. 265.
3. Nick Kukich interview.
4. NA: RG 226, Entry 108, Box 71, Folder GB 1–49.
5. Hibbert, p. 75.
6. Davies, pp. 153–157.
7. Hibbert, p. 80.
8. Hibbert, p. 81.
9. NA: RG 226, Entry 108, Box 389, Folder GB 23.
10. NA: RG 226, Entry 108, Box 75, Folder GB 750. The editor of the paper was Agile Tasi, who lived and studied in the United States before returning to Albania.
11. NA: RG 226, Entry 108, Box 72, Folder GB 625.
12. NA: RG 226. Entry 108, Box 73, Folder GB 850.
13. NA: RG 226, Entry 108, Box 72, Folder GB 625.
14. Hoxha, *Anglo-American Threat*, p. 58; Quayle, *Speak*, p. 277.
15. NA: RG 226, Entry 108, Box 81, Folder GB 350.
16. NA: RG 226, Entry 108, Box 72, Folder GB 450.
17. Quayle, *Speak*, p. 270.
18. Agnes Jensen Mangerich, *Albanian Escape: The True Story of U.S. Army Nurses Behind Enemy Lines* (Lexington: The University Press of Kentucky Press, 1999). Note: I discovered the remains of the Dakota C-53 in the village of Çestie in 1994. I brought a piece of the plane home to Agnes Jensen Mangerich. The following year I accompanied her family to the site.
19. Report of Capt. Lloyd B. Smith, 29 March 1944. Provided by Smith to author.
20. Anthony Quayle, *Eight Hours from England* (London: William Heinemann Ltd., 1945), p. 64. Quayle wrote two books dealing with Albania: the novel *Eight Hours From England* and his biography *A Time to Speak*.
21. Nick Kukich interview.
22. NA: RG 226, Entry 190, Box 178, Folder 1383.
23. The Quayle Report, February 28, 1944. Nick Kukich files. The account of Carapizzi's murder is based on both, and on interviews with Nick Kukich.
24. Quayle, *Speak*, p. 276.
25. NA: RG 226, Entry 154, Box 178, Folder 1383.
26. NA: RG 226, Entry 136, Box 22, Folder 236.
27. Nick Kukich interview.
28. NA: RG 226, Entry 154, Box 178, Folder 1383.
29. The Quayle Report.
30. Quayle, *Speak*, pp. 279–301.
31. Sterling Hayden, *Wanderer* (New York: Alfred A. Knopf, Inc., 1963; reprint, Dobbs Ferry, NY: Sheridan House, 1998), p. 325.
32. Nick Kukich interview.

Chapter 3

1. Joan Fultz Kontos, *Red Cross, Black Eagle: A Biography of Albania's American School* (New York: Columbia University Press, 1981), pp. 171–173.
2. NA: RG 226, Entry 154, Box 14, Folder 181.
3. James W. Hudson, *Beyond OSS* (Publish America, Baltimore, 2004), p. 48.
4. Hudson, p. 67.
5. NA: RG 226, Entry 136, Box 34, Folder 388.
6. NA: RG 266, Entry 154, Box 16, Folder 232.
7. NA: RG 266, Entry 154, Box 16, Folder 235.
8. Hudson, p. 244.
9. NA: RG 226, Entry 136, Box 34, Folder 388.
10. NA: RG 266, Entry 154, Box 14, Folder 181.
11. James Hudson email interview.
12. NA: RG 226, Entry 154, Box 8, Folder 119.
13. Kostas Routsis kept a diary, which was forbidden, and expanded it in 1946. The accounts of his experiences are based on those documents and on personal interviews conducted by the author.
14. NA: RG 226, Entry 154, Box 17, Folder 237.
15. Kostas Routsis notes and interview.
16. NA: RG 226, Entry 154, Box 17, Folder 237.
17. NA: RG 226, Entry 108, Box 72, Folder GB 450.

18. NA: RG 226, Entry 108, Box 71, Folder GB 350.
19. NA: RG 226, Entry 108, Box 72, Folder GB 500.
20. NA: RG 226, Entry 108, Boxes 71, 74, Folders GB 350, 1300.
21. NA: RG 226, Entry 108, Box 72, Folder GB 400.
22. NA: RG 226, Entry 108, Box 76, Folder GB 1900.
23. NA: RG 226, Entry 108, Box 75, Folder GB 1450.
24. NA: RG 226, Entry 108, Box 75, Folder GB 750.

Chapter 4

1. Federal Writers' Project of the WPA, *The Albanian Struggle In the Old World and New* (Boston: The Writer, Inc., Publishers, 1939), p. 88.
2. *Ibid.*, pp. 91–92.
3. NA: RG 226, Entry 108B, Box 33, Folder 305.
4. NA: RG 226, Entry 154, Box 16, Folder 232.
5. NA: RG 226, Entry 136, Box 34, Folder 336.
6. Hibbert, pp. 118–119.
7. NA: RG 226, Entry 154, Box 17, Folder 238.
8. *Ibid.*
9. *Ibid.*
10. Nick Kukich interview.
11. Jon Halliday, *The Artful Albanian: The Memoirs of Enver Hoxha* (London: Chatto & Windus, Ltd., 1986), p. 352.
12. Hibbert, p. 148.
13. NA: RG 226, Entry 136, Box 34, Folder 335.
14. NA: RG 226, Entry 108B, Box 33, Folder 305.
15. *Ibid.*
16. NA: RG 226, Entry 108, Box 73, Folder GB 825.
17. NA: RG 226, Entry 154, Box 17, Folder 238.
18. NA: RG 226, Entry 154, Box 17, Folder 237.
19. *Ibid.*
20. Kostas Routsis interview.
21. NA: RG 226, Entry 136, Box 34, Folder 366.
22. NA: RG 226, Entry 154, Box 17, Folder 237.
23. *Ibid.*

Chapter 5

1. NA: RG 226, Entry 154, Box 16, Folder 229.
2. NA: RG 226, Entry 154, Box 17, Folder 238.
3. Nick Kukich interview.
4. *Ibid.*
5. *Ibid.*
6. *Ibid.*
7. Lt. John O'Keefe File. Museum of World War II, Natick, MA.
8. NA: RG 226, Entry 16, Box 34, Folders 366–368.
9. NA: RG 226, Entry 154, Box 17, Folder 238.
10. Kukich interview.
11. *Ibid.*
12. NA: RG 226, Entry 154, Box 17, Folder 238.
13. NA: RG 226, Entry 108B, Box 33, Folder 306.
14. Amery, p. 266.
15. NA: RG 226, Entry 136, Box 34, Folder 366.
16. Kostas Routsis journal.
17. NA: RG 226, Entry 136, Box 34, Folder 366.
18. *Ibid.*
19. NA: RG 226, Entry 136, Box 34, Folder 366.
20. NA: RG 226, Entry 154, Box 17, Folder 237.
21. NA: RG 226, Entry 154, Box 8, Folder 119.

Chapter 6

1. O'Keefe File.
2. NA: RG 226, Entry 108, Box 78, Folder GB 2700.
3. Nick Kukich interview.
4. NA: RG 226, Entry 210, Box 476, Folder 10.
5. NA: RG 226, Entry 108B, Box 33, Folder 307.

6. O'Keefe File.
7. Nick Kukich interview.
8. NA: RG 226, Entry 108B, Box 7, Folder 107.
9. NA: RG 226, Entry 136, Box 34, Folder 370.
10. O'Keefe File.
11. *Ibid.*
12. NA: RG 226, Entry 108B, Box 33, Folder 307.
13. O'Keefe File.
14. NA: RG 226, Entry 136, Box 34, Folder 370.
15. Nick Kukich interview.
16. Hibbert, p. 189.
17. Nick Kukich interview.
18. NA: RG 226, Entry 136, Box 34, Folder 368. There is no record of Brennan's reply. Stefan did not get to Washington until May 1945, when he was discharged from the U.S. Army.
19. Kostas "Gus" Routsis journal.
20. NA: RG 226, Entry 136, Box 19, Folder 199.
21. Kostas "Gus" Routsis journal.
22. NA: RG 226, Entry108B, Box 33, Folder 307.
23. NA: RG 226, Entry 139, Box 40, Folder 303.

Chapter 7

1. Memhet Shehu, *Lufta per Çlirimin e Tiranes (The Battle to Liberate Tirana)* (Tirana, Albania: "8 Nentori" Publishing House, 1978), p. 5.
2. NA: RG 226, Entry 210, Box 476, Folder 10.
3. Hibbert, p. 217.
4. Nick Kukich interview.
5. NA: RG 226, Entry 139, Box 40, Folders 294–303: "A General Picture of Tirana." Stephen Peters.
6. *Enver Hoxha 1908-1985* (Tirana, Albania: Institute of Marxist-Leninist Studies, 1986), p. 31.
7. Kukich interview.
8. Kemp, *No Colours or Crest*, pp. 97–98.
9. Smiley, pp. 56–57.
10. Kukich interview.
11. Shehu, pp. 25–28.
12. Shehu, pp. 46.

13. NA: RG 226, Entry 108B, Box 7, Folder 107.
14. Kukich interview.
15. Hibbert, p. 214.
16. Kukich interview.
17. *Ibid.*
18. Hibbert, p. 214.
19. O'Keefe File.
20. Shehu, p. 68.
21. *Ibid.*, pp. 69–73.
22. NA: RG 226, Entry 136, Box 22, Folder 236.
23. NA: RG 226, Entry 108B, Box 34, Folder 308.
24. Shehu, p. 78.
25. NA: RG 226, Entry 108B, Box 34, Folder 308.
26. NA: RG 226, Entry 108B, Box 7, Folder 107.
27. NA: RG 226, Entry 136, Box 22, Folder 236.
28. *Ibid.*
29. *Ibid.*
30. *Ibid.*

Chapter 8

1. NA: RG 226, Entry 136, Box 22, Folder 236.
2. Enver Hoxha, *Laying the Foundations of the New Albania* (Tirana, Albania: The "8 Nentori" Publishing House, 1984), pp. 510–512.
3. Nick Kukich interview.
4. NA: RG 226, Entry 108B, Box 34, Folder 308.
5. Kostas "Gus" Routsis Journal.
6. NA: RG 226, Entry 136, Box 22, Folder 236.
7. *Ibid.*
8. *Dielli*, December 23, 1944.
9. NA: RG 226, Entry 108B, Box 34, Folder 308.
10. *Ibid.*
11. O'Keefe File, World War II Museum, Natick, MA. Dilfiruze Banush was a woman friend of O'Keefe's who worked for Radio Tirana. She wrote in English to O'Keefe when he was in Rome recovering from an appendix operation. One letter that survived is dated April 28, 1945. It reads: "Hello, Keefe! I am sure that your betrothed

wouldn't have written you as many letters as I have, and to think that I was so indifferent while you were here enjoying the best of health. Captain Stefan stopped on the street today to tell me the good news of your operation. Gee, but you certainly were born with a shirt on, as the Albanians say! Well, now it's all over and let's not think about it. He said that you would recover in about 3 weeks and you'd come here. Do you really want to return to this blessed place? Would it not be better to return to the old Kentucky home, Keefe? No such luck, eh? I saw the boys working in the back garden today, they were laboring under the hot sun with their forks and spades just in their trunks. I shouted at them, 'Hey, kids, do you need any help?' And they shouted back, 'Sure, plenty to do here!' I got such a kick. Oh, Keefe, you can't imagine what it means to me to exchange a few words with Americans. Do you know what a nostalgie [sic] I have when I pass your Mission? Then I see that beloved flag of stars and stripes flying in the breeze, Keefe, my eyes just fill with tears. I think of my school days when I used to say every morning: 'I pledge allegiance to my flag....' Do you remember, Keefe? God, it all seems like a happy dream that will never come true. Have you a nice nurse to take care of you? Is she pretty, Keefe? Italian girls are pretty snappy. Hope you fall in love with one of them. It's the best remedy for all ailments, especially in springtime, don't you think? My lessons are going well. The blond across the way who seems to be sympathized by everyone is anxious to learn English. Do you suspect any home-breakers around here? Many of the women don't like her much. Too strong competition, I guess. But where's the target? That's what I can't get at. What a mystery! If I detect any more news about her I'll be sure to let you know. Interested? Won't we have fun when you come back! You won't sit in the corner so taciturn anymore, Keefe. I'll take you and show you off to the gals. Would you like that? Albanian girls are very faithful and good housewives. Better than your Americans who live four months with you and then quarrel over cold coffee and show you the door so coolly. We shall talk it over when you return. Is there anything I can send you, Keefe? If there is, just let me know and I shall gladly send it. Be happy, Keefe, and drop me a line if you can. I shall look forward very eagerly to your letters. Dilfiruze Banush." Ms. Banush, according to sources at Radio Tirana, was arrested as a spy sometime after 1946 when O'Keefe and the American OSS left the country. She was sent to prison where she died.

12. Edward E. Nichols Memoir, provided by his son Ned.

13. Kukich interview.

14. NA: RG 226, Entry 139, Box 40, Folders 294–303: "General Picture." Peters.

15. Ismail Kadare, *Albanian Spring: The Anatomy of Tyranny* (Saqi Books, London 1995), pp. 117–120.

16. NA: RG 226, Entry 139, Box 40, Folder 294–303: "General Picture." Peters.

17. *Ibid.*

18. NA: RG 226, Entry 108B, Box 34, Folder 309.

19. NA: RG 226, Entry 139, Box 40, Folders 294–303: "General Picture." Peters.

20. NA: RG 226, Entry 180, Box 73, Folder 185.

21. NA: RG 226, Entry 136, Box 19, Folder 200.

22. NA: RG 226, Entry 136, Box 22, Folder 236.

23. NA: RG 226, Entry 139, Box 40, Folders 294–303: "General Picture." Peters.

24. *Ibid.*

25. NA: RG 226, Entry 210, Box 289, Folder 2.

26. NA: RG 226, Entry 154, Box 16, Folder 230.

27. NA: RG 226, Entry 108B, Box 7, Folder 107.

28. NA: RG 226, Entry 99, Box 33, Folder 1.

29. NA: RG 226, Entry 108B, Box 7, Folder 107.

30. Kukich interview.

31. Robert Lee Wolff, *The Balkans in Our Time* (Cambridge, MA: Harvard University Press, 1956), p. 338.

32. NA: RG 226, Entry 139, Box 40, Folders 294–303: "General Picture." Peters.

33. NA: RG 226, Entry 136, Box 19, Folder 200.
34. Kukich interview.
35. NA: RG 226, Entry 154, Box 7, Folder 113.

Chapter 9

1. Kukich interview.
2. *Ibid.*
3. Kontos, p. 182.
4. *Ibid.*, p.183.
5. NA: RG 226, Pers. 19, Box 30.
6. *Boston Globe,* March 11, 1951.
7. Kukich interview.
8. Gus Routsis interview.
9. Halliday, p. 352.
10. Hoxha, *Anglo-American Threat,* pp. 350–352.
11. Hibbert, p. 230.

Bibliography

Agolli, Dritero. *The Man with the Gun.* Tirana, Albania: The "8 Nentori" Publishing House, 1983.

Alia, Ramiz. *Our Enver.* Tirana, Albania: The "8 Nentori" Publishing House, 1988.

Amery, Julian. *Sons of the Eagle: A Study in Guerilla War.* London: MacMillan & Co. Ltd., 1948.

Blau, George E. *Invasion Balkans!: The German Campaign in the Balkans, Spring 1941.* Shippensburg, PA: Burd Street Press, 1997.

Brown, Anthony Cave. *Wild Bill Donovan: The Last Hero.* New York: Times Books, 1982.

Cervi, Mario. *The Hollow Legions: Mussolini's Blunder in Greece, 1940-1941.* Garden City, NY: Doubleday & Company, Inc., 1971.

Ciano, Count Galeazzo. *The Ciano Diaries 1939-1943.* Garden City, NY: Doubleday & Company, Inc., 1946.

Corvo, Max. *The OSS in Italy 1942-1945: A Personal Memoir.* New York: Praeger, 1990.

Davies, Brigadier Edmund Frank ("Trotsky"). *Illyrian Venture.* London: The Garden City Press, Ltd., 1952.

Durham, Edith. *High Albania.* Boston: Beacon Press, 1985. (First published by Edward Arnold, London, 1909.)

Enver Hoxha 1908-1985. Tirana, Albania: Institute of Marxist-Leninist Studies, 1986.

Federal Writers' Project. *The Albanian Struggle in the Old World and New.* Boston: The Writer, Inc., 1939.

Fischer, Bernd J. *Albania at War 1939-1945.* West Lafayette, IN: Purdue University Press, 1999.

Halliday, Jon, ed. *The Artful Albanian: The Memoirs of Enver Hoxha.* London: Chatto & Windus, 1986.

Hayden, Sterling. *Wanderer.* New York: Alfred A. Knopf, Inc., 1963. Reprint, Dobbs Ferry, NY: Sheridan House, 1998.

Hibbert, Reginald. *Albania's National Liberation Struggle: The Bitter Victory.* London and New York: Pinter Publishers, 1991.

Hoxha, Enver. *The Anglo-American Threat to Albania.* Tirana, Albania: The "8 Nentori" Publishing House, 1982.

_____. *The Khrushechevites.* Tirana, Albania: The "8 Nentori" Publishing House, 1984.

_____. *Laying the Foundations of the New Albania.* Tirana, Albania: The "8 Nentori" Publishing House, 1984.

_____. *The Superpowers.* Tirana, Albania: The "8 Nentori" Publishing House, 1986.

_____. *The Titoites.* Tirana, Albania: The "8 Nentori" Publishing House, Tirana, 1982.

Hudson, James W. *Beyond OSS.* Baltimore: Publish America, 2004.

Huot, Louis. *Guns for Tito.* New York: L.B. Fischer, 1945.

Kadare, Ismail. *The General of the Dead Army.* Tirana, Albania: The "8 Nentori" Publishing House, Tirana, 1983.

_____. *Albanian Spring: The Anatomy of Tryanny.* London: Saqi Books, 1995.

Kasneci, Lefter. *Steeled in the Heat of Battle.*

Tirana, Albania: The "Naim Frasheri" Publishing House, 1966.
Katz, Robert. *The Battle for Rome*. New York: Simon & Schuster, 2003.
Kemp, Peter. *No Colours or Crest*. London: Panther Books, 1960. (First published in Great Britain by Cassell & Co., Ltd., 1958.)
Kennedy, Robert M. *Hold the Balkans!: German Antiguerrilla Operations in the Balkans, 1941-1944*. Shippensburg, PA: White Mane Books, 2000.
Kontos, Joan Fultz. *Red Cross, Black Eagle: A Biography of Albania's American School*. New York: Columbia University Press, 1981.
Maclean, Fitzroy. *Eastern Approaches*. London: Jonathan Cape, 1949.
Mangerich, Agnes Jensen. *Albanian Escape: The True Story of U.S. Army Nurses Behind Enemy Lines*. Lexington: The University of Kentucky Press, 1999.
Mazower, Mark. *Inside Hitler's Greece: The Experience of Occupation, 1941-1944*. New Haven, CT: Yale University Press, 1995.
The OSS: America's First Intelligence Agency. Washington, DC: Central Intelligence Agency.
Owen, Major General David Lloyd. *The Long Range Desert Group 1940-1945: Providence Their Guide*. London: George G. Harrap & Co., Ltd., 1980.
Peters, Stephen. "Ingredients of the Communist Takeover in Albania." In *The Anatomy of Communist Takeovers*, edited by Thomas T. Hammond. New Haven and London: Yale University Press, 1975.
Puto, Arben. *From the Annals of British Diplomacy*. Tirana, Albania: The "8 Nentori" Publishing House, 1981.
Quayle, Anthony. *Eight Hours from England*. London and New York: White Lion Publishers, 1973. (First published in the United Kingdom by Willian Heinemann Ltd., 1945.)
____. *A Time to Speak*. London: Barrie & Jenkins, 1990.
Roosevelt, Kermit. *The Overseas Targets: War Report of the OSS*. Vol. 2. New York: Walker Publishing Co., 1976.
Shehu, Mehmet. *Lufta per Çlirimin e Tiranes (Battle for the Liberation of Tirana)*. Tirana, Albania: "8 Nentori" Publishing House, 1978.
Smiley, David. *Albanian Assignment*. London: Chatto & Windus, The Hogarth Press, 1948.
Smith, Denis Mack. *Mussolini's Roman Empire*. New York: The Viking Press, 1976.
Tilman, H.W. *When Men & Mountains Meet*. Cambridge, UK: University of Cambridge Press, 1946.
Vickers, Miranda, and James Pettifer. *Albania: From Anarchy to a Balkan Identity*. New York: New York University Press, 1997.
White, Leigh. *Balkan Caesar: Tito Versus Stalin*. New York: Charles Scribner's Sons, 1951.
Williams, Heather. *Parachutes, Patriots, and Partisans: The Special Operations Executive and Yugoslavia, 1941-1945*. Madison: The University of Wisconsin Press, 2003.
Wolff, Robert Lee. *The Balkans in Our Time*. Cambridge, MA: Harvard University Press, 1956.

Index

Adams, Philip 48, 64
Albanian National Liberation Army (ANLA) 102, 139, 151, 160, 163, 178, 188
Alimerko, Hito 86
Alimerko, Pasho 86
Alimerko, Reuf 86
Amery, Capt. Julian 1, 29, 115, 191, 193, 199, 201
Antonescu, Gen. Ion 182
Antonio Gramsci Battalion 33, 160
Arch Street Tavern 82–83, 119, 155
Armenians 51, 66–67, 76–77, 98, 146

Balli Kombëtar, Balli (BK) 2–3, 6, 12–13, 21–24, 27–29, 31, 35–36, 46, 56, 64, 67, 73–74, 77, 86–87, 91, 102, 107, 121, 131, 140–41, 154, 158, 163–64, 176–78, 180, 186–87, 190, 192n
Banush, Dilfiruze 202n, 203n
Bari 8, 11, 13, 18–19, 23, 33, 41–42, 45, 49–50, 52–54, 58–61, 63, 66, 68, 70, 86, 91–94, 99, 101–3, 107–13, 115–17, 122, 124, 126–27, 129–30, 132–34, 141, 147, 153, 156, 160, 170, 177–79, 182, 190, 194
Berat 2, 7, 53–53, 66, 73, 90, 95, 124–25, 132–36, 142, 154, 156–59, 175, 190
Biçaku, Aziz 45–46
Boston 7, 39–41, 67, 80–85, 95, 116, 132, 162, 166, 176, 189–90, 194–95
Brennan, Earl 134–35, 179, 189, 202
Brindisi 71, 111
Brussels 141

Cairo 22–23, 63, 111
Carapizzi (Karapiçi), Ismail 13, 17–19, 25, 37, 43, 45, 47, 51, 53–60, 200
Carlo 125, 131
Carroll, Madeleine 39, 65, 190
Çela, Agim 73
Çela, Xhelil 7, 13, 45, 51, 53, 55–56, 59, 66, 71–73, 180
Chekani, Sgt. George 120
Churchill, Sir Winston 26, 166
Ciano, Count Galeazzo 144, 176
CINC (Enver Hoxha codename, pronounced "Chink" by Stefan and others) 101, 112, 119
Çitaku, Colonel Ramadan 95, 103, 107–8, 170
Communist Party of Albania (CPA) 1–3, 6, 13, 18, 25, 27, 31, 77, 87, 93, 103, 108–9, 117, 140–42, 190
Congress of Përmet 90, 94
Corvo, Max 19, 144

Dajti Hotel 138, 158, 160–61, 169, 171, 173, 184
Dajti Mountain 7, 146, 182
Davies, Brigadier E.F. "Trotsky" 12, 24, 35–37, 45–46, 58, 139
Dixon, Charlie 41
Dixon, Jack 41
Doda, Salim 111–12, 117, 121
Donovan, Gen. William 22, 26, 177, 188
Duffy, Lt. Gavan B. Duffy 52
Dukat 7, 13, 21–22, 37, 45, 51–53, 55–56, 58–59, 62, 66–76, 85–87, 134, 180, 191

Index

Durrës 9, 15, 17, 28, 47, 51, 66, 147, 151, 174
Duskanoviç, Ali (Ali Mali) 93, 108

Eastwood, Capt. Stan 148
Elbasan 7, 27, 66, 75, 124, 147–50, 153, 157, 175

Faja, Baba 29, 158, 170
Feder, Sid 159–60, 162
Field, Maj. Gerry 21, 31, 34, 42–43, 56, 180
Fier 51, 66, 76–77, 96, 132
First (1st) Partisan Division 129
Fronti Nacional Çlirimtar (FNC) 25, 27, 112, 118, 124, 137, 140, 163, 164, 166–67, 177
Fultz, Harry T. (Code names Gates, Plak) 8, 11, 13, 23, 25–26, 48, 54, 56–57, 63–66, 69–70, 72, 75, 84, 86, 88–90, 93–94, 96, 99–103, 105, 108–9, 112–18, 122, 126, 128, 131, 134–35, 142, 150, 153–54, 161, 165, 175, 178, 180–83, 186–88, 192–93, 197
Fultz School (American Vocational School, AVS) 11, 13, 64, 72, 75, 107, 111, 129, 131, 142, 197
Furst, Peter 172

Gelany, George 163
German Army (1st Mountain Division, 104th Jaeger Division, 297th Infantry Division, 22nd Corps.) 33, 50, 67, 76–77, 94, 98, 144, 159, 161
Ghegs 28
Gjirokastër 17, 104, 141, 197
Gloucester 39–41
Grama Bay 7, 49–50, 52, 57, 60–62, 66, 96, 104
Gramsci, Antonio 33, 161

Halliday, Jon 91, 191
Hamid, Xhevit 71–73
Hamilton, (Sterling Hayden) Capt. John 11, 39, 41, 60, 65
Hansen, Art 40
Hayden, Sterling 7, 11, 39–41, 43, 60–62, 65, 83–84, 144, 190, 193–96, 200
Helmës 90, 92–93, 95, 101, 103–6, 108–9, 111–13, 115–16, 132, 140, 190–91
Hibbert, Reginald 1, 21, 33, 47, 86, 91, 130, 138, 148, 192–93, 199, 200–2, 204

Hollywood 39, 41, 190, 194
Hoxha, Enver 1–3, 5–7, 9, 11–13, 24–32, 35–36, 45–47, 49, 59, 64–65, 72, 78, 85, 87–98, 101–4, 106–21, 125, 127–36, 139–43, 150, 154–66, 168–91, 192n, 193–94, 197, 199, 200–2, 204
Hoxha, Kadri 178, 188
Hoxha, Nexhmije 97, 197
Hoxha, Tahir (Code name X) 73
Hudson, Capt. James W. (Code name Bill) vii, 7–8, 11, 63, 65–75, 85, 102, 104, 116, 121–22, 156, 193–94, 186, 200

Infante, Gen. Adolfo 34, 44, 144
Italian Army 2, 32, 45, 139, 144

Jacobs, Joseph E. 183, 186–88
Johan, Paul 163

Kadare, Ismail 168–69, 203
Kali, Mysli 55–56, 58–59
Karaburun Peninsula 2, 5, 7, 15, 44, 191
Keko, James 163
Kemp, Maj. Peter 29–31, 143–44, 191, 199, 202
Kolasin 78
Korçë 7, 29, 32, 77, 80, 85, 87, 98, 98, 110, 132, 141–42, 158, 163–64, 176, 179, 197
Koshena, Maliq 86–87
Kukich, Lieutenant Nick R. (Code name Galba) vii, 6, 8, 11–12, 19, 33, 38–39, 42–44, 49, 51–57, 59–61, 65–69, 71–72, 84–86, 91, 97, 103–4, 106–15, 119–20, 122, 124–32, 134, 139, 142–44, 147–48, 150, 153–55, 158–59, 161–62, 164–65, 169, 171–73, 175, 178, 180–86, 189–90, 194, 196, 199–204
Kupi, Abas 12–13, 28–29, 35–37, 90–91, 94, 102, 113–15, 126, 140
Kyrias, Sgt. Vangel N. (Code name Matioti) 111–12, 116–17, 120, 128, 131–32, 153, 156, 178

Labinot 2, 27, 29, 142
Laconia, N.H. 7, 11, 26, 80–82, 160, 162–63, 188, 195
Legaliteti 2–3, 12–13, 23–24, 28, 31, 35
Lëvizja Nacional-Çlirimtare (LNÇ) 27–29, 56–57, 88–89, 96, 99
Llupa, Nusret (Code name Pietro) 73
Long Range Desert Group (LRDG) 6, 24, 72, 127–28, 146, 148–49

Los Angeles 194–95
Lushnje 52
Lyon, Maj. Marcus 108, 110–11, 113–14, 158, 161

Maleshova, Sejfulla 170
Mantho, Cpl. Robert 179
Mboria, Tefik 176
McAdoo, Dale (Code name Tank) 11, 15, 17, 19, 22–23, 25, 33, 35, 37, 43–45, 49, 51, 53–59, 66, 84
McLean, Maj. Billy 12–13, 27, 29–31, 35–36, 114–15, 143
Meto, Hodo 44–45, 53, 66, 75
Metro, Navy Seaman Angelo (Code name Angel) 85, 95–96, 99, 196
Mihailovic, Gen. Draza 35
Moisiu, Spiro 91, 96, 124, 127
Muço, Skënder 56, 87, 107, 191–92
Mushqeta 148, 149, 157, 159
Mussolini, Benito 18–19, 27–29, 34, 48, 54, 83, 144, 158, 160, 176

Ndreu, Dali 153
Nichols, Lt. Col Arthur 46, 58
Nichols, Sgt. Edward E. 164–65, 203
Nishani, Omer 93, 95, 97, 109, 114, 134, 158–59, 165, 170, 176
Nosi, Maj. Frederick 103, 107, 110, 187

Odriçan 65, 72, 87, 90, 95–97, 101, 104, 116, 120–22, 124, 127, 132, 140, 190
Office of Strategic Services (OSS) 2–3, 5–8, 11–13, 15, 17, 19, 22–28, 30–36, 38–39, 41–42, 44, 46–50, 53, 57, 59–61, 63–78, 84–86, 88, 91, 94–98, 100, 102–3, 106, 108–9, 111, 113–14, 116–23, 132, 134, 136–37, 140, 149, 151, 160–61, 164, 166, 169, 174, 176–77, 179–80, 182–84, 186–87, 189–96, 199, 103
O'Keefe, Lieutenant John H. (Code name Venol, Mazzini) 12, 97, 103–4, 111–13, 119–20, 122, 124–28, 132, 134, 148, 153–54, 161, 164–65, 169, 181, 183, 186, 188, 191, 196, 201–3
Oliver, Capt. J.F.P. 129, 146–48
Omari, Bahri 176, 185
Omari, Fahrije 176
Orahood, Don 17, 19, 42
OSS *see* Office of Strategic Services
O'Toole, Lawrence 40–41
Owen, Col. David Lloyd 128

Palmer, Lt. Col. Alan 96–97, 103, 115, 127, 161
Përmet 2, 7, 90–91, 93–94, 105, 132, 142, 187
Peters, Sgt. Stephen 12, 140, 166–70, 172–73, 176, 181, 196, 202–3
Peza (village) 27, 111, 120, 147
Peza, Myslim 12, 29, 119–21, 126, 146, 158, 197
Pogradec 7, 75
Puto, Arben 1

Qepi, Hodo 59n
Quayle, Maj. Anthony 1, 7, 11–12, 19, 21, 34, 42–43, 49, 51–53, 55–62, 65–66, 193, 196, 199–200

Rome 13, 33, 135, 159, 169, 172, 177–80, 185–86, 188, 202
Roosevelt, Pres. Franklin D. 26, 166
Roosevelt, Kermit 25, 38, 199
Rosenberg, Morris 160
Routsis, Cpl. George 8, 104, 111, 116, 132, 134
Routsis, Cpl. Kostas "Gus" vii, 8, 12, 71, 73–74, 101, 104, 106, 109, 161, 121–22, 132–34, 138–39, 145, 152, 159, 161, 190, 194, 196, 200–2, 204

Saranda 7, 21–22, 51, 66, 76, 122
Sazan Island 15, 21
Seaview 2, 7, 11–13, 15, 19, 21, 24, 31, 33–35, 37, 42–45, 47, 49–50, 52–55, 57–58, 60–62, 65–75, 85–86, 96, 104–5, 107–8, 116, 180
Shehu, Fiqret 161
Shehu, Mehmet 1–2, 7–8, 12, 29–31, 47, 119–20, 126, 128–32, 134–36, 138–39, 142–51, 158, 161, 168, 170, 182, 188, 197, 202
Shkodër 7, 9, 47, 66, 148, 168
Shtab 106, 112–13, 117, 124, 127, 129, 132, 135, 154–55, 180
Simollari, Semeon 194
Skanderbeg 16, 131
Skanderbeg Square 144–45, 158, 166
Smiley, Capt. David 1, 27, 29–32, 35–36, 46, 114–15, 143, 191, 193, 199, 202
Smith, Capt. Lloyd 53, 193, 200
Smith, Maj. Victor 146
Spahiu, Colonel Bedri 96, 103, 127
Special Operations Executive (SOE) 3,

11–13, 19, 21–27, 29–31, 33, 35, 42, 47, 50, 52, 66, 85–87, 91, 96, 100–1, 103, 106, 108–9, 113–14, 143, 146, 180, 191–92, 199
Stalin, Joseph 5, 25, 27, 94, 102, 117, 160, 165–66, 182–83
Stefan, Eftim 80–81
Stefan, Capt. Thomas (Code name Art) vii, 6–8, 11–12, 26, 65–66, 68, 72, 80–97, 99–103, 105–9, 112–13, 115–19, 121–22, 124, 127–28, 130, 132–35, 144, 150, 154–55, 158–64, 169–71, 173, 175, 177–86, 188–95, 202–3
Steffo, Sgt. George 97, 116

Tassi, Cpl. Milton 116, 120, 126
Thanas, Christo 163
Thanas, Sgt. Spiro 116, 132
Thornton, Maj. M.J. 146
Tilman, Maj. Bill 31–32
Tirana 1–2, 7–8, 12, 24, 27–28, 36, 45–47, 49, 53–56, 64, 66, 77, 83, 86, 93, 103, 111, 119–20, 124, 126, 128–32, 134–36, 138, 140–51, 153–59, 161–70, 175–81, 183–88, 190, 192n, 193, 197, 197, 199, 202–3
Tito, Joseph Broz 13, 35, 60, 78, 93–94, 108, 140, 160, 166, 168, 171

Tolie, Pfc. Albert 85, 96, 99, 161
Tosks 28
Tragjas 7, 67–68, 85–86
Trap, Judge Harry E. 163
Tromara, Kol 176, 185

UNRRA 174–75, 181, 187–88

Vatra 176
Vlora 7, 9, 13, 15, 17–18, 21–22, 34, 45, 51, 53–55, 58, 61, 66, 68–69, 72–73, 75–77, 86, 134, 156, 174, 176, 188, 192
Vrioni, Lillian 184
Vrioni, Lulu 178, 184, 190–91, 195, 197
Vrioni, Qemal 176, 178, 185

Washington, D.C. 4, 64, 69, 128, 134–35, 163, 172, 179, 188–89, 197, 199
Watrous, Maj. Eliot 66, 180
Wheeler, Lt. Col. Norman 86–87

Xoxe, Koçi 9, 97, 158–59, 163, 165, 171, 175, 197

Zog, King Ahmed 13, 17, 24, 27–28, 36, 64, 91, 94, 111, 121, 140, 141, 158, 167, 177, 187, 197

www.ingramcontent.com/pod-product-compliance
Ingram Content Group UK Ltd.
Pitfield, Milton Keynes, MK11 3LW, UK
UKHW041959140426
5217IPUK00015B/872